Corpus-based Studies in Specialized Discourses

Linguistic Insights

Studies in Language and Communication

Edited by Maurizio Gotti,
Emeritus Professor,
University of Bergamo (Italy).

Volume 313

PETER LANG
Lausanne - Berlin - Bruxelles - Chennai - New York - Oxford

Francisco Alonso-Almeida / Begoña Bellés-Fortuño (eds.)

Corpus-based Studies in Specialized Discourses

PETER LANG
Lausanne - Berlin - Bruxelles - Chennai - New York - Oxford

Bibliographic information published by the Deutsche Nationalbibliothek
The Deutsche Nationalbibliothek lists this publication in the Deutsche Nationalbibliografie; detailed bibliographic data is available on the Internet at http://dnb.d-nb.de.

Library of Congress Cataloging-in-Publication
A record in the CIP catalog has been requested for this book of the Library of Congress.

The editors gratefully acknowledge the support provided by the Departamento de Filología Moderna, Traducción e Interpretación at the Universidad de Las Palmas de Gran Canaria and the Departament d'Estudis Anglesos at Universitat Jaume I. They also deeply appreciate the sponsorship from the Ministerio de Economía y Competitividad through the project 'Identificación y análisis de las estrategias metadiscursivas en artículos científicos en español e inglés' (reference FFI2016-77941-P).

ISSN 1424-8689
ISBN 978-3-0343-4261-2 (Print)
E-ISBN 978-3-0343-5377-9 (E-PDF)
E-ISBN 978-3-0343-5378-6 (E-PUB)
DOI 10.3726/b22316

Published by Peter Lang Group AG, Lausanne, Switzerland

info@peterlang.com - www.peterlang.com/

Table of Contents

FRANCISCO ALONSO-ALMEIDA / BEGOÑA BELLÉS FORTUÑO

Universidad de Las Palmas de Gran Canaria / Universitat Jaume I

Introduction to Corpus-based Studies in Specialized Discourses

The study of specialized discourses has gained significant traction within applied linguistics, driven by the need to understand how language operates within specific professional and academic contexts. As specialized discourses encompass a wide range of fields, from medicine to engineering to the humanities, it is crucial to explore the distinct linguistic features and rhetorical strategies that characterize these domains. This volume, "Corpus-based Studies in Specialized Discourses," aims to shed light on these unique linguistic phenomena through rigorous corpus-based research methodologies. Corpus-based studies offer a systematic approach to analyzing large collections of texts, allowing researchers to uncover patterns and trends that might not be apparent through traditional qualitative methods. By using corpora, researchers can quantitatively assess linguistic features such as lexical density, metadiscourse markers, and rhetorical structures, providing a more nuanced understanding of how language functions in specialized contexts. This methodological rigor is particularly valuable in examining how language varies across different academic and professional fields, contributing to a comprehensive view of specialized discourses (*Biber, Conrad, & Reppen, 1998*; *Flowerdew, 2012*).

One of the central themes in the study of specialized discourses is the concept of metadiscourse, which refers to the ways in which writers organize their texts, engage with readers, and convey their stance. Metadiscourse markers, such as transitions, frame markers, and engagement markers, play a crucial role in making texts coherent and persuasive (*Hyland, 2005*). They help bridge the gap between the writer and reader, facilitating comprehension and fostering a collaborative construction of knowledge. Understanding the use of metadiscourse across different disciplines is essential for improving academic writing and enhancing communication within specialized fields (*Crismore, Markkanen, & Steffensen, 1993*; *Hyland & Jiang, 2021*). Another key area of focus is the rhetorical structure of research articles, particularly introductions. Introductions are pivotal in establishing the context of a study, presenting background knowledge, identifying research gaps, and justifying the research. Analyzing the rhetorical moves and steps within introductions can reveal how researchers from different fields construct their arguments and establish credibility. This knowledge is invaluable for teaching academic writing, as it helps students and novice researchers understand the conventions of their specific disciplines (*Swales, 1990*; *Swales & Feak, 2004*; *Ozturk, 2007*).

The customization of vocabulary software to reflect local and institutional wordlists is another innovative approach discussed in this volume. By aligning vocabulary learning tools with the specific needs of learners in different regions, educators can provide more relevant and effective language instruction. This approach underscores the importance of considering local educational contexts and cultural nuances in language teaching and learning (*Nation, 2001*; *Coxhead, 2018*). Pragmatic competence, or the ability to use language appropriately in different social contexts, is also a critical component of specialized discourses. Studies on pragmatic strategies, such as expressing disagreement or using euphemisms, highlight the challenges that learners face in mastering the socio-cultural norms of communication in academic and professional settings (*Thomas, 1983*; Rodríguez Velasco & Ainciburu, this volume; *Taguchi, 2019*). Addressing these challenges through explicit instruction can enhance learners' communicative competence and ensure their success in specialized fields (*Kasper & Rose, 2002*; *Bardovi-Harlig, 2020*).

Altogether, "Corpus-based Studies in Specialized Discourses" offers a comprehensive exploration of the linguistic and rhetorical features that characterize specialized discourses. Through a series of methodically conducted corpus-based studies, this volume provides valuable insights into the ways language operates within different academic and professional domains. The findings presented here have significant implications for teaching, research, and practice, making this volume an essential resource for scholars and educators in applied linguistics and related fields. In the first chapter, María Paula Roverso and Julia T. Williams Camus explore the rhetorical structures of research article (RA) introductions in two medical subfields: neurology and pediatrics. English, as the predominant language of scientific communication, necessitates that researchers publish their work in English for broader visibility and recognition. The analysis of RA discourse, particularly introductions, has garnered significant interest over the past three decades within the field of English for Specific Purposes (ESP). Introductions are pivotal sections where authors establish their credibility, present background knowledge, identify research gaps, and justify their studies. This chapter employs a modified version of Swales' Creating a Research Space (CARS) model to analyze 60 RA introductions, split evenly between neurology and pediatrics. The study focuses on articles published in top-tier English-language journals from North America, the UK, and Europe during 2017–2018, resulting in a corpus of 22,370 tokens. The analysis reveals that most neurology and pediatrics introductions follow the CARS model, with frequent cyclical patterns of Moves 1 (establishing a territory) and 2 (establishing a niche) before presenting the study in Move 3 (occupying the niche). The study's findings underscore the significance of understanding subdiscipline-specific rhetorical patterns for pedagogical purposes. The consistency in following the CARS model suggests its utility as a pedagogical tool for teaching academic writing in medical contexts.

The subsequent chapter by Begoña Bellés-Fortuño and Lucía Bellés-Calvera deals with the metadiscourse patterns in research articles (RAs), specifically examining the disciplinary and cross-cultural variations of engagement markers. The evolution of academic writing over the past few decades has transitioned from an objective, impersonal mode of communication to a more interactive and dynamic process. This shift has highlighted the importance of metadiscourse, which encompasses self-reflective expressions that negotiate interactional meanings and establish connections with readers. Previous studies have shown that researchers from various linguistic backgrounds use metadiscoursal elements to disseminate disciplinary knowledge and contribute to the construction of scientific discourse. National culture and local academic norms significantly influence these elements, as evidenced by comparisons of RAs written by non-native English speakers from countries like Spain, Greece, Sweden, Finland, Turkey, Iran, and Korea, with those authored by English or American researchers.

This chapter addresses the need for further investigation into the metadiscourse conventions deployed in English and Spanish RAs. It aims to understand how academic writing in these two languages compares by analyzing engagement markers in RAs from three fields: Medicine, Engineering, and Linguistics. The study's significance lies in its comparison of papers published in international journals in two of the world's most widely used languages, focusing on how writers construct persuasive arguments and foster inclusive relationships with their readers. The research is conducted within the framework of the IAMET project, which compiled a large contrastive corpus of Spanish and English journal articles from various disciplines. Using METOOL, a newly developed corpus tool software, the study identifies and labels engagement markers across distinct categories. The analysis is grounded in the taxonomies proposed by Mur Dueñas (2011) and Salas Valdebenito (2015), with a focus on personal asides, questions, imperatives, and directives.

The findings reveal that engagement markers are more prevalent in Linguistics articles compared to Medicine and Engineering. English RAs generally exhibit higher occurrences of these markers than their Spanish counterparts, though personal asides and questions are more common in Spanish medical RAs. The use of personal pronouns, rhetorical questions, and imperatives varies across disciplines, reflecting different approaches to engaging readers and establishing credibility. The chapter concludes that understanding these variations has important pedagogical implications for teaching academic writing and can help scholars publish in both English and Spanish. Future research could expand on these findings by analyzing a broader range of disciplinary fields and developing tools to track language evolution patterns and enhance discourse comprehension.

This third chapter, entitled "Logical Metadiscursive Markers in Research Papers Written in English: A Corpus-based Approach" by

Elena Quintana-Toledo and Margarita Esther Sánchez-Cuervo, focuses on the pivotal role of logical metadiscursive markers in the construction and dissemination of scientific knowledge through research articles. Recognizing these articles as fundamental tools for scientific communication, the chapter highlights the shift from viewing scientific discourse as impersonal and objective to understanding it as inherently interactive and interpersonal. Logical metadiscursive markers, such as additive, contrastive, and consecutive linkers, are instrumental in this process, as they help to connect various parts of the text, guiding readers through complex arguments and facilitating comprehension. The chapter emphasizes the importance of these markers in organizing academic texts and enhancing reader engagement. Building on Hyland's model of metadiscourse, which classifies these markers within the interactive dimension, the authors argue that transition markers not only provide structural coherence but also reflect the writer's consideration of the reader's cognitive and processing needs. This dual function underscores the markers' role in both structuring discourse and fostering a collaborative construction of knowledge between writer and reader.

A key asset of this chapter is its corpus-based approach, which involves a detailed analysis of research articles from three distinct disciplines: Linguistics, Engineering, and Medicine. By examining the frequency and function of logical metadiscursive markers across these fields, the chapter provides insights into disciplinary variations in academic writing practices. The findings reveal that while additive markers are most prevalent across all disciplines, the use of contrastive and consecutive markers varies significantly, reflecting different rhetorical strategies and epistemological approaches. Furthermore, the chapter's methodological rigor is evident in its comprehensive corpus and meticulous annotation process, which ensures the reliability and validity of the results. This systematic analysis not only contributes to our understanding of metadiscourse in academic writing but also offers practical implications for improving the clarity and persuasiveness of research articles. In short, the chapter underscores the significance of logical metadiscursive markers in enhancing the readability and rhetorical effectiveness of academic texts. By bridging the gap between writer and reader, these markers play a crucial role in the dynamic process of scientific communication, making this chapter an essential contribution to the study of specialized discourses.

The chapter "Lexical Diversity and Lexical Density of Metadiscourse Devices in Academic English Papers on Linguistics, Engineering, and Medicine" by María Luisa Carrió-Pastor and Hanna Skorczynska focuses on the complex interaction between academic English papers, metadiscourse, lexical diversity, and lexical density. While most studies on lexical diversity and density focus on second language vocabulary acquisition, this chapter investigates these measures within metadiscourse devices across three distinct fields: engineering, linguistics, and medicine. These fields represent hard sciences (engineering), soft sciences (linguistics), and a combination of both (medicine). The authors aim to fill a research gap by examining two underexplored measures – lexical diversity (the variety of different words used) and lexical density (the proportion of lexical items) – within metadiscourse in academic papers. The objectives are threefold: first, to determine if lexical density and diversity vary across specific fields of knowledge and rhetorical markers (textual and interpersonal); second, to explore the relationship between the frequencies of rhetorical markers and lexical measures; and third, to investigate the correlation and frequency of lexical diversity and density across different domains.

Lexical density measures the proportion of content words to the total number of words, offering insight into the informational content of texts. Content words include nouns, verbs, adjectives, and adverbs, while function words encompass articles, pronouns, prepositions, and conjunctions. Higher lexical density indicates more information-packed texts. Conversely, lexical diversity assesses the variety of different words used, calculated through the type-token ratio (TTR). Both measures provide a comprehensive view of the linguistic richness and complexity in academic discourse. Metadiscourse, key in linking interactions between writers and readers within the same discourse community, encompasses two main categories: textual (interactive) and interpersonal (interactional) metadiscourse. Textual markers manage the flow of information, guiding readers through the content, while interpersonal markers engage readers in the argument, reflecting the writer's stance. These categories are further divided into subcategories such as logical markers, code glosses, frame markers, evidentials, hedges, boosters, attitude markers, engagement markers, and self-mentions. The analysis revealed significant differences in the use of metadiscourse markers and lexical measures across disciplines. Linguistic papers exhibited the highest lexical diversity and lowest lexical density, indicating a wider variety of words with less repetition. In contrast, medical papers showed the highest lexical density and lowest lexical diversity, reflecting the specialized nature of medical research with frequent repetition of specific terms. Engineering papers displayed intermediate values in both measures. Linguists used more textual and interpersonal markers, guiding readers through complex arguments with a variety of rhetorical strategies. Medical researchers relied less on metadiscourse markers, possibly due to the established structure and specificity of medical journals. The use of boosters and attitude markers in medical papers suggests a trend towards a more assertive presentation of findings.

The study confirms that lexical density and diversity are sensitive to different academic domains. Linguists employ a broader vocabulary with less repetition, while medical researchers use more content-specific terms with higher repetition. The frequency and use of metadiscourse markers also vary significantly, reflecting different rhetorical strategies and traditions in academic writing across disciplines. These findings contribute to our understanding of linguistic complexity in academic discourse and highlight the importance of metadiscourse in shaping reader engagement and comprehension. Future research should explore these patterns in other domains such as architecture, law, and economics to further elucidate the ways academic communication varies across fields. Analyzing frequency, accuracy, and complexity of words can provide additional insights into the interplay between lexical measures and metadiscourse in academic writing.

In the fifth chapter titled "Interactive Metadiscourse Markers in Abstracts Written by Undergraduate Students," Carme Bach and Maria Dolors Cañada Pujols study the nuances of abstract writing by undergraduate students, focusing on their use of interactive metadiscourse markers and the correlation between these markers and the rhetorical structure of the texts. This research addresses a significant gap in the literature, as most studies on abstracts focus on texts produced by expert researchers rather than student writers. The chapter is especially pertinent in the Spanish context, where a 2007 law mandated that all undergraduate and master's programs include a final thesis project, thus making abstract writing a universal academic practice in Spain. The abstract, an essential academic genre, functions to concisely inform readers about the contents of an article, helping them decide whether to read the full text. This genre shares characteristics with other academic discourses such as lectures and literature reviews. Abstracts can vary in their structure – descriptive, structured, or informative – and their function encompasses indexing texts for databases, orienting readers about the content, and persuading them to read further. The chapter highlights the importance of understanding the abstract's functions to appreciate its rhetorical organization fully.

Bach and Cañada Pujols adopt a comprehensive approach to examining the abstracts by integrating macrotextual and microtextual analyses. At the macrotextual level, they identify seven rhetorical moves: introduction, aims, methodology, results, conclusions, structure, and limitations. The latter two are emerging moves, indicating a blend of student and researcher identities in the writers. Their analysis reveals that the most frequent moves are aims, methodology, and introduction, often characterized by excessive detail not typical of professional abstracts. Microtextually, the chapter focuses on interactive metadiscourse markers as classified by *Hyland (2005)* – transition markers, frame markers, evidentials, and definitional contexts – with an addition of metadiscursive nouns. The analysis shows a predominant use of frame markers, especially metadiscursive nouns, which help create coherence in the text. Transition markers are mainly used for contrast and consequence, aiding in the logical flow and justification of research.

One significant finding is that student writers often confuse the features of an abstract with those of an introduction, leading to the inclusion of structural and limitations moves. This confusion impacts their use of verb tenses and structural markers, indicating a lack of full understanding of the genre's situational parameters. The chapter also notes the use of sequencing discourse markers, predominantly in the results move, and the presence of definitional contexts, especially in the introduction and methodology moves, suggesting an attempt to make the text accessible to readers. The benefits of this chapter are manifold. It provides a detailed description of the linguistic and rhetorical features of abstracts written by undergraduate students, highlighting areas where their understanding of the genre is still developing. By identifying the specific metadiscourse markers and rhetorical moves used by students, the chapter offers insights into their discursive competence and areas for improvement. This analysis can inform teaching practices, helping educators guide students in mastering the abstract genre. Additionally, the chapter contributes to the broader field of academic writing by comparing student-produced texts with those of expert researchers, offering a situated understanding of genre acquisition and the development of academic literacy skills. Overall, the chapter underscores the importance of explicit instruction in academic writing, particularly in the production of abstracts, to ensure that students develop a sophisticated understanding of genre conventions and rhetorical strategies. This research not only fills a gap in the literature but also provides practical recommendations for enhancing student writing in academic contexts.

In the subsequent chapter "Metadiscourse in Classroom Discourse: An Analysis of Interactive Markers in CLIL Seminars," Lucía Bellés-Calvera examines the use of interactive metadiscourse markers in Content and Language Integrated Learning (CLIL) seminars, specifically comparing the disciplines of Humanities and Health Sciences. The internationalization of education and the need for multilingual competencies have prompted the European Union to encourage the learning of multiple foreign languages, thereby integrating English into various educational levels. CLIL, a pedagogical approach that uses an additional language for teaching subject content, is a focal point of this study due to its dual emphasis on content mastery and language proficiency. CLIL courses present unique challenges and opportunities for both educators and students. The implementation of these programs requires careful planning, teacher training, and assessment to ensure effective learning outcomes. While much research has focused on written academic texts and lectures, there is a gap in understanding students' spoken discourse in seminar settings. This chapter aims to fill this gap by analyzing the use of metadiscourse markers – linguistic devices that help structure discourse and engage the audience – in project-based seminars conducted in English.

The study investigates first-year History undergraduate students and third-year Medicine undergraduate students at a Spanish university. The analysis is based on authentic recorded seminars, which provides a realistic context for examining how students use metadiscourse to organize their speech and interact with their audience. By focusing on interactive markers such as transitions, frame markers, endophoric references, evidentials, and code glosses, the research aims to uncover differences in the use of these markers across the two disciplines. The methodological approach includes recording seminar sessions, transcribing them, and creating a corpus for analysis. The study employs *Hyland's (2005)* interpersonal model of metadiscourse, which categorizes interactive markers into several types. The corpus consists of 17,506 words from two project-based seminars, one in History and one in Medicine. This comparative analysis reveals that transitions are the most frequently used interactive markers in both fields, indicating a need to establish explicit relationships between discourse units.

In History seminars, students rely heavily on additive transitions and contrastive markers. In contrast, Medicine students use a broader range of transitions, including consecutive markers. Frame markers, which help structure speech, are more prevalent in History seminars, where students frequently use sequencing markers to organize their presentations. Medicine students also use frame markers but with a focus on indicating the objectives and limitations of their research. Endophoric references, which refer to other parts of the text, are similarly used in both fields, often pointing to tables, figures, or previously mentioned information. Evidentials, which cite external sources, are predominantly found in Medicine seminars, reflecting the research-oriented nature of the discipline. Code glosses, which explain or elaborate on terms, are used to a comparable extent in both fields, although Medicine students demonstrate a slightly higher frequency. The chapter concludes that the use of metadiscourse markers in CLIL seminars is influenced by the context and content of the disciplines. The findings highlight the importance of transitions and frame markers in organizing discourse and enhancing comprehension. The study underscores the need for CLIL instructors to provide scaffolding techniques that address both cognitive and linguistic demands, ensuring that students can effectively communicate academic content.

This piece of research has significant pedagogical implications. By identifying common interactive resources in CLIL settings, educators can better understand students' discourse preferences and areas needing improvement. The study suggests incorporating prompts on content and language structure and providing academically oriented materials to improve communicative competence in the target language. Despite its limitations, including the small sample size and focus on only two disciplines, this chapter offers valuable insights into CLIL classroom practices and sets the stage for future research on interpersonal metadiscourse in other academic fields.

In the chapter "Engagement Markers in Medical Recipes: Evidence from G.U.L. MS Hunter 93 (T.4.10)," Ivalla Ortega-Barrera and Elena Quintana-Toledo explore the use of engagement markers in John de Feckenham's "Booke of Soueraigne Medicines," a sixteenth-century medical manuscript. Engagement markers, which are linguistic devices that explicitly address readers to focus their attention or include them as participants in the discourse, are a crucial component of metadiscourse. Metadiscourse itself is the way language reflects on itself, indicating how discourse participants and the texts are related. The study situates itself within the broader context of reflexivity in language, particularly as it relates to metadiscourse in scientific communication. This research area has grown significantly over the past three decades, examining various genres and languages. The authors reference significant contributions from scholars such as Hyland, who emphasized writing as a form of social engagement, placing importance on authorial presence, audience awareness, and the organization of discourse to ensure effective communication.

Ortega-Barrera and Quintana-Toledo's research focuses on engagement markers, which are essential for understanding the dialogic nature of discourse. These markers include personal pronouns, directives, and other linguistic devices that involve the reader in the text. The study aims to provide insights into how such markers function in early English medical writing, which often tailored its style to the intended audience, reflecting changes in scientific thought and rhetoric over time. The manuscript under study, "H93," is attributed to the medical tradition and contains 739 recipes aimed at restoring health. Written in the vernacular, it bridges the transition period in England where standardization and vernacularization were underway. The recipes are categorized into sections like title, ingredients, preparation, application, storage, and efficacy, each with specific linguistic features. The analysis reveals that directives, particularly imperative clauses, are the most prominent engagement markers in H93. Imperatives directly instruct the reader on how to prepare and apply remedies, marking the social distance between the authoritative writer and the reader. These directives are classified into physical acts, guiding readers through empirical actions in the real world.

In addition to imperatives, obligation modals are prevalent. These modals align the writer's goals with those of the reader, implying an obligation to follow the prescribed procedures to achieve the desired outcomes. The use of deontic modals in H93 reinforces the instructive nature of the recipes, framing therapeutic recommendations that the reader is expected to follow. Person markers, especially the second-person pronouns "you" and "thou," and their possessive forms, are extensively used to establish a direct relationship between the writer and the reader. These pronouns address the reader explicitly, enhancing the force of the directives. The coexistence of "you" and "thou" in the text reflects the linguistic evolution of the period. The first-person singular pronoun "I" and the third-person singular pronoun "he" (along with "his" and "him") are also employed to indicate authorial presence and interpersonal distance. The study concludes that the use of engagement markers in H93 serves to instruct and guide readers through the preparation and application of medical recipes, reflecting an authoritative voice aimed at ensuring compliance and effective communication. This initial research lays the groundwork for further studies on metadiscursive elements in medical recipes from different periods, offering a deeper understanding of historical scientific discourse and its interactional strategies.

In the ninth chapter, "Customizing vocabulary software to reflect local and institutional English wordlists," Arthur McNeill explores the integration of local wordlists into vocabulary software to enhance its effectiveness for learners of English as a second language. McNeill argues that while global frequency lists are useful for guiding vocabulary growth, they may not fully address the specific needs of learners in different regions. This chapter details the customization of the Lexical Frequency Profiler (LFP) software to reflect four English wordlists developed by the Hong Kong Education Department for various educational stages. The Hong Kong wordlists comprise 5,000 words tailored to local educational needs, developed through teacher consultations and assessments of existing corpora, including the British National Corpus and the Academic Wordlist. The customization aimed to align the LFP software with these local lists, facilitating more relevant and effective vocabulary learning.

The original LFP software measures lexical richness by categorizing words into frequency-based levels, which can be limiting for intermediate learners whose curricula might not align with global frequency lists. McNeill suggests that by incorporating local wordlists, the LFP can become a more useful tool for learners globally, aiding them in both academic and general language acquisition. A study involving undergraduate and postgraduate students demonstrated the benefits of customized LFP software. Undergraduate students, after using LFP to analyze their texts, significantly improved their lexical richness in revised drafts by substituting higher-frequency words with more advanced vocabulary. This exercise not only enhanced the quality of their writing but also encouraged conscious engagement with vocabulary, promoting unfamiliar word acquisition. In contrast, postgraduate students, whose initial drafts already showed high lexical richness due to discipline-specific vocabulary, benefited more from feedback on grammar and syntax. McNeill concludes that localized wordlists can significantly support the teaching and learning of English worldwide. The chapter highlights the importance of understanding local educational needs and integrating them into vocabulary software like LFP, thus providing learners with a valuable tool for developing their productive vocabularies in contextually relevant ways.

In "The expression of disagreement of Chinese students in a foreign language: writing emails to their Spanish lecturer," David Rodriguez Velasco and María Cecilia Ainciburu investigate the pragmatic strategies employed by Chinese students when disagreeing with their Spanish lecturers via email. The study emphasizes the importance of pragmatic competence, which encompasses understanding both pragma-linguistic and socio-pragmatic factors crucial for appropriate communication in a foreign language. The authors point out that pragmatic strategies are often not explicitly taught, leading to direct and sometimes inappropriate expressions of disagreement in academic settings. The research analyzes 135 emails written by senior Chinese students of Spanish at Heilongjiang International University, focusing on the macro and microstructure of these emails, including subject lines, greetings, self-identification, disagreement strategies, farewells, and signatures. The findings reveal that a considerable number of students omitted essential elements like subject lines and self-identification, indicating a lack of awareness of their importance in academic communication. Most students used direct disagreement strategies with minimal mitigation, which, combined with emotional expressions and a lack of deference, made their emails unsuitable for the academic context.

The study highlights the need for explicit instruction in the sociocultural norms of virtual communication in academia, as the ways students interact with their teachers can vary significantly across cultures. By providing empirical data and a detailed analysis, this chapter contributes to the understanding of pragmatic competence in language learning and underscores the necessity of integrating pragmatic instruction into language curricula to better prepare students for effective communication in academic and professional settings.

In the subsequent chapter, "Intensification and Euphemisms in American Opinion Articles about Weinstein's Accusations," Conchi Hernández Guerra explores how intensification and euphemisms are used in American media to report on the high-profile Harvey Weinstein trial. This case, which gained significant global attention due to the prominence of Weinstein and the severe nature of the accusations, provides a fertile ground for analyzing how language can shape public perception. Hernández Guerra's study focuses on the personal choices of writers in employing intensifiers, which reflect cultural nuances and authorial biases. Intensifiers can exaggerate or manipulate events, thus revealing the underlying subjectivity in supposedly objective reporting. The chapter also examines euphemisms, which, although not intensifiers per se, serve to present information in an ironically softened manner, often to avoid offensive descriptions. The chapter begins with a discussion on the importance of intensification and how it has been traditionally classified into amplifiers and downtoners. It draws on a broad range of literature, including works by Quirk (1987), Zhiber (2019), and Palmer (2001), to frame the analysis of how intensifiers function in reinforcing the expression and affecting the reader's perception. The empirical data for the study comprises ten articles from various

American online sources, published between October 2017 and December 2018. The analysis reveals that intensification in these articles is achieved more through lexical choices than through semantic or idiomatic expressions. However, the overall use of intensifiers is relatively low, with the repetition of specific terms like "sexual harassment" contributing to the perceived intensity of the reports.

Euphemisms are frequently used to veil the harsh realities of the accusations, substituting more neutral or polite terms for offensive or blunt language. This strategy serves to mitigate the severity of the described actions, reflecting a reluctance to confront the brutal nature of the offenses directly. The chapter provides detailed examples from the analyzed corpus, highlighting how euphemisms such as "unwanted sexual attention" or "unwelcome advances" are employed to soften the impact of the allegations. The chapter concludes that the use of intensifiers and euphemisms in American opinion articles about Weinstein's accusations reflects the broader cultural and legal context. The American media tends to balance between reporting the facts and maintaining a certain level of decorum, which often results in a nuanced presentation of highly charged topics. This study underscores the importance of critically examining the language used in media to understand the subtle ways in which it can influence public perception and discourse. By examining the linguistic strategies used in these articles, Hernández Guerra's chapter contributes to a deeper understanding of how language functions in the media, particularly in cases involving sensitive and controversial issues. The findings highlight the need for media literacy and critical thinking skills to navigate and interpret the complex layers of meaning in news reporting.

The last chapter by Francisco J. Álvarez-Gil and Marta Isabel González-Blanco focuses on the translation of deontic modal verbs from Nicolas de Blegny's 1682 work, *Le Remède Anglois pour la Guérison des Fièvres*, into English. The study compares deontic modals in both the original French text and its English translation, aiming to identify discrepancies and analyze how modality—specifically deontic, dynamic, and epistemic—was rendered. Drawing on previous research, the authors examine the shifts in modality type, the translation strategies used, and the possible implications of these shifts. The study highlights the role of modality in both languages, particularly how deontic modality often conveys authority, and how its translation may alter the tone and meaning of the text. The analysis also explores the translator's role in balancing the imposition of authority with linguistic and cultural expectations of the target audience. This chapter ultimately contributes to understanding how translation choices impact the preservation or transformation of modal meaning across languages by conveying specific nuances, which often rely on social and cultural aspect.

In conclusion, the comprehensive exploration of specialized discourses presented in "Corpus-based Studies in Specialized Discourses" underscores the importance of understanding the unique linguistic features and rhetorical strategies employed across various professional and academic domains. By deploying corpus-based research methodologies, the volume offers valuable insights into how language functions in specialized contexts, revealing patterns and trends that enhance our understanding of effective communication within these fields. The chapters demonstrate the utility of metadiscourse markers, the rhetorical structures of research articles, customized vocabulary tools, and pragmatic strategies, all of which contribute to the development of academic writing and professional communication skills. This volume not only enriches the field of applied linguistics but also provides practical implications for educators, researchers, and practitioners, emphasizing the necessity of explicit instruction and tailored tools to support learners in mastering the conventions of their specific disciplines.

References

Bardovi-Harlig, K. (2020). *Pragmatics and language teaching: Bringing pragmatics and pedagogy together*. Wiley-Blackwell.

Biber, D., Conrad, S., & Reppen, R. (1998). *Corpus linguistics: Investigating language structure and use*. Cambridge University Press.

Crismore, A., Markkanen, R., & Steffensen, M. S. (1993). Metadiscourse in persuasive writing: A study of texts written by American and Finnish university students. *Written Communication, 10*(1), 39–71.

Coxhead, A. (2018). Vocabulary and ESP. In B. Paltridge & S. Starfield (Eds.), *The handbook of English for specific purposes* (pp. 115–132). Wiley-Blackwell.

Flowerdew, L. (2012). *Corpora and language education*. Palgrave Macmillan.

Hyland, K. (2005). *Metadiscourse: Exploring interaction in writing*. Continuum.

Hyland, K., & Jiang, F. (2021). *Academic discourse and global publishing: Disciplinary persuasion in changing times*. Routledge.

Kasper, G., & Rose, K. R. (2002). *Pragmatic development in a second language*. Blackwell.

Nation, I. S. P. (2001). *Learning vocabulary in another language*. Cambridge University Press.

Ozturk, I. (2007). The textual organization of research article introductions in applied linguistics: Variability within a single discipline. *English for Specific Purposes, 26*(1), 25–38.

Swales, J. M. (1990). *Genre analysis: English in academic and research settings*. Cambridge University Press.

Swales, J. M., & Feak, C. B. (2004). *Academic writing for graduate students: Essential tasks and skills* (2nd ed.). University of Michigan Press.

Taguchi, N. (2019). Second language acquisition and pragmatics: An overview. In N. Taguchi (Ed.), *The Routledge handbook of second language acquisition and pragmatics* (pp. 1–15). Routledge.

Thomas, J. (1983). Cross-cultural pragmatic failure. *Applied Linguistics, 4*(2), 91–112.

MARÍA PAULA ROVERSO / JULIA T. WILLIAMS CAMUS

Universidad de Cantabria / Universidad de Cantabria

Rhetorical Structure of Research Article Introductions in Two Medical Subfields

1. Introduction

English is undoubtedly the language most widely used in science for the transmission of knowledge and dissemination of scientific discoveries. Therefore, researchers from different areas of knowledge feel obliged to present their research articles (RAs) in journals published in English if they want their articles to gain more visibility and recognition from researchers and institutions worldwide (*Mur-Dueñas, 2016*). In the last three decades, there has been a growing interest in analysing discourse in research articles. Many scholars in the field of English for Specific Purposes (ESP) have focused on the different sections of the RA. For example, several have investigated the abstract (*Amnuai, 2019*; *Salager-Meyer, 1990*; *Samraj, 2005*); others have centred their studies on different aspects of introductions (*Bruce, 2014*; *Cortés, 2013*; *Samraj, 2002*; *Swales, 1981, 1990, 2004*); on the methods section (*Cotos, Huffman & Link, 2017*); on the results section (*Lim, 2010*; *Williams, 1999*); and on the conclusions (*Holmes, 1997*; *Soler-Monreal, 2016*; *Bunton, 2005*). Moreover, there are articles that have analysed other aspects of the RA such as the most relevant lexical items (*Cardinali, 2015*; *Mur Dueñas, 2016*).

According to *Swales (1990)*, "introductions are known to be troublesome, and nearly all academic writers admit to having more difficulty with getting started on a piece of academic writing than they have with its continuation" (p. 137). He explains that writers have to decide on different aspects of how to present background knowledge, their attitude and stance. Introductions are the space in which writers present themselves to the research community and they are crucial because it is here that they have not only to save their own face and appear as credible researchers, but also to protect other researchers' face when citing and evaluating previous literature in the field. It is, therefore, important to study and analyse the most relevant aspects of RA introductions for pedagogical purposes. *Dudley-Evans (2000)* argues that ESP theory should be based on the text, but taking into account that texts vary according to discipline. The analysis of the rhetorical structure of medical RA introductions has been addressed in greater or lesser detail in studies describing the complete rhetorical structure of general medicine RAs (*Skelton, 1994*; *Nwogu, 1997*; *Li & Ge, 2009*; *Fryer, 2012* and *Davis, 2015*). Medicine is a broad discipline consisting of many subdisciplines and these may need to be studied separately, since disciplinary variation has been found in fields such as engineering (*Kanoksilapatham, 2012*) or environmental science (*Samraj, 2002*). However, to our knowledge, no study has compared RA introductions in different subfields of medicine. Therefore, the aim of the present study is to examine the rhetorical structure of two such subfields: neurology and paediatrics.

With the results obtained from this research, we hope to shed light on the field of ESP and help students and professionals in medicine to read and interpret other researchers' studies and to write up their own. The results can indicate the rhetorical structures most commonly used in these subdisciplines and can suggest which linguistic realizations are employed most in the different moves. This paper is organized as follows. Section 2 presents the main methodological aspects, the description of the corpus created and the methods applied to carry out the analysis. Section 3 summarizes the principal results obtained in each subdiscipline and the comparison of the two. Finally, Section 4 concludes the paper and presents the possible pedagogical implications.

2. Corpus Description and Methodology

For the purpose of this study, we created a corpus of sixty RA introductions in two different biomedical subdisciplines: neurology and paediatrics. We searched the Scimago Journal and Country Rank website for the English language journals with the best positions for the two subfields in North America, the United Kingdom and Europe. For selection, the journals had to allow free access to all, or some, articles and they had to belong to the general areas of neurology and paediatrics. For neurology, the selected journals were *JAMA Neurology* (JN) from the United States of America, *Journal of Neurology* (JON) from Germany, *The Lancet Neurology* (TLN) from the United Kingdom, and for paediatrics: *JAMA Pediatrics* (JP) from the United States of America, *The European Journal of Pediatrics* (TEJOP) from Germany and *BMC Pediatrics* (BMCP) from the United Kingdom. To avoid variation in time and to reflect the latest trend in the genre across the world, the corpus was restricted to a period of two years: only articles published in the years 2017 and 2018 were selected. Although the six journals publish different types of texts such as reviews, comments, editorials, among others, only articles presenting original research were considered for this study.

For the selection of the introductions, we downloaded all the free access articles from 2017 and 2018 in each journal and randomly selected 10 texts from each. The native language and nationality of the authors was not taken into account, because the aim was to observe the tendencies in each subdiscipline and not to search for differences in the writing of native and non-native speakers. We then created the corpus by extracting the sixty introductions: thirty for neurology (10,788 tokens) and thirty for paediatrics (11,582 tokens). Thus, the total corpus is made up of 22,370 words or tokens. It should be noted that, for the creation of this corpus, we selected the sections placed immediately after the abstract of the article and before the section of methods because this section did not always appear under the subtitle of *Introduction* and in some it was labelled *Background.*

For the analysis of the rhetorical structure of the RA introductions of the two subdisciplines, we adapted Swales' model (*Figure 1*) by selecting features from the CARS model (1990, 2004) and from *Swales and Feak (2012)* and by redefining a step we thought useful for our study. These decisions were taken according to the needs that arose in the analysis of the different texts.

Creating a Research Space model (1990 – 1994 – 2004)
Move 1 – Establishing a research territory (citations required)
Step 1A by showing that the general research area is important, central, interesting, problematic or relevant in some way (optional)
Step 1B by introducing and reviewing items of previous research in the area (obligatory)
Move 2 – Establishing a niche (citations possible)
Step 1A Indicating a gap or need
Step 1B Question-raising
Step 2 (optional) Presenting positive justification
Step 3 Continuing own research [this study]
Move 3 – Occupying the niche / Presenting the present work
Step 1 – (obligatory) Announcing present research descriptively and/or purposively
Step 2* – (optional) Presenting research questions or hypotheses
Step 3 – (optional) Definitional clarifications
Step 4 – (optional) Summarizing methods
Step 5 – (PISF**) Announcing principal outcomes
Step 6 – (PISF) Stating the value of the present research
Step 7 – (PISF) Outlining the structure of the paper
* Steps 2-4 are not only optional but less fixed in their order of occurrence than the others
** PISF: Probable in some fields, but unlikely in others

Figure 1. CARS model modified for this study

For Move 1, we included the two steps proposed by *Swales and Feak (2012)* in a model for students because we considered them to be more appropriate for our study: an optional Step 1A that contributes to establishing the territory by showing that the topic is relevant, central or problematic; and an obligatory Step 1B, where writers review the literature by citing previous research in the field. These two steps contribute to the establishment of the territory within the field of study and introduce and create the space of the following movement. For Move 2, we maintained Step 1A from the model of 2004 to indicate that there is a gap in the field, and we added the word need since some articles express this gap in this way. We also maintained Step 2 from the model of 2004 to present a positive justification for doing the study. We included Step 1B of question-raising from 1990 and redefined steps from previous models as a new Step 3 where authors indicate that the new study represents a continuation of the same authors' previously published research. This may occur in the biomedical field because of the complexity of some research and restrictions in length imposed by journals. Finally, in Move 3, we maintained the seven steps from the model of 2004 for a more complete analysis.

For the rhetorical structure analysis, the sixty introductions were printed and analysed manually by coding each move and step. They were then saved in a .docx format as tables with the sentences separated to classify the different moves and steps digitally (See Sample texts 1 and 3). After classification, the frequencies of the moves and steps were calculated and the two subdisciplines were compared for the frequency and order of the moves.

Classification of moves and steps was performed by top-down analysis through a careful reading of each introduction to distinguish changes in the topic to aid coding. The study combines quantitative and qualitative methods: it compares the frequency of use of the different moves and steps in the two subdisciplines and it describes the rhetorical move structure of the RA introductions.

3. Results

3.1. Neurology

Table 1 summarizes the different rhetorical structure patterns found in the thirty introductions in neurology.

Table 1. Rhetorical structure in the neurology introductions

	Nº of articles	%
Articles that follow Swales' CARS model		
M1 – M2 – M1 – M2 – M1 – M2 – M3	8	26,67 %
M1 – M2 – M3	6	20 %
M1 – M2 – M1 _ M2 – M3	6	20 %
M1 – M2 – M1 – M2 – M1 – M2 – M1 – M2 – M3	3	10 %
M1 – M2 – M1 – M2- M1 – M2 – M1 – M3	1	3,33 %
M1 – M2 – M1 – M2 – M1 – M3	1	3,33 %
M1 – M2 – M1 – M3	1	3,33 %
M1 – M2 – M1 – M2 – M1 – M2 – M1 – M2 – M1 - M3	1	3,33 %

Continued

Table 1. *Continued*

M1 – M2 – M1 – M2 – M1 – M2 – M1 – M2 – M1 – M2 – M3	1	3,33 %
M1 – M2 – M1 – M2 – M1 – M2 – M1 – M2 – M1 – M2 – M1 - M3	1	3,33 %
Articles that do not follow Swales' CARS model		
M1	1	3,33 %
Total number of articles	30	

The neurology introductions analysed seem to be rather conventional, since most of them follow the model proposed by *Swales (1990, 2004)*. In this study, it was found that six RA introductions in neurology follow the strict M1-M2-M3 pattern and twenty-three introductions alternate Moves 1 and 2 establishing the territory and the gap before the occupation of the niche with Move 3 (*Del Saz Rubio, 2011*). The most frequent pattern, found in eight articles, was one in which three M1–M2 cycles appeared before M3. Other frequent cyclical patterns had two M1–M2 cycles (six articles) and four cycles (three articles) before M3, while other multiple cycles or combinations occurred only once. This cyclicity accords with the results obtained by previous researchers (*Crookes, 1986*; *Swales, 1990*). For instance, *Crookes (1986)* observed that the length of the introductions can affect cyclicity, as he found that the longest introductions presented the greatest cyclic variation. Sample text 1 contains an example of the analysis of one of the RA introductions in neurology that follows the strict CARS M1-M2-M3 pattern.

Sample text 1

JON - 17		
Diagnosis of Guillain–Barre′ syndrome in children and validation of the Brighton criteria	Move	Step
The Guillain–Barre′ syndrome (GBS) is a clinical diagnosis, supported by the results of the cerebrospinal fluid (CSF) and nerve conduction studies (NCSC) [1].	1	1A
Recognition of GBS is *important* to start treatment and monitoring as soon as possible.	1	1A
Accurate diagnostic criteria for GBS *are also required* to determine background incidence rates and to conduct vaccine safety studies.	1	1A
For this purpose, criteria for GBS were developed in 1978 by the National Institute of Neurological and Communicative Disorders and Stroke (NINDS) and updated in 1990 [2].	1	1B
In response to the H1N1 vaccination campaign in 2009 and its possible relation with GBS, new case definitions for GBS *were developed by the Brighton Collaboration*, an international collaboration sponsored by the World Health Organization to improve vaccine safety monitoring [3].	1	1B
Previous studies have validated the Brighton criteria in cohorts of adult patients with GBS from South Korea and The Netherlands [4, 5].	1	1B
The Brighton criteria *also require* validation for GBS in children, which may differ considerably from GBS in adults [6].	2 2	1A 1B
In 2011 the Brighton criteria were validated in children from India, but the clinical presentation of GBS in India is not the same as in a Western country.	2	1A
Therefore, in this study, we describe in detail the clinical presentation and course of GBS in children, focussing on the key diagnostic characteristics, *and validate* the Brighton criteria for pediatric GBS.	3	1

Only one article does not follow the CARS model. This introduction simply establishes the territory of the field being investigated, characterizes the phenomenon studied and defines important aspects by means of Move 1, but it does not make use of Moves 2 and 3 to establish and occupy a niche. However, when continuing reading the article, it was found that there was an overlap between the Introduction and Methodology sections, since statements characteristic of these moves were present in the Methods section. Sample text 2 shows the extract containing these statements (underlined).

Sample text 2 (JN-3)

Methods In a recent screen of 358 children with EEs, we identified 3 novel KCNB1 variants (approximately 1 %), all of which were found to be de novo.[18] We subsequently collected data from 13 additional patients from research and diagnostic sources who were reported to carry a de novo novel KCNB1 variant not present in public databases. In this article, we describe the phenotypic and genetic characteristics of these patients. In addition, we collected more information about 10 patients who were described previously. For 3 of the 10 patients in previously published articles, the authors have provided updated information for the current article. We present the available information on 26 patients for a broad overview of the phenotypic and genetic variability and similarities. Statistical tests were performed using $\chi2$ 2 × 2 contingency tables; the significance of the enrichment of de novo mutation was calculated using a $\chi2$ goodness-of-fit test. A 2-sided $\chi2$ test with $P <.05$ determined statistical significance. Collection of data procedures agreed with the local ethics guidelines at the different institutes.	Move 2 Step 3 Move 3 Step 1 Move 3 Step 1

In the methodological description, the authors use a Move 2-Step3-type statement to express that the study is the continuation of the author's previously published research. They also introduce the new study descriptively in two statements that are typical of Step 1 in Move 3 of introductions and marked by the present tense verbs in contrast to the past tense narrative of the Methods.

As regards Move 1 (*Table 2*), all the introductions of the three journals of neurology made use of Step 1A to contextualize the study and twenty-seven introductions used Step 1B to mention previous research by other authors that investigated related topics.

As can be observed in *Table 2*, in Move 2, twenty-four of the thirty neurology introductions established a gap in the field by means of Step 1A. In addition, sixteen made use of Step 1B where authors raised questions or made hypotheses about the phenomenon being studied. Step 2 was used in eleven introductions to present a positive justification for performing the study and only three articles included a Step 3 to express the continuation of previous research by the authors.

Table 2. Moves and steps in the neurology introductions

		JAMA Neurology		**Journal of Neurology**		**The Lancet**	
Move 1	1A	10/10	100 %	10/10	100 %	10/10	100 %
	1B	9/10	90 %	9/10	90 %	9/10	90 %
Move 2	1A	8/10	80 %	7/10	70 %	9/10	90 %
	1B	4/10	40 %	7/10	70 %	5/10	50 %
	2			5/10	50 %	6/10	60 %
	3			1/10	10 %	2/10	20 %
Move 3	1	9/10	90 %	10/10	100 %	10/10	100 %
	2					4/10	40 %
	3						
	4	1/10	10 %	1/10	10 %	1/10	10 %
	5						
	6	1/10	10 %			1/10	10 %
	7						

For Move 3, except for text JN-3 commented on above (Sample text 2), all the introductions in neurology presented the new study descriptively or introduced the aims by means of Step 1. Four introductions included Step 2 to present the research questions or hypotheses. Only three introductions summarized methodological aspects employed in the study by using Step 4 and only two articles established the value of the investigation by means of Step 6. It should be noted that Steps 3, 5 and 7 were not present in any of the RA introductions in neurology for definitional clarifications, main results or specification of the article structure.

With regard to the order of the moves and steps, all the introductions started with Move 1 and twenty-seven began with Step 1A. The other three displayed minor variations. One of the articles started with Step 1B without presenting a more general contextual statement:

(1) Recent studies have proposed a potential link between celiac disease (CD) and ALS [1, 2], and suggest that sensitivity to gluten (GS) may occur in a subgroup of patients, who may then benefit from a gluten-free diet (GFD) [2]. (JON-19)

Another variation combined Steps 1A and 1B in the opening sentence, characterizing the phenomenon being studied and supporting this with data obtained in previous research.

(2) Cognitive impairment in multiple sclerosis can occur from the earliest stages of the disease and its prevalence can exceed 80% in some studies of secondary progressive multiple sclerosis (SPMS). [1,2] (TLN-22)

The third variation involved including in the general opening a reference to the problematic nature of the phenomenon investigated:

(3) Falls aetiology in people with Parkinson's disease (PD) is complex and multi-dimensional. (JON-15)

This was considered a blend of Step 1A from Move 1 with Step 1A from Move 2, since the purpose of the study was to through light on the complexity by identifying features to distinguish different patient risks.

Finally, all the neurology introductions, except (JN-3), presented Move 3, which always appeared at the end of the introduction after Moves 1 and 2 in a single cycle or multiple cycles.

3.2. Paediatrics

Table 3 summarizes the rhetorical structure of the RA introductions in paediatrics.

Table 3. Rhetorical structure in the paediatrics introductions

	Nº of articles	%
Articles that follow Swales' CARS model		
M1 – M2 – M1 – M2 – M3	8	26,67 %
M1 – M2 – M1 – M2 – M1 – M2 – M3	6	20 %
M1 – M2 – M3	5	16,67 %
M1 – M2 – M1 – M2 – M1 – M2 – M1 – M2 – M1 – M2 – M1 – M2 – M3	3	10 %
M1 – M2 – M1 – M3	2	6,67 %
M1 – M2 – M1 – M2 – M1 – M2 – M1 – M2 – M3	1	3,33 %
M1 – M2 – M1 – M2 - M1- M2 – M1 – M3	1	3,33 %
M1 – M2 – M1 _ M2 – M1 – M3	1	3,33 %
M1 – M2 – M1 – M2 – M1 – M2 – M1 – M2 – M1 – M3	1	3,33 %
M1 – M2 – M1 – M2 – M1 – M2 – M1 – M2 – M1 – M2 – M3	1	3,33 %
Articles that do not follow Swales' CARS model		
M1 – M2 – M1 – M2 – M1 – M2 – M1 – M2 – M1 – M2 – M1 – M2	1	3,33 %
Total number of articles	30	

All the articles, except one, followed, in some way, the CARS model. Only five introductions presented the strict M1-M2-M3 pattern without cyclicity and the others combined Moves 1 and 2 before the occupation of the niche. The most frequently used pattern, found in eight introductions, had two M1–M2 cycles before the third move, while six introductions included three M1–M2 cycles before Move 3. Overall, twenty-four of the thirty introductions in paediatrics displayed cyclicity of Moves 1 and 2 to a greater or lesser extent. These results are consistent those of *Crookes (1986)* and the association of cyclicity with text length. Sample text 3 illustrates the analysis of a paediatrics introduction that follows the strict CARS M1-M2-M3 pattern.

Sample text 3

TEJOP-48		
Renal function in neonates with twin-twin transfusion syndrome treated with or without fetoscopic laser surgery	Move	Step
Twin-twin transfusion syndrome (TTTS) is a serious complication that occurs in *10–15 %* of monochorionic twin pregnancies and results from unbalanced inter-twin blood transfusion through placental vascular anastomoses [1].	1	1A
TTTS is detected by prenatal ultrasound and *is characterized* by the presence of polyhydramnios in the recipient twin due to hypervolemia and polyuria, and oligohydramnios in the donor due to hypovolemia, renal hypoperfusion, and oliguria.	1	1A
TTTS can be treated antenatally with serial amnioreduction, but the optimal treatment is coagulation of the vascular anastomoses with fetoscopic laser surgery [2].	1	1A
Laser surgery is associated with a significant reduction in perinatal *morbidity and mortality* [3].	1	1A
As a result of the increase in perinatal survival, *attention is now shifting* toward short-term and long-term morbidity in survivors.	1	1A
Several small studies in TTTS not treated with laser surgery reported various renal complications in donor twins after birth, caused by impaired renal perfusion, including histological renal changes such as hypovascularisation and microangiopathy *[4–8]*.	1	1B
Whether postnatal renal dysfunction also occurs in twins affected by TTTS treated with laser surgery *is not well known, as only few small studies* have been published *to date [9, 10*].	2	1A
The aim of this retrospective study is to investigate the short-term postnatal renal function in a large cohort of TTTS twins treated with laser surgery (laser group), compared to a group of TTTS twins treated conservatively with either serial amnioreduction or expectant management (non-laser group) and evaluate potential risk factors such as incomplete laser surgery and donor status.	3	1

Only one paediatrics introduction did not follow the CARS model as it lacked a Move 3. After a critical review of relevant studies on the relationship between arterial and venous blood gas (ABG and VBG, respectively) levels, the authors state a hypothesis but only in general terms (Move 2 Step 1B):

> (4) Understanding the level of agreement between arterial and venous lactate, and how this agreement changes as these values increase, *will demonstrate* whether VBGs *could act* as a surrogate for ABGs; or alternatively, an ABG *should* always *be sought* to confirm a venous measurement when identifying sepsis in children. (TEJOP-46)

However, this was not signalled as a Move 3 through the characteristic markers, such as *this/ the present study* or first-person reference (*Swales, 1981*, p. 76) to indicate it as the hypothesis to be tested.

As in the anomalous neurology introduction, an overlap was found between the Introduction and Methods sections since the description of the study appeared at the start of the Methods section, which also included the main objective, as shown in sample text 4:

Sample text 4

Methods This was a retrospective, cohort study of paediatric intensive care patients over the course of three years and four months between June 2012 and October 2015.	Move 3 Step 1
The setting was the PICU department of a large London-based hospital, with an annual intake of approximately 650 patients a year. Data was collected from the trust's online electronic patient database ("iCLIP") or from patient paper notes. As this was a service evaluation, with no study interventions or deviations from usual practice, neither consent nor ethical approval was required.	
The inclusion criteria encompassed children with sepsis, neutropenic sepsis and septic shock (≤17 years of age), who had a VBG taken first, then an ABG taken after within one hour. The lactate and pH values measured by each method were analysed. Premature infants, patients admitted without sepsis and those who received a fluid bolus between the two blood gas samples were excluded from this study. The main objective was to assess the level of agreement between arterial and venous lactate and pH measurements through calculating the mean difference (MD) with 95 % limits of agreement (LOA) (mean difference ± 1.96× standard deviation). This data was then used to construct two Bland-Altman plots, one being mean lactate vs difference in lactate and the other being mean pH vs difference in pH.	Move 3 Step 1

Table 4 summarizes the different moves and steps present in the paediatrics RA introductions. All the introductions included Step 1A from Move 1 to contextualize the topic or the phenomenon studied before the development of the article, and all, except one, introduced other previous research in the area by means of Step 1B.

Table 4. Moves and steps in the paediatrics introductions

		JP		**TEJOP**		**BMCP**	
Move 1	1A	10/10	100 %	10/10	100 %	10/10	100 %
	1B	9/10	90 %	10/10	100 %	10/10	100 %
Move 2	1A	9/10	90 %	10/10	100 %	9/10	90 %
	1B	5/10	50 %	2/10	20 %	3/10	30 %
	2	3/10	30 %	3/10	30 %	1/10	10 %
	3	1/10	10 %	1/10	10 %		
Move 3	1	10/10	100 %	9/10	90 %	10/10	100 %
	2	2/10	20 %	1/10	10 %	2/10	20 %
	3						
	4	2/10	20 %				
	5						
	6	1/10	10 %			1/10	10 %
	7						

In Move 2, twenty-eight of the thirty introductions established a gap in knowledge in a Step 1A, indicating something that had not previously been investigated, or a need to study a specific issue or phenomenon. Step 1B was included in ten introductions to raise questions about the topic and Step 2 appeared in seven introductions to present a positive justification for carrying out the study. Only two articles indicated that the present study was a continuation of the authors' previous research by means of Step 3.

For Move 3, all the introductions, except one, included Step 1 to present the study descriptively or purposively. Only five articles made use of Step 2 to present research questions or the hypothesis to be tested in the study. Steps 4 and 6 were employed in only two introductions to summarize the methods and to express the importance of the study. As in the neurology texts, Steps 3, 5 and 7 were not present in any of the paediatrics introductions.

With regard to the order of steps and moves, all the RA introductions in paediatrics opened with Move 1, twenty-seven with step 1A and one with 1B.

> (5) Stunting in under-five children has been established as a risk factor for reduced intellectual performance and job productivity in later life, particularly when this stunting occurs in the first 2 years of life [1]. (BMCP-53)

Another introduction started with a combination of Steps 1A and 1B, thus establishing the phenomenon to be studied and referring to data obtained in previous research:

> (6) One-third of American children are overweight or obese,[1] which is associated with significant negative health outcomes. [2-8] (JP-33)

A final variation was seen in an introduction that included Step 1A from Move 2 immediately after Step 1A from Move 1, thus characterizing the phenomenon studied and indicating a lack of conclusive evidence:

> (7) Adequate water intake is essential for health, but any benefit for weight management remains unclear. (JP-40)

This gap is clearly picked up in Move 3 in the aim of the study:

> (8) The aim of this study was to compare the effects of recommending consumption of 8 cups of water per day on weight loss in adolescents with overweight or obesity during a 6-month weight-reducing diet. (JP-40)

Finally, in all the paediatrics introductions, except (TEJOP-46), Move 3 is always located at the end after Moves 1 and 2 either as a single cycle or in multiple cycles.

3.3. Comparison of the Two Subfields

Figure 2 compares the rhetorical structure employed in the RA introductions in neurology and paediatrics. The results show no differences between the two subdisciplines, which follow the CARS model. Most introductions present one or more M1–M2 cycles to establish the territory and existing gaps in knowledge to motivate new research, and then introduce the study in Move 3. A relatively small number of introductions, six in neurology and five in paediatrics, follow the M1-M2-M3 pattern. Those that display this pattern tend to be shorter than those exhibiting greater cyclicity of Moves 1 and 2 before the occupation of the niche (*Crookes, 1986*; *Swales, 1990*). Only one introduction in each subdiscipline was found to deviate from the CARS model by omitting one or more moves. In these cases, statements similar to those that occur in the missing moves were located in the methods section, which suggests that there exists a degree of overlap between Move 3 and the opening of this section.

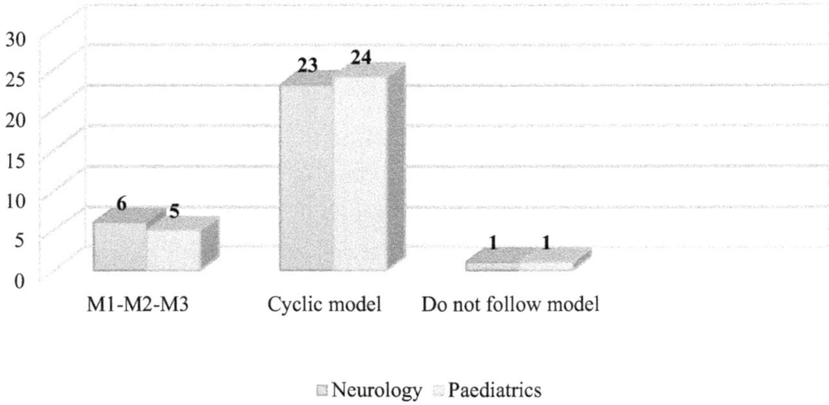

Figure 2. Comparison of the order of the rhetorical structure in neurology and paediatrics

Figure 3 compares the two subdisciplines in relation to the frequency of the patterns of cyclicity. The most frequent were the two- and three-cycle patterns, which overall were each used in 14 introductions, the former occurring eight times in paediatrics and six in neurology with the figures reversed for the three-cycle pattern. Other longer multiple-cycle patterns were those with four and six cycles, each occurring overall in four introductions: the four-cycle pattern was used three times in neurology and only once in paediatrics and these figures were reversed for the six-cycle pattern.

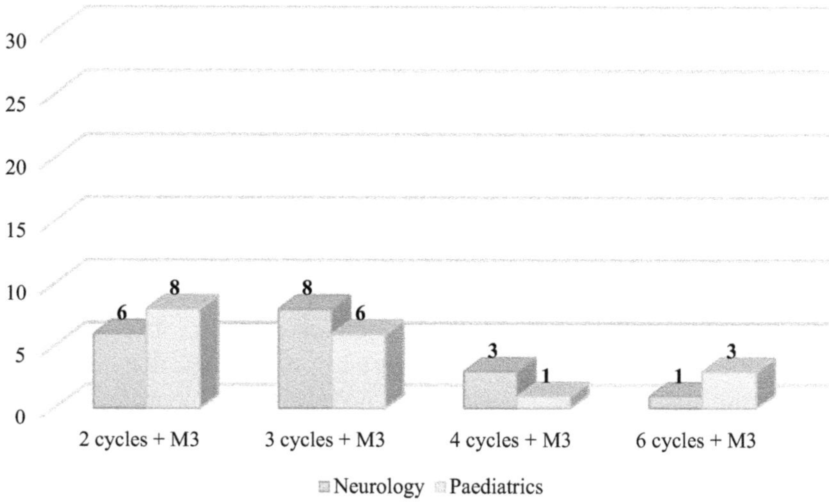

Figure 3. Most frequent patterns of cyclicity in neurology and paediatrics

Table 5 gives the data for moves and steps for neurology and paediatrics RA introductions. All make use of Move 1 to establish the territory and all, except one neurology text (JN-3) establish a niche in the research field. Move 3 is present in all the introductions except one in each field (JN-3 and TEJOP-46). In general, therefore, the introductions in both subdisciplines present the obligatory moves proposed by *Swales (1990, 2004)*.

Within Move 1, all the introductions begin by situating the research and establishing the importance of the topic studied (*Samraj, 2002*). This is achieved through Step 1A, which contextualizes the phenomenon being investigated indicating that it is relevant, interesting or challenging in some way (*Swales & Feak, 2012*). Moreover, most include Step 1B to introduce and evaluate previous related research in the field. In this case, a small difference was observed between the two subfields in that one paediatric but three neurology introductions did not make explicit use of this step. This does not mean that the writers did not refer to previous research, but that numerical citations were appended to general statements with no overt mention of the cited authors, studies, reports or findings included in the text, i.e. Step 1A-type statements supported by parenthetical or superscript numbers.

Within Move 2, Step 1A, which indicates a lack of knowledge or a problematic aspect that needs to be addressed, was slightly more frequent in paediatrics than in neurology introductions (twenty-eight versus twenty-four). In contrast, the neurology texts made more use of Step 2B to raise questions and to hypothesize than the paediatrics texts (sixteen versus eleven). More neurology introductions presented a positive justification for the study in a Step 2 (eleven versus seven). Step 3, as defined in this study to indicate a continuation of the authors' own previous research, was relatively rare, present in three neurology and two paediatrics introductions. It should be noted that the neurology study lacking Moves 2 and 3 was also an extension of the authors' previous research as made clear in the Methods section (see Sample text 1).

For Move 3, a descriptive or purposive statement introducing the new study was identified in all the neurology and paediatrics introductions except the two anomalous texts, where these statements were located in the Methods. This supports the obligatory nature of Step 1 (*Swales, 1990*). Of the other steps, four neurology and five paediatrics introductions included Step 2 to present research questions to be addressed or hypotheses to be tested; three neurology and two paediatrics texts described methodological aspects in Step 4; and two introductions in each subdiscipline used Step 6 to make a positive evaluation of the contribution of the study. These results confirm the optionality of these Steps (*Swales, 1990*). Steps 3, 5 and 7 were absent from the introductions in both subdisciplines. This may be attributed to the strong adherence to the IMRAD model in biomedical RAs. Definitions, selection criteria and classification details are characteristic of the Methods section. Specific results are less likely to be foregrounded in the introduction than the overall significance of the study (as seen in the few instances of Step 6). Finally, the rigid IMRAD format, which has been referred to as a "straitjacket" that stifles "personality and sparkle" (*Lock, 1988*, p. 156), makes specification of the article structure unnecessary in medical RAs.

Table 5. Moves and steps in RA introductions of neurology and paediatrics

	Neurology		Paediatrícs	
	N° of introductions	%	N° of introductions	%
Move 1	30/30	100 %	30/30	100 %
Step1A	30/30	100 %	30/30	100 %
Step 1B	27/30	90 %	29/30	96,67 %
Move 2	29/30	96,67 %	30/30	100 %
Step 1A	24/30	80 %	28/30	93,33 %
Step 1B	16/30	53,33 %	10/30	33,33 %
Step 2	11/30	36,67 %	7/30	22,33 %
Step 3	3/30	10 %	2/30	6,67 %
Move 3	29/30	96,67 %	29/30	96,67 %
Step 1	29/30	96,67 %	29/30	96,67 %
Step 2	4/30	13,33 %	5/30	16,67 %
Step 3				
Step 4	3/30	10 %	2/30	6,67 %
Step 5				
Step 6	2/30	6,67 %	2/30	6,67 %
Step 7				

4. Discussion

This study had as its main aim to analyze and compare the rhetorical structure of the RA introductions of two medical subdisciplines: neurology and paediatrics. We decided to work with RA introductions because it is the section in which authors have to present themselves as credible researchers, introduce other authors in the field, demonstrate that the topic is relevant and that there is a need or gap to be filled to justify the present study. In this sense, introduction sections have been viewed as "essentially exercises in public relations" (*Swales, 1984*, p. 82).

The results show that most introductions in both subdisciplines reflect Swales' CARS model (1990, 2004) both overall and, in many cases, its rhetorical structure components. The findings have important pedagogical implications in the design of activities and ESP courses for medical students and professionals in the field. The regularity in the rhetorical structure allows guidelines to be established since, as *Biber et al. (2007, p.* 40) point out, "[p]rototypes are particularly valuable in educational and training contexts to help novices learn to understand and produce a genre that is new to them". These prototypes should provide typical patterns for each subdiscipline, so that learners have the opportunity to work with the rhetorical structures and learn to identify and use them when writing their own articles (*Swales, 1990*). Working with genre in class with such texts can be really meaningful and help students to improve their analytical skills by focusing on the specific generic features that they will actually have to read or write (*Dudley-Evans, 2000*, p. 10). In ESP courses for non-native speakers with time constraints on their learning needs, it is important that they should become familiar with the genre-specific rhetorical structure of the texts in their discipline (*Dudley-Evans, 2000*).

To conclude, this study has shown that the rhetorical patterns in the introduction sections of neurology and paediatrics RAs generally conform to the model proposed by *Swales (1990*, *2004)* and the results indicate that with certain reservations, such as the optional Steps 3, 5 and 7 in Move 3, the model can serve as a useful pedagogical tool for interdisciplinary instruction on genre in biomedical contexts.

References

Amnuai, W. (2019). Analyses of rhetorical moves and linguistic realizations in accounting research article abstracts published in international and Thai-based journals. *SAGE Open, 9*(1), 1–9. https://doi.org/10.1177/2158244018822384.

Biber, D., Connor, U., & Upton, T. A. (2007). *Discourse on the move: Using corpus analysis to describe discourse structure*. Amsterdam, Netherlands: John Benjamins Publishing Company.

Bruce, I. (2014). Expressing criticality in the literature review in research article introductions in applied linguistics and psychology. *English for Specific Purposes, 36*, 85–96. https://doi.org/10.1016/j.esp.2014.06.004.

Bunton, D. (2005). The structure of PhD conclusion chapters. *Journal of English for Academic Purposes, 4*(3), 207–224. https://doi.org/10.1016/j.jeap.2005.03.004.

Cardinali, R. F. (2015). Uso de sustantivos evaluativos en artículos de investigación en inglés: un estudio de corpus. In M. Pascual (Ed.), *La evaluación en el discurso científico: Aportes a la comprensión del diálogo de pares* (pp. 93–108). San Luis, Argentina: Nueva Editorial Universitaria. Available at: http://www.neu.unsl.edu.ar/wp-content/uploads/2018/03/La-Evaluacion-en-el-Discurso.pdf.

Cortés, V. (2013). The purpose of this study is to: Connecting lexical bundles and moves in research article introductions. *Journal of English for Academic Purposes, 12*(1), 33–43. https://doi.org/10.1016/j.jeap.2012.11.002.

Cotos, E., Huffman, S., & Link, S. (2017). A move/step model for methods sections: Demonstrating rigour and credibility. *English for Specific Purposes, 46*, 90–106. https://doi.org/10.1016/j.esp.2017.01.001.

Crookes, G. (1986). Towards a validated analysis of scientific text structure. *Applied Linguistics, 7*(1), 57–70. https://doi.org/10.1093/applin/7.1.57.

Davis, R. H. (2015). *A genre analysis of medical research articles*. PhD thesis.

Del Saz Rubio, M. M. (2011). A pragmatic approach to the macro-structure and metadiscoursal features of research article introductions in the field of Agricultural Sciences. *English for Specific Purposes, 30*(4), 258–271. https://doi.org/10.1016/j.esp.2011.03.002.

Dudley-Evans, T. (2000). Genre analysis: A key to a theory of ESP? *Ibérica, 2*, 3–11.

Fryer, D. (2012). Analysis of the generic discourse features of the English-language medical research article: A systemic-functional approach. *Functions of Language, 19*(1), 5–37.

Holmes, R. (1997). Genre analysis, and the social sciences: An investigation of the structure of research article discussion sections in three disciplines. *English for Specific Purposes, 16*(4), 321–337. https://doi.org/10.1016/S0889-4906(96)00038-5.

Kanoksilapatham, B. (2012). Structure of research article introductions in three engineering subdisciplines. *IEEE Transactions on Professional Communication, 55*(4), 294–309. https://doi.org/10.1109/TPC.2012.2223252.

Li, L., & Ge, G. (2009). Genre analysis: Structural and linguistic evolution of the English-medium medical research article (1985–2004). *English for Specific Purposes, 28*(2), 93–104.

Lim, J. M. H. (2010). Commenting on research results in applied linguistics and education: A comparative genre-based investigation. *Journal of English for Academic Purposes, 9*(4), 280–294. https://doi.org/10.1016/j.jeap.2010.10.001.

Lock, S. (1988). Structured abstracts. *British Medical Journal, 297*, 156.

Mur-Dueñas, P. (2016). Self-reference in research articles across Europe and Asia: A review of studies. *Brno Studies in English, 42*(1), 71–92. https://doi.org/10.5817/BSE2016-1-4.

Nwogu, K. (1997). The medical research paper: Structure and functions. *English for Specific Purposes, 16*(2), 119–138.

Salager-Meyer, F. (1990). Discoursal flaws in Medical English abstracts: A genre analysis per research- and text-type. *Text – Interdisciplinary Journal for the Study of Discourse, 10*(4), 365–384. https://doi.org/10.1515/text.1.1990.10.4.365.

Samraj, B. (2002). Introductions in research articles: Variation across disciplines. *English for Specific Purposes, 21*(1), 1–17. https://doi.org/10.1016/S0889-4906(00)00023-5

Samraj, B. (2005). An exploration of a genre set: Research article abstracts and introductions in two disciplines. *English for Specific Purposes, 24*(2), 141–156. https://doi.org/10.1016/j.esp.2002.10.001

Skelton, J. (1994). Analysis of the structure of original research papers: An aid to writing original papers for publication. *British Journal of General Practice, 44*(387), 455–459.

Soler-Monreal, C. (2016). A move-step analysis of the concluding chapters in computer science PhD theses. *Ibérica, 32*, 105–132. http://hdl.handle.net/10251/80709.

Swales, J. M. (1981). *Aspects of article introductions.* Birmingham, United Kingdom: The University of Aston, Language Studies Unit.

Swales, J. (1984). Research into the structure of introductions to journal articles and its application to the teaching of academic writing. In R. Williams & J. Kirkman (Eds.), *Common grounds: Shared interests in ESP and communication studies* (pp. 77–86). New York: Pergamon Press.

Swales, J. M. (1990). *Genre analysis: English in academic and research settings*. Cambridge: Cambridge University Press.

Swales, J. M. (2004). *Research genres: Explorations and applications.* Cambridge: Cambridge University Press.

Swales, J. M., & Feak, C. B. (2012). *Academic writing for graduate students: essential tasks and skills* (3rd ed.). Ann Arbor: University of Michigan Press.

Williams, I. A. (1999). Results section of medical research articles: Analysis of rhetorical categories for pedagogical purposes. *English for Specific Purposes, 18*(4), 347–366. https://doi.org/10.1016/S0889-4906(98)00003-9.

BEGOÑA BELLÉS-FORTUÑO / LUCÍA BELLÉS-CALVERA

Universitat Jaume I / Universitat de València

Metadiscourse Patterns in Research Articles: Disciplinary and Cross-cultural Variations of Engagement Markers

1. Introduction

Over the last decades, academic writing has undergone a significant evolution, departing from its former characterization as an objective and impersonal form of communication. Instead, it is now recognized as an interactive and dynamic process wherein writers actively engage with readers, employing linguistic resources to convey disciplinary knowledge (*Crismore et al., 1993*; *Hyland, 2005*; *Jiang & Hyland, 2018*; *Penris & Verspoor, 2017*). At the core of academic writing lies the concept of metadiscourse, which encompasses self-reflective expressions used to negotiate interactional meanings and establish connections with readers, as noted by *Hyland (2005)*.

Previous studies indicate that researchers with diverse linguistic backgrounds employ metadiscoursal elements for two primary purposes: (a) disseminating disciplinary knowledge and (b) contributing to the construction of scientific discourse. Some scholars suggest that writers' decisions in this regard might be shaped by national culture and the norms prevailing within their local academic communities. This potential influence has been explored by analyzing research articles written in English by non-native scholars from several nations, such as Spain (*Aguilar & Khan, 2022*; *Carrió-Pastor, 2016*; *Pérez Llantada, 2007*), Greece (*Moreti, 2019*), Sweden (*Bergqvist, 2020*), Finland (*Mauranen, 1993*), Turkey (*Köroğlu, 2018*), Iran (*Khalili & Aslanabadi,*

2014; *Golmohammadi et al., 2014*), and Korea (*Chang, 2015*). These investigations commonly involve comparing these articles with those authored by English or American authors. Consequently, it becomes apparent that cultural differences could impact academic conventions, depending on the language employed (*Crismore & Abdollehzadeh, 2010*; *Dafouz-Milne, 2008*; *Hyland et al., 2022*; *Mur-Dueñas, 2011*; *Ozdemir & Longo, 2014*). In this sense, variations in the use of linguistic features, such as personal pronouns, hedges, negations, counterclaims, proclaims, conjunctions, and reporting verbs may be identified (*Abasi, 2012*; *Jiang, 2020*).

With this in mind, there is a need for further investigation into the metadiscoursal conventions employed in English and Spanish research articles (RAs) as this is one of the most popular genres for the dissemination of knowledge in academia (*Swales, 1990*). This study seeks to understand how academic writing is (dis)similar in English and Spanish by analysing engagement markers in research articles addressing three areas of study, including Medicine, Engineering and Linguistics. for interactional features of metadiscourse (i.e., stance and engagement). The study is significant as it compares papers published in well-known international journals in two of the most used languages around the world. By focusing specifically on engagement markers, we seek to shed light on how writers construct persuasive arguments and foster inclusive relationships with their readers. This research not only contributes to our understanding of academic writing practices but also has practical implications for language teaching and scholarly communication in diverse academic contexts.

The current study is carried out within the frame of the IAMET project[1] where a large contrastive corpus of Spanish and English journal articles from different disciplines has been gathered. Concepts such as systematicity and the problems of parallel corpora also find their place in this study (*Aijmer, 1997*; *Salkie, 1995*, *1997*), we intend to take a similarity assessment (*Chesterman, 1998*) as understood by contrastive linguistics in terms of the number of shared and distinctive features in

1 *IAMET Project is a competitive project granted by the Spanish Ministry of Economy and Competitivity, its acronym stands for: Identification and analysis of rhetoric elements in Spanish and in English: study of metadiscoursive strategies.

English and Spanish markers in journal articles in terms of their degree of feature matching (*Tversky, 1977*). The study of Research Article (RA) journal publications through contrastive linguistics can aid specialised writers, novel researchers and university students in the reading and understanding of a shaped RA. To carry out the analysis newly specific corpus tool software which has been developed in the frame of the aforementioned project called METOOL has been used. Along with previous authors who have largely studied Discourse Markers (DMs) (*Fraser, 1987, 1999*; *Schiffrin, 1987*), we agree on DMs having a core meaning; being this meaning strongly context-dependent rather than semantic (*Bellés-Fortuño, 2008, 2016*). Following systemic functional linguistics (*Halliday & Matthiesen, 2004*), the three dimensions or relational functions of language are the basis for the diverse classification of markers existing (*Bellés-Fortuño, 2017*) where the relevant focus of analysis lies in the relations established between writer-text and writer-reader.

Before delving into our analysis, we provide an overview of the theoretical framework guiding our study and review the existing literature on metadiscourse in academic writing.

2. Literature Review

Research articles have been regarded as a key genre in scholarly life. In academic discourse, persuasion plays a pivotal role, with scholars adopting unique perspectives and anticipating their audience's reactions to their ideas (*Deroey, 2015; Hyland, 2001, 2004*). This persuasive aspect extends to both written and spoken academic communication (e.g., *Hyland & Guinda, 2012*) because research claims often require explicit persuasion to ensure consensus. To enhance the accessibility of their findings, researchers strive to foster interaction in their discourse, aligning their stance with the audience's expectations (*Scotto di Carlo, 2015; Hyland, 2010*). Linguistic tools for academic persuasion are commonly categorized under evaluation (Hunston & Thompson, 2000) and appraisal (*Martin & White, 2005*).

One prominent framework for analyzing academic interaction is *Hyland's (2005)* interpersonal model of metadiscourse. This model can be subdivided into two different dimensions: (a) interactive and (b) interactional. Interactive resources (e.g. transitions, frame markers, endophoric markers, evidentials, and code glosses markers) refer to how discourse is organised based on writers' assumptions about readers' background knowledge, needs, and cultural expectations (*Hyland, 2005*). On the other hand, interactional resources (e.g. hedges, boosters, attitude markers, self-mentions and engagement markers) have to do with how writers engage with the content by evaluating or commenting on propositions, thus revealing their attitudes and stance in discourse. Out of the variety of rhetorical devices, engagement markers are the focus of our study since they are pivotal not only for establishing a connection with readers but also for directing their attention to support the writer's viewpoints (*Hyland, 2001*; *Hyland & Jiang, 2016*; *Jiang & Ma, 2018*). According to Hyland (2005), they serve as a means through which writers acknowledge the readers' presence, guide them through explanations, and actively involve them in the argument. *Hyland* (2001) points out that written communication is meant to be successful provided that a meaningful dialogue with the readers can take place. In essence, engagement markers foster a dialogic interaction, facilitating the connection between writers and readers in a broad textual discourse and enabling writers to anticipate reader responses. Following *Mur-Dueñas' (2011)* model, four main features are used by writers to engage readers, namely personal asides, questions, imperatives and directives.

Hyland's (2005) and *Mur-Dueñas' (2011)* frameworks are also applicable to the analysis of academic spoken discourse, where immediate feedback and engagement can be provided (*Qiu & Jiang, 2021). Martín del Pozo (2014)* and *Bellés-Calvera (2021)* explored the use of these metadiscoursal devices in Content and Language Integrated Learning settings with bilingual and multilingual speakers enrolled in different disciplinary courses.

Despite the existing research, there has been a noticeable scarcity of comparative studies examining the linguistic features of research articles across multiple disciplinary areas in both English and Spanish. Given that research articles in fields such as medical, engineering and linguistics cater to distinct audiences, an investigation into the usage of engagement markers would provide insights into reader-oriented characteristics and deepen our comprehension of cultural divergences within this genre. Therefore, this paper seeks to explore the following research questions (RQs):

RQ(1). What are the frequency, forms and functions of engagement features used in medical, engineering and linguistic research articles written in English and Spanish?

RQ(2). What similarities and differences can be observed among the three disciplines?

An account of the corpus and the fields of study examined is given in the section below. The methodological foundations and the procedures followed for the analysis of the corpus will also be provided.

3. Corpus and Method

3.1. Data Collection

For this study, aiming at exploring disciplinary and cross-cultural variations of the interpersonal dimension in English and Spanish research articles, it was necessary to review and compile corpora (*Carrió-Pastor, 2020*). Initially, an examination of available corpora in both English and Spanish languages was undertaken to assess their suitability for analyzing discourse markers. Notable Spanish corpora include the Corpus del español actual (CEA), Corpus de Referencia del Español Actual (CREA), and Corpus de aprendices de español (CAES), among others. Similarly, prominent English corpora comprise the British National Corpus (BNC), Corpus of Contemporary American English (COCA), corpora hosted by the Centre for English Corpus Linguistics at the University of Leuven, and the like. Upon identifying available corpora, it was considered that it would be more advantageous to compile and analyse our own corpus. This approach allowed us to identify discourse markers within three specialised areas of scientific articles relevant to this project: medicine, engineering, and linguistics.

Hence, the corpus for this study encompasses two academic macro-corpora, one in English and the other in Spanish, with each subdivided into the aforementioned disciplines. The Engineering corpus is composed of 64 texts in English and 65 in Spanish, reaching 684,743 and 654,214 words respectively. The medical corpus covers a broad range of specialised areas, such as dermatology, oncology, paediatrics or medical education, to name but a few. The English sub-corpus, made up of 108 texts, includes 371,548 words, whereas the Spanish sub-corpus amounts to 421,674 words with 76 research articles. As for the Linguistics corpus, 636,620 words have been identified in 80 articles of the English sub-corpus; however, its Spanish equivalent is characterized by a lower number of words and manuscripts, as seen *Table 1* below. It should be noted that all these publications were taken from renowned journals as reported by indicators like the Journal Citation Report or Scopus.

Table 1. Sub-corpora and fields of study

	English corpus		**Spanish corpus**	
	No. of words	**Texts**	**No. of words**	**Texts**
Engineering	684,743	64	654,214	65
Medicine	371,548	108	421,674	76
Linguistics	636,620	80	592,321	56
Total	1,692,911	252	1,668,209	197

These corpora were imported into METOOL, a newly developed software originating from a research project funded by the Spanish Ministry of Economy, Industry and Competitiveness (FFI2016-77941-P Project: Identification and analysis of metadiscourse strategies in Spanish and English research articles). METOOL, designed at the Research Institute for Information and Language Processing (University of Wolverhampton), serves for the labeling and identification of metadiscoursal markers. To prevent linguistic interference, this tool was replicated for each language variant. Consequently, research articles authored by native

English speakers were stored in the English version of the software, while access to articles in Spanish was facilitated through the Spanish variant of the platform.

3.2. Data Analysis

The analytical framework employed in this study is based on the taxonomies arising from the studies conducted by *Mur Dueñas (2011)* and *Salas Valdebenito (2015)*. In so doing, elements such as evidentials, logical markers, frame markers, and engagement markers were considered together with other metadiscoursal devices. For the identification of these categories, which was feasible thanks to the use of colours (*Carrió-Pastor, 2020*), different labels were incorporated in the engine to simplify the tagging process. However, in the study presented here, the focus is on engagement markers, particularly on personal asides, questions, imperatives and directives.

3.3. Procedure

Teamwork among ten researchers from the Universitat Politècnica de València, Universitat Jaume I, Universidad de Las Palmas de Gran Canaria, and the University of Wolverhampton was necessary to select the corpora. Once the corpora were assembled, the METOOL software was customized to suit the specific requirements of the corpus collection and analysis, with functionalities being incorporated and updated as the project progressed. Upon completion of the tool development, the compiled corpora and the list of discourse markers were integrated into the software. These linguistic features, previously classified, were then labeled across various categories and subcategories outlined in the theoretical frameworks established by *Hyland (2005)* and *Mur-Dueñas (2011)*. Additional features, such as unique colour coding for each category and options to denote the negative, neutral, or positive polarity of textual markers, were implemented for identification purposes.

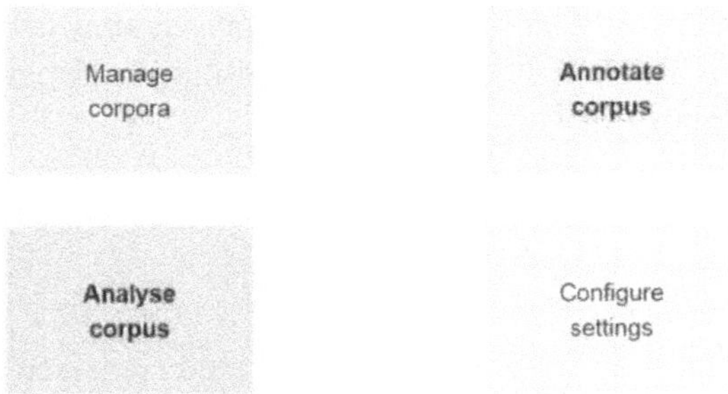

Figure 1. METOOL corpus analysis software homesite

The English corpus was labeled thanks to the allocation of tagging tasks among the project team members. Similarly, the Spanish corpus was labelled following the same procedure, with all markers and categories introduced into the tool. After both corpora were tagged, serving as the foundation for evolving the tool into a discourse marker analyser for academic texts, quantitative analyses were conducted on cases. Examples were extracted from texts based on discipline, verifying the accuracy of each researcher's annotation of the corpus.

The next section will present the key findings regarding the occurrence of engagement markers in research articles dealing with medicine, engineering and linguistics.

4. Results and Discussion

This section is devoted to analysing the linguistic features that academic writers use to express engagement in research articles published in English and Spanish. As shown above in the framework, the features used to express such interactional relationships in the text are personal asides, questions, imperatives and directives.

Figure 2 below shows the number of occurrences of engagements markers in both the English and the Spanish corpora. The findings reveal that there are differences in the use of engagement markers (i.e.

personal references, questions, imperatives and directives), with occurrences in the field of Linguistics outnumbering those in Medicine and Engineering.

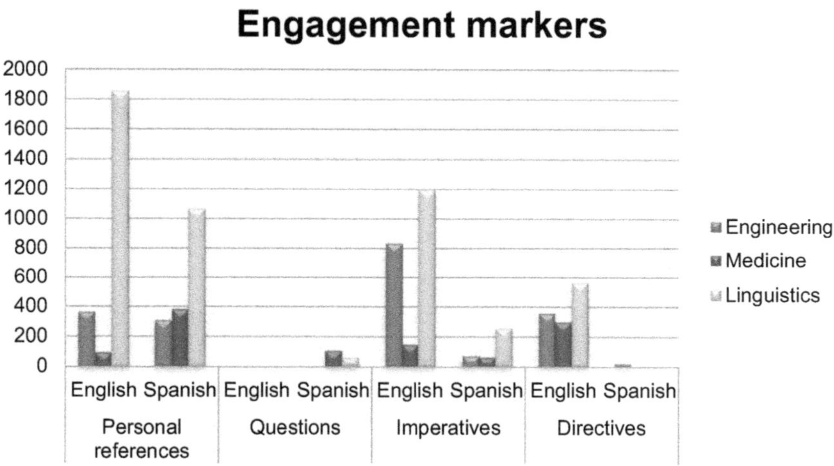

Figure 2. Frequency of engagement markers in the English and Spanish sub-corpora

As regards the English corpus, personal asides appear to be the most recurrent category in Linguistics articles, followed by imperatives, directives and questions. Within the Engineering sub-corpus, imperatives are the preferred metadiscoursal feature in written productions where English is the vehicular language, whilst the incidence of personal references and directives declines to a certain extent, occupying the second and third position respectively. In contrast, the number of engagement markers drops significantly in medical research articles, with directives being the most common category in medical research articles; other regular items are imperatives and personal asides. There was no occurrence of questions as an engagement feature in the English corpus. These results may be attributed to the nature of research articles, which may be perceived as formal pieces of text that should keep impersonal constructions.

On the other hand, the Spanish corpus is characterised by a lower incidence of metadiscoursal devices. In this case, personal asides are highly used in the three fields under study, being much more frequent in Linguistics as opposed to Medicine and Engineering. The same applies for imperatives, but in this case Medicine with the lower occurrence of markers. When it comes to questions, these are non-existent in Engineering but can be found in Medicine and Linguistics. Surprisingly, writers of medical research articles are likely to use more of these devices compared to scholars addressing linguistic issues. As for the absence of directives, we may relate this finding to cross-cultural differences in the standards of academic writing.

4.1. Personal Asides

Addressing the reader in a direct way is a clear sign that the writer acknowledges the active role of a potential audience. However, the use of first-person pronouns is notable in the corpus, particularly within linguistics (e.g. we, us, one, our, me, note that, you, my) and engineering texts (One, our, we, us, you, me). Unlike these two domains where second-person pronouns are also evident, they are remarkably absent in medical articles (e.g. one, our, we, us). It should also be noted that the reduction in the occurrence of personal asides in engineering and medical texts indicates a reluctance among writers to establish direct and personal rapport with their readers, as reported by *Hyland and Jiang (2016)*. As with the English corpus, first-person pronouns can be observed in linguistics (e.g. nos, nosotros, -mos, nuestra, nuestro), engineering (e.g. -mos, nos) and medicine (e.g. nuestro, nuestra, nosotros, -mos). Nonetheless, third-person pronouns are also common in the three areas (e.g. le, su, sus).

First-person and indefinite pronouns are used by scholars to make the readers participate actively in their argument. Evidence may be found in the examples below:

(1) The OLS coefficient indicates that for every grade point increase in F1 and F2, **one** may expect a reduction of 0.113 and 0.0518, respectively. (Engineering)

(2) As **our** health care system evolves and there are more care options, urgent care serves as a community navigator [. . .] (Medicine).

(3) As **we** have seen, corpus based keyword analysis has already been utilized [. . .] (Linguistics).
(4) Por los resultados obtenidos **podemos** concluir que los compuestos que se extraen [. . .] (Engineering).
(5) Según **nuestra** hipótesis, las subordinadas encabezadas [. . .] (Linguistics).

In example (1), the first-person pronoun "one" is used to establish a connection between the writer and the reader, suggesting a shared understanding and involvement in the subject matter. This fosters a sense of collaboration and mutual engagement, where the reader is invited to interpret the findings alongside the writer.

Example (2) demonstrates the use of "our" to create a sense of inclusivity and shared responsibility. By referring to "our health care system," the writer positions themselves as part of the collective effort to understand and address issues within the healthcare system. This not only engages the reader but also emphasizes a collective perspective on the topic.

In (3), the writer uses "we" to imply shared knowledge or experiences between themselves and the reader. By stating "As we have seen," the writer acknowledges the reader's participation in the discussion, reinforcing the idea of collaboration and joint exploration of the topic.

Example (4) employs the first-person plural pronoun "nuestra" (our) to assert ownership or involvement in the research process. This helps establish credibility and authority, indicating that the conclusions drawn are based on collective analysis and interpretation.

Finally, in (5), the writer uses "nuestra" (our) to introduce a hypothesis, implying a shared perspective or assumption between the writer and the reader. This creates a sense of involvement and investment in the argument, encouraging the reader to consider the hypothesis in the context of their shared understanding.

Overall, the strategic use of first-person or indefinite pronouns in academic writing serves to foster a sense of connection, collaboration, and shared understanding between the writer and the reader, enhancing the overall effectiveness of the communication.

4.2. Questions

As previously mentioned, questions addressed directly to the reader are relatively uncommon in research articles within fields like medicine, engineering, and linguistics. Several reasons may explain this when publishing in the English language, such as formality, focus or standards. Generally speaking, academic writing in these fields typically maintains a formal and objective tone. Addressing the reader directly with questions may be perceived as too informal or conversational, potentially undermining the credibility and professionalism of the research. In addition, research articles in these disciplines prioritise presenting data, analysis, and interpretations. Authors aim to convey information efficiently and objectively, focusing on the research findings rather than engaging the reader with rhetorical questions. Thus, while engagement with the reader can be effective in other contexts, such as persuasive writing or educational materials, it may not align with the expectations of the academic audience in these disciplines.

When addressing the reader in Spanish, the occurrence of questions may be higher in research articles. Due to cultural norms, Spanish speakers have a more direct and expressive communication style compared to English. As a result, authors writing in Spanish may feel more comfortable using rhetorical questions to engage readers and stimulate their interest. Apart from that, the fact that the Spanish language offers greater flexibility in sentence structure and word order compared to English may allow authors to seamlessly integrate questions into their writing without disrupting the flow or coherence of the text.

(6) **¿Por qué** esa escasez de investigaciones sociolingüistas detalladas sobre un fenómeno que ha contado con tanta atención al otro lado del océano y al que, incluso por estos lares, se han acercado diversos dialectólogos**?** (*Why this scarcity of detailed sociolinguistic research on a phenomenon that has received so much attention on the other side of the ocean and to which, even on these shores, various dialectologists have approached?*) (Linguistics).

The use of direct questions in Example 6, "¿Por qué esa escasez de investigaciones sociolingüistas detalladas sobre un fenómeno que ha contado con tanta atención al otro lado del océano y al que, incluso por estos lares, se han acercado diversos dialectólogos?", can be explained by the long tradition of engaging through dialogue and inquiry in academic writing. In Spanish culture, rhetorical questions are often used to stimulate critical thinking and invite readers to reflect on complex issues. Likewise, by posing the question, the author highlights the need for further investigation and invites readers to contemplate potential explanations or solutions. Hence, these rhetorical strategies are deeply rooted in the conventions of Spanish academic writing and contribute to a more interactive and engaging discourse.

4.3. Imperatives

In research articles dealing with linguistics, medicine, and engineering, imperatives are occasionally used to convey instructions or recommendations to the reader. However, their usage and prevalence vary across disciplines due to differences in writing conventions, rhetorical styles, and the nature of the subject matter.

In linguistics research articles, imperatives may be employed to instruct readers on how to conduct experiments or analyses. For example, researchers might use imperatives to guide readers through the steps of data collection, analysis, or interpretation. Common verbs used in imperatives in linguistics articles include: consider, note that, see, suppose, notice, possible, argument, and assume. In Spanish, the most recuent verbs are: analizar, valorar, poder, pensar, or tener, among others. However, the first person is also used to give this imperative sense (e.g. recordemos, dejemos, pensemos, analicemos).

As for medicine, imperatives are often used to provide recommendations or guidelines for clinical practice or research methodology. For instance, authors may use imperatives to suggest diagnostic procedures, treatment protocols, or preventive measures. Common verbs found in imperatives in medical articles include: consider, see and assume, whereas in Spanish the use of the verbs is similar to that of linguistics (e.g. poder, valorar, tener, aportar, analizar, ser, recordar, dejar)

Turning to engineering research articles, imperatives are commonly employed to outline procedures, protocols, or methodologies for conducting experiments or implementing solutions. Engineers may use imperatives to specify steps for designing, building, testing, or troubleshooting systems or devices. Common verbs used in imperatives in engineering articles involve: see, consider, note that, notice, suppose, assume, and indicate.

In certain contexts where clear, concise instructions or recommendations are needed, imperatives can be effective in conveying information and guiding readers through complex processes or procedures.

(7) However, consider the possibility that a patient has an acute care need, calls EMS, but does not need hospital based services [. . .] (Medicine).
(8) Notice that it is not important if the first calculation [. . .] (Engineering).

In Example 7 the reader's attention is directed to a specific scenario where some kind of action should be taken. Then, Example 8 is characterized by the use of "Notice" to draw attention to a particular point or observation. It prompts the reader to pay attention to the fact that the first calculation mentioned is not significant or relevant to the discussion. This imperative is employed to guide the reader's interpretation of the information presented and to emphasize the importance of focusing on the subsequent calculations that are more pertinent to the topic at hand.

Regarding differences between Spanish and English research articles in the use of imperatives, it is worth mentioning that both languages may use imperatives for similar purposes, such as giving instructions, providing guidance, or emphasizing key points. However, there may be subtle variations in the frequency or tone of imperative usage due to differences in cultural norms, writing conventions, and linguistic nuances between the two languages.

4.4. Directives

As regards directives, items such as "should", "need to", "must", "consider" and "note that" are commonly used to convey recommendations, requirements, or important observations. The same occurs in Spanish with verbs like "tener" or "considear". These directives serve to guide readers' understanding of the research findings and implications. Evidence may be found in example 9 where "should not be applied" indicates specific actions or precautions that should be taken into account in medical practice or research.

(9) LET should not be applied to mucous membranes because [...] (Medicine).

In engineering research articles, similar directives like "must", "should", "need to", "propose", and "may" are prevalent. In Spanish research articles these correspond to "notar", "ser", "tener" or "calcular". These directives often outline requirements, recommendations, or suggestions for implementing engineering solutions or interpreting experimental results. In this case, phrases like the ones in Example 10 highlight important considerations or potential variations in engineering analyses or methodologies. When it comes to Example 11, the verb "notar" (to notice) is conjugated in the imperative form "Nótese" to instruct or urge the reader to take note of a particular detail or aspect mentioned in the text. This helps ensure clarity and comprehension.

(10) Those interpreting these results should keep in mind that participants were aware [...] (Engineering).
(11) Nótese que la intensidad de los mapas varía según [...] (*Notice that the intensity of the maps varies according to [...]*) (Engineering).

Apart from the directives mentioned above, "seem" is also commonly used to convey recommendations, observations, or interpretations of linguistic phenomena. In Spanish, the items identified involve "como" and "tener que". These directives help guide readers' understanding of linguistic theories, analyses, or empirical findings, as can be seen in examples 12 and 13.

(12) A successful analysis, we think, should have the following properties [...] (Linguistics).
(13) Aunque en este último se reconozcan, como es bien sabido, géneros, tópicos, modelos, escuelas, movimientos, corrientes, tendencias e influencias de todo tipo, cada obra de arte [...] (*Although in the latter, it is recognized [...]*) (Linguistics).

While there may be some variations in the specific directives used across different disciplines and languages, the overall function of these directives remains consistent: to provide guidance, recommendations, or observations to readers and to enhance clarity and precision in conveying research findings and implications. Additionally, the choice of directives may also reflect disciplinary conventions, research methodologies, or cultural norms prevalent in each field.

5. Conclusion

All in all, this paper has been concerned with the identification of engagement markers in three fields of study, namely medicine, engineering and linguistics. To this end, this study stemmed from the following research questions:

> RQ(1). What are the frequency, forms and functions of engagement features used in medical, engineering and linguistic research articles written in English and Spanish?
> RQ(2). What similarities and differences can be observed among the three disciplines?

As for RQ(1), the findings indicate that there is a higher number of engagement markers in articles related to the field of Linguistics, followed by Engineering and Medicine, being more recurrent in the discourse produced by native speakers of the English language. When addressing the similarities and differences among the three disciplines, as specified in RQ(2), it has been observed that the incidence of engagement markers in the English corpus is higher than those devices encountered in the Spanish corpus. Nonetheless, personal asides and questions happen to be more common in medical research written in Spanish.

Limitations in this study should be acknowledged. The tool itself has inherent constraints, and ongoing efforts are directed towards implementing improvements, including server migration and refining coordination methods for tagging. A broader range of disciplinary fields and a more extensive corpus could have potentially enhanced the generalisability of results. As regards pedagogical implications, metadiscoursal elements may be identified based on proficiency levels in a foreign language, aligning with the Common European Framework of Reference for Languages (CEFR) levels. This information could be progressively incorporated into foreign language teaching materials following text analysis to identify the most commonly used markers at each proficiency level.

From a professional perspective, the study of engagement markers in this context may be helpful for scholars and faculty members who seek to publish in both languages since linguistic and cultural factors may have an impact on the use of specific patterns in academic texts. By learning how to incorporate these elements in specialised academic discourse, publication opportunities in high-impact factor journals could increase. Thus, further research could be focused on developing the tool for the analysis of language variations at a synchronous level, potentially aiding in identifying language evolution patterns accelerated by global communication and external language influences. Another potential application could deal with the classification of those metadiscourse elements that enhance discourse comprehension, attractiveness, and persuasiveness, offering effective communication strategies for professionals such as advertisers, politicians, and others requiring daily communication skills.

5.1. Funding

The authors acknowledge having received funding from the Spanish Ministry of Economy. Grant ID FFI2016-77941-P: Identification and analysis of metadiscourse strategies in Spanish and in English – Identificación y análisis de las estrategias metadiscursivas en artículos científicos en español e inglés.

References

Abasi, A. (2012). The pedagogical value of intercultural rhetoric: A report from a Persian-as-a-foreign-language classroom. *Journal of Second Language Writing, 21*(3), 195–220.

Aguilar-Pérez, M., & Khan, S. (2022). Metadiscourse use when shifting from L1 to EMI lecturing: Implications for teacher training. *Innovation in Language Learning and Teaching, 16*(4–5), 297–311.

Aijmer, K. (1997). I think an English modal particle. In T. Swan & O. J. Westvik (Eds.), *Modality in Germanic languages* (pp. 1–47). Berlin/New York: Mouton de Gruyter.

Bellés-Calvera, L. (2021). *Multilingual education: a contrastive analysis in humanities, social sciences and health sciences* (Doctoral dissertation, Universitat Jaume I).

Bellés-Fortuño, B. (2008). A spoken academic discourse contrastive study: Discourse markers in North-American and Spanish lectures/ Un estudio comparativo en el discurso académico hablado: los marcadores discursivos en el género de la clase magistral norteamericana y española. *RESLA*. Logroño: Asociación Española de Lingüística Aplicada.

Bellés-Fortuño, B. (2016). Academic discourse markers: A contrastive analysis of the discourse marker then in English and Spanish lectures. *Verbeia, 1*, 57–78.

Bellés-Fortuño, B. (2018). Evaluative language in medical discourse: A contrastive study between English and Spanish university lectures. *Languages in Contrast, 18*(2). https://doi.org/10.1075/lic.15018.bel.

Bergqvist, H. (2020). Swedish modal particles as markers of engagement: Evidence from distribution and frequency. *Folia Linguistica, 54*(2), 469–496.

Carrió-Pastor, M. L. (2016). A contrastive study of interactive metadiscourse in academic papers written in English and in Spanish. In F. Alonso-Almeida, L. Cruz García, & V. González Ruiz (Eds.), *Corpus-based studies on language varieties* (pp. 89–114). Peter Lang.

Carrió-Pastor, M. L. (2020). Conocer la lengua a través de los corpus: La herramienta METOOL, retos para el análisis de los marcadores discursivos. *Pragmalingüística, 28*, 255–274.

Chang, J. Y. (2015). A comparison of the first-person pronoun I in NS and Korean NNS corpora of English argumentative writing. *English Teaching, 70*(2), 3–31.

Chesterman, A. (1998). *Contrastive functional analysis*. Amsterdam/ Philadelphia: John Benjamins.

Crismore, A., & Abdollehzadeh, E. (2010). A review of recent metadiscourse studies: The Iranian context. *Nordic Journal of English Studies, 9*(2), 195–219.

Crismore, A., Markkanen, R., & Steffensen, M. S. (1993). Metadiscourse in persuasive writing: A study of texts written by American and Finnish university students. *Written Communication, 10*(1), 39–71.

Dafouz-Milne, E. (2008). The pragmatic role of textual and interpersonal metadiscourse markers in the construction and attainment of persuasion: A cross-linguistic study of newspaper discourse. *Journal of Pragmatics, 40*(1), 95–113.

Deroey, K. L. B. (2015). Stance and engagement in lectures: A corpus-based analysis of academic discourse. *Journal of English for Academic Purposes, 20,* 29–47. https://doi.org/10.1016/j.jeap.2015.05.002

Fraser, B. (1987). Pragmatic formatives. In J. Verschueren & M. Bertucelli-Papi (Eds.), *The pragmatic perspective* (pp. 179–192). Amsterdam/Philadelphia: John Benjamins.

Fraser, B. (1999). What are discourse markers? *Journal of Pragmatics, 31*, 931–952.

Golmohammadi, S., Suluki, S., Daneshmand, F., & Salahshoor, F. (2014). Socio-cognitive perspective to the analysis of the strategic features of the discussion section of research articles in applied linguistics: Native vs. non-native researchers. *Procedia-Social and Behavioral Sciences, 98*, 604–613.

Halliday, M., & Matthiessen, C. (2004). *An Introduction to Functional Grammar* (3rd ed.). London: Arnold.

Hunston, S., & Thompson, G. (Eds.). (2000). *Evaluation in text: Authorial stance and the construction of discourse: Authorial stance and the construction of discourse*. Oxford University Press, UK.

Hyland, K. (2001). Bringing in the reader: Addressee features in academic articles. *Written Communication, 18*(4), 549–574. https://doi.org/10.1177/0741088301018004005

Hyland, K. (2004). *Disciplinary discourses: Social interactions in academic writing*. University of Michigan Press.

Hyland, K. (2005). *Metadiscourse*. London: Continuum.

Hyland, K. (2010). Metadiscourse: Mapping interactions in academic writing. *Nordic Journal of English Studies*, *9*(S2), 125–143.

Hyland, K., & Guinda, C. S. (Eds.). (2012). *Stance and voice in written academic genres*. Basingstoke: Palgrave Macmillan.Hyland, K., & Jiang, F. K. (2016). We must conclude that…: A diachronic study of academic engagement. *Journal of English for Academic Purposes, 24*, 29–42.

Hyland, K., Wang, W., & Jiang, F. K. (2022). Metadiscourse across languages and genres: An overview. *Lingua, 265*, 103205.

Jiang, F. K. (2020). A diachronic multi-dimensional investigation into the stylistic features in academic discourse. *Foreign Language Teaching and Research, 5*(5), 663–673.

Jiang, F. K., & Hyland, K. (2018). Nouns and academic interactions: A neglected feature of metadiscourse. *Applied Linguistics, 39*(4), 508–531.

Jiang, F. K., & Ma, X. (2018). 'As we can see': Reader engagement in PhD candidature confirmation reports. *Journal of English for Academic Purposes, 35*, 1–15.

Khalili, A., & Aslanabadi, M. (2014). The use of metadiscourse devices by non-native speakers in research articles. *Journal of Applied Linguistics and Applied Literature: Dynamics and Advances, 2*(2), 21–34.

Köroğlu, Z. (2018). A study on metadiscoursive interaction in the doctoral dissertations of the native speakers of English and the Turkish speakers of English. *Journal of Language and Linguistic Studies, 14*(3), 396–404.

Martín del Pozo, M. A. (2014). *Aproximación lingüístico didáctica al discurso académico de la clase magistral en la formación del profesorado en contextos universitarios bilingües* (Doctoral dissertation, Tesis doctoral. Universidad Complutense de Madrid).

Martin, J. R., & White, P. R. R. (2005). *The language of evaluation: Appraisal in English.* London, UK: Palgrave Macmillan.

Mauranen, A. (1993). Contrastive ESP rhetoric: Metatext in Finnish-English economic texts. *English for Specific Purposes, 12*, 3–22. https://doi.org/10.1016/0889-4906(93)90024-I

Moreti, K. (2019). *A rhetorical analysis of discussion sections in MA dissertations in English: A corpus-based comparison between native and non-native writers* (Doctoral dissertation, Aristotle University of Thessaloniki).

Mur-Dueñas, P. (2011). An intercultural analysis of metadiscourse features in research articles written in English and in Spanish. *Journal of Pragmatics, 43*(12), 3068–3079.

Ozdemir, N. O., & Longo, B. (2014). Metadiscourse use in thesis abstracts: A cross-cultural study. *Procedia-Social and Behavioral Sciences, 141*, 59–63.

Penris, W., & Verspoor, M. (2017). Academic writing development: A complex, dynamic process. In M. Verspoor, K. de Bot, & W. Lowie

(Eds.), *Future research directions for applied linguistics* (pp. 215–242). New York: Routledge.

Pérez-Llantada, C. (2007). Native and non-native English scholars publishing research internationally: A small-scale study on authorial (in)visibility. *Journal of Applied Linguistics, 4*(2), 217–238.

Qiu, X., & Jiang, F. K. (2021). Stance and engagement in 3MT presentations: How students communicate disciplinary knowledge to a wide audience. *Journal of English for Academic Purposes, 51*, 100976.

Salas Valdebenito, M. (2015). Una propuesta de taxonomía de marcadores metadiscursivos para el discurso académico-científico escrito en español. *Revista signos*, *48*(87), 95–120.

Salkie, R. (1995). INTERSECT: A parallel corpus project at Brighton University. *Computer and Texts, 9*, 4–5.

Salkie, R. (1997). Naturalness and contrastive linguistics. In E. Lewandowska-Tomaszcyk & P. J. Melia (Eds.), *Practical applications in language corpora* (pp. 297–312). Lödz: Lödz University Press.

Schiffrin, D. (1987). *Discourse markers.* Cambridge: Cambridge University Press.

Scotto di Carlo, G. (215). Stance in TED talks: Strategic use of subjective adjectives in online popularization. *Ibérica, 29*, 201–222.

Swales, J. M. (1990). *Genre analysis: English in academic and research settings.* Cambridge: Cambridge University Press.

Tversky, A. (1977). Features of similarity. *Psychological Review, 84*(4), 327–352. https://doi.org/10.1037/0033-295X.84.4.327

ELENA QUINTANA-TOLEDO / MARGARITA ESTHER SÁNCHEZ-CUERVO

Universidad de Las Palmas de Gran Canaria / Universidad de Las Palmas de Gran Canaria

Logical Metadiscursive Markers in Research Papers Written in English: A Corpus-based Approach[1]

1. Introduction

The creation of scientific knowledge is an eminently social practice which involves individuals engaged in exchanging their ideas and reaching agreements in a principled way in the specific contexts of their disciplines (*Hyland, 2005a*, *2004*; *Swales, 1993*, *1990*). Research articles occupy a privileged position not only among the existing means to disseminate that knowledge and to preserve it for the future, but also among the genres that academics have at their disposal for scientific communication. It is not surprising, then, that research articles have attracted considerable attention from scholars interested in their rhetorical organisation for more than three decades now.

The traditional view of scientific discourse as impersonal and objective is being gradually superseded by another which emphasises its interpersonal nature. In fact, extensive research supports the idea that academic genres and research articles in particular are examples of interactional discourse (*Álvarez-Gil & Domínguez-Morales, 2018*; *Alonso-Almeida &*

1 This paper is part of the research project "Identification and analysis of metadiscourse strategies in Spanish and English research papers", grant FFI2016-77941-P (Ministerio de Economía, Industria y Competitividad). This grant is hereby gratefully acknowledged.

Carrió-Pastor, 2017; *Cao & Hu, 2014*; *Livnat, 2012*; *Lorés-Sanz, Mur-Dueñas & Lafuente-Millán, 2010*; *Hyland, 2008, 2005a*, 2005b, *2004*). In this regard, *Jiang and Ma (2019, p.* 43) affirm that "[s]uccessful academic texts are built not simply on the writers' plausible representation of external reality, but perhaps more importantly on their engagement with readers in the joint construction of academic discourse while persuading them of the relevance and value of their research". Involvement is probably one of the most conspicuous features of rhetorical interaction in discourse, but there are others which undoubtedly deserve scholarly attention, even though they have not been conventionally taken to have an impact on writer-reader relationships in metadiscourse taxonomies. A case in point is logical markers which have been previously referred to as text connectives (*Vande Kopple, 1985*), logical connectives (*Crismore, Markkanen & Steffensen, 1993*; *Hyland, 2004*), connectors (*Mauranen, 1993*), logical markers (*Dafouz-Milne, 2003*), or transition markers (*Hyland, 2005a*). In contrast to circumstance and stance adverbials, for example, *Biber et al. (1999*, p. 765) describe their function as "connective" as "[t]hey make explicit the relationship between two units of discourse" and further highlight their frequent occurrence in academic prose, being by far the most frequent type of adverbial in this register.

Logical metadiscursive markers are standardly classified as interactive, which in practice means that they have an explicit text-organising function (*Vande Kopple, 1985*; *Crismore, Markkanen & Steffensen, 1993*; *Mauranen, 1993*; *Hyland, 1999, 2004*; *Dafouz-Milne, 2003*). Yet, this fact does not undermine their potential for materialising the strategic interaction between writers and readers, too, as noted by some authors like *Hyland (2005a)* and *Hyland and Tse (2004)*. Pursuing this line of research, they argue that "all metadiscourse is interpersonal in that it takes account of the reader's knowledge, textual experiences and processing needs" (*Hyland, 2005a*, p. 41; *Hyland & Tse, 2004*, p. 161). As other interactive metadiscourse features, logical markers may not only provide precise guidance as for how the connections between stretches of discourse should be interpreted, but also relevant information about, for instance, what the writer wishes to prioritise in the presentation of material (*Hyland & Jiang, 2020*). Consequently, it would be also possible to assign them with interpersonal functions in terms of authorial positioning and reader involvement.

This paper analyses the three kinds of transition markers indicating additive, contrastive and consecutive relations in three types of academic research articles which belong to the disciplines of Linguistics, Engineering and Medicine. Following *Hyland's (2005a*, p. 50) classification, the markers establish the following relations:

(a) Additive linkers add elements to an argument and comprise items like "and", "further", "in addition", "moreover", "furthermore", or "by the way".
(b) Comparative linkers include arguments of two types: similar, with items like "similarly", "likewise", "equally", "in the same way", or "correspondingly"; or different, with items such as "in contrast", "however", "but", "on the contrary", or "on the other hand".
(c) Consecutive linkers also establish two types of relations that reflect, firstly, whether a conclusion is drawn or justified, as in "thus", "therefore", "consequently", or "in conclusion"; and whether an argument is countered, as in "admittedly", "nevertheless", "anyway", "in any case" or "of course".

Section 2 of this study reviews background literature on logical connectives and their place within models of metadiscourse. Previous studies where connectives are studied across disciplines are also referred to in this section. The corpus and methodology used for this research are described in Section 3. After conducting the analysis, Section 4 examines the frequency of each marker in the three disciplines and which ones are preferred. Section 5 offers some conclusions as regards the presence of these metadiscourse transition markers in the research fields selected.

2. Logical Connectives and the Interpersonal in Metadiscourse

Metadiscourse, understood as an indicator of social interaction and engagement in academic writing, can be realised through a countless number of features which allow writers to organize their texts and to show their stance both towards the information itself and towards potential readers. One such feature involves transition markers which "are mainly conjunctions and adverbial phrases which help readers interpret pragmatic connections between steps in an argument" (*Hyland, 2005a*, p. 50). They belong to the interactive dimension in *Hyland's (2005a, 2005b)* model of metadiscourse where they are classified together with other resources such as frame markers, endophoric markers, evidentials and code glosses. Generally speaking, their roles transcend the mere text-structuring functions to further mark writers' a priori assumptions about readers' processing abilities.

Crismore, Markkanen and Steffensen (1993) stand as one of the first studies that identify the value of logical connectives as metadiscourse markers. These authors partially follow *Vande Kopple's (1985)* ideas regarding their use, which account for the connections that can be established between the different parts of a whole text. *Hyland (2005a,* p. 34) notes, however, that the criterion used by *Crismore, Markkanen and Steffensen (1993)* to include items into this category is syntactic rather than functional, leading to a major inadequacy of their framework as subordinating conjunctions would not count as metadiscourse. In this sense, *Hyland (2005a,* p. 35) emphasises the need to take the polyfunctional nature of connectives as a guiding principle so as to be able to trace their metadiscoursal traits.

As much theorising on metadiscourse functions and taxonomies, *Hyland (2005a, pp.* 45–48) also relies on concepts borrowed from Systemic Functional Linguistics to accommodate the aforementioned polyfunctional nature of connectives into his metadiscourse model. As a matter of fact, this framework offers interesting insights into the dimensions associated to the conjunctive relations which may be expressed by connectives. According to the system of CONJUNCTION developed by *Halliday and Matthiessen (2004,* pp. 540–548), they are said to express three main types of relations: (i) elaboration, (ii) extension and (iii) enhancement. Within elaboration, connectives allow for reformulation or clarification. Extension applies when connectives are used to add new information or some sort of variation, frequently "by contrast or by qualification" (*Eggins, 2004,* p. 47). Enhancement involves connectives which contribute to unfolding the meaning of a previous

sentence "in terms of dimensions such as time, comparison, cause, condition or concession" (*Eggins, 2004*, p. 48).
A cross-cutting distinction is then made between "external" and "internal" conjunctive relations (*Halliday & Hasan, 1976*, p. 240; *Martin, 1992*, p. 180), which *Thompson (2013*, p. 227) rightly summarises as follows: "external conjunction is viewed as constructing relations between states of affairs in the world, whereas internal conjunction sets up relations between discourse segments". Echoing *Martin's (1992, p.* 180) words, *Hyland (2005a*, p. 45) establishes the link between the polyfunctional character of connectives and the external/internal relations by positing that connectives "can function to either connect steps in an exposition (internal), organizing the *discourse* as an argument, or they can connect activities in the world outside the text (external), representing *experiences* as a series of events". In other words, cohesion as manifested by the use of connectives may be subject to something internal or external to the communicative situation itself. While internal cohesion has to be looked at as belonging to the interpersonal in language, external cohesion is construed as being related to the experiential metafunction of language.

Within metadiscourse studies specifically, the idea that cohesive devices like connectives may contribute to building authorial stance is supported by *Hyland and Tse (2004)*, *Hyland (2005a, 2010)* and *Mur-Dueñas (2009)*. *Hyland (1998, 2004)* and *Dafouz-Milne (2008)* do not readily embrace this view as they still observe a clear distinction between textual and interpersonal dimensions of metadiscourse. Nevertheless, there is an implicit sense of audience attached to the use of connectives in their models, where it is also assumed that their purpose goes beyond signalling syntactic relations of addition, result or contrast. What is more, *Hyland (1998)* and *Dafouz-Milne (2008)* highlight the persuasive effect writers achieve thanks to their rhetorical choices regarding connectives, among other metadiscourse resources. Persuasion is certainly an indication of authorial projection into academic texts as well as of the writers' intention to convince their readers of the validity of their claims. In this light, it can he hardly disputed that connectives can play an important part in showing the writers' positioning with respect to the unfolding text and its audience. Drawing on the relationship between cohesion and the expression of evaluative meaning, *Degaetano-Ortlieb (2015)* examines how certain evaluative expressions can fulfill both textual and interpersonal metafunctions in scientific writing. This author analyses two types of evaluative meanings, i.e. obviousness and importance, and their impact on the expression of concessive and consecutive relations respectively. *Thompson (2005)*, on his part, makes a strong case for giving more prominence to the interpersonal meanings which can be realised by "internal" conjunction, and so he puts forwards a model which is articulated around the notions of audience awareness, on the one hand, and authorial stance, on the other. Categories in the former are oriented towards the 'you' of the exchange, in that they signal the speaker or writer's awareness of the addressee's potential beliefs and expectations. The other categories "are more oriented toward the 'I', in that they express aspects of the speaker or writer's stance toward the information being exchanged, in term of appraisal (Martin, 2000), modal validation or speech-act justification" (*Thompson, 2005, p.* 785–786).

2.1. Disciplinary Variation in Interactive Metadiscourse: Connectives

Since our aim is to describe how members of three different disciplines, i.e. linguistics, engineering and medicine, use connectives in research papers, concepts such "disciplinary culture" or "discourse community" must be brought to the foreground. *Becher and Trowler (2001*, p. 24) stress the importance of academic texts in this sense; they note that "academics engage with their subject matter and the narratives they develop are important structural factors in the formulation of disciplinary cultures". The concept is used here to refer to the set of principles, attitudes and codes of behaviour which have been devised by members who represent a particular discipline. *Swales (1990*, pp. 24–32) concurs with *Becher and Trowler (2001)* in that the texts produced by the members of a discipline are central in the configuration of disciplinary groups, but he uses the term "discourse communities", where discourses are taken as a vehicle for guaranteeing communication among members as well as for achieving a common set of goals. In Swales' view, being able to engage in the discourses of a disciplinary community somehow grants membership to that community. *Hyland (2004)* does not seem to agree completely with the disciplinary homogeneity that can be inferred from *Becher's and Trowler's (2001)* notion of "disciplinary culture", or even with the disciplinary constraints proposed in *Sullivan (1996)*. It may be too risky to assume that there is a general consensus as for disciplinary practices and as for how that consensus critically determines disciplinary behaviour. Rather than adhering to a more restrictive way of thinking, *Hyland (2004*, pp. 10–11) posits that "disciplines might be seen as systems in which multiple beliefs and practices overlap and intersect".

In their seminal work, *Becher and Trowler (2001)* suggest a classification of academic disciplines according to cultural and sociological parameters. They are divided into four groups: (i) hard pure disciplines, where pure sciences like chemistry or physics are included; (ii) soft pure disciplines, which involve humanities, i.e. history or English; (iii) hard applied disciplines, which have to do with technologies, i.e. engineering; and (iv) soft applied disciplines, where social sciences are covered, i.e. education or management. Knowledge production and management is different in each category, for example, while in hard pure fields knowledge is cumulative and mainly concerned with universals, in soft pure disciplines it is iterative and concerned with peculiarity. In hard applied sciences, knowledge is used to create products and/or techniques; in soft applied fields, in contrast, it is used to develop protocols.

Becher's and Trowler's (2001, p. 39) hard/soft and pure/applied distinctions are probably the most influential ones, even though the authors admit that it is not always easy to establish clear-cut boundaries between categories. In any case, their classification is systematic and may be a useful tool to identify disciplinary features in texts. In fact, *Cao and Hu (2014*, p. 16) observe that these variations across disciplines have inspired much research in interactive and interactional metadiscourse studies.

As for connectives, which is our concern in this paper, *Peacock (2010)* looks into linking adverbials which express contrast/concession, result/inference, addition and apposition in science (chemistry, computer science, materials science and neuroscience) or non-science (economics, language and linguistics, management and psychology) research articles. Linking adverbials in all semantic categories are less frequent in science, being chemistry where they are used less often. Differences in semantic categories have been attested across disciplines within both science and non-science: contrast/concession and apposition adverbials abound in psychology, and the same happens with result/inference adverbials in economy, and with addition adverbials in language and linguistics. As for functions, this study confirms a large part of the results in *Biber et al. (1999)* and adds an extra function to the use of contrast/concession, addition and apposition adverbials, that of making and/or strengthening claims as well.

Khedri et al. (2013) analyse interactive metadiscourse in research article abstracts in the fields of applied linguistics and economics drawing on *Hyland's (2005a)* interpersonal proposal. Although both these fields are in the broad domain of soft sciences, sharp differences were found in how writers use transitions in one field and the other. Abstracts written by economists reveal a higher occurrence of this type of markers, which may reflect the writers' intention to reduce ambiguity. In addition, the transitions mostly used in applied linguistics are additive, which may point to an authorial interest in simplifying the exposition of arguments. This lies in opposition to what is found in economics abstracts as writers have a tendency to use more contrastive markers. In a later work, *Khedri and Kritsis (2018)* scrutinise introductions to applied linguistics and chemistry research articles. This time evidentials, hedges and boosters outnumber transitions, which are more common in applied linguistics than in chemistry. Applied linguistics introductions exhibit a more discursive rhetorical style, while in chemistry the use of transitions seeks clarity and precision.

Hyland and Jiang (2020) also investigate interactive metadiscourse, but in this case from a diachronic standpoint. Their aim is to map changes in interactions in academic writing in a time span of fifty years, from 1965 to 2015. Applied linguistics and sociology research articles are taken as representative of soft sciences, and electrical engineering and biology are representative of hard sciences. Their corpus-based approach clearly differs from others taken so far when researching connectives as interactive metadiscourse markers: taking as reference the findings in *Biber et al. (1999)* in relation to the use of these two markers in academic prose and conversation, the authors made the decision not to include "and" and "or" in their counts. In the end, "and" and "or" come to "represent the default options for marking conjunctive relations of addition and alternation rather than conscious rhetorical strategies for signalling particular writer intensions" (*Hyland & Jiang, 2020*). Their own findings show that interactive features seem to have increased in a more or less uniform way across the four disciplines in the past fifty years. This fact makes manifest that in general they are gaining relevance as a means to attain academic persuasion. Transitions and evidentials are the most frequent of all categories, but transitions have fallen throughout the years in all disciplines except for applied linguistics. The decrease observed in hard sciences and sociology may be due to the fact that there is probably no need to mark explicitly the lines of arguments as readers may recover the connections inferentially. Research papers in applied linguistics have changed substantially over the years: the growth of empirical studies has motivated that arguments tend to be less narrative and more transitions are needed so as to build elaborate lines of reasoning. Additive markers occur more often than contrastive and concessive ones, and besides marking addition, they are also used to emphasise information, and so, they are seen as signalling attitudinal information in terms of truth or importance.

3. Corpus and Methodology

The present research is part of the national research project called "Identification and Analysis of Metadiscourse Strategies in Spanish and English" (IAMET). The research articles (henceforth RAs) selected are part of a larger corpus which is still being annotated by a group of researchers from several Spanish Universities. It is a dynamic corpus and, although most RAs in English have been tagged by now, the analysis conducted reflects the results obtained in November 2019. The general corpus comprises complete RAs in English and Spanish in the fields of linguistics, engineering and medicine. They were randomly selected during a timespan which ranges from 2014 to 2017 and were taken from several international high-impact scientific journals ranked in JCR or similar tools of evaluation. The compilers had to choose articles where the author is a native speaker of either English or Spanish, the languages used in the article. When there was multiple authorship, at least one of the authors must be a native speaker.

The logical markers have been tagged manually and identified by means of METOOL, a tool designed to calculate the number of metadiscourse elements in the corpora selected. After tagging all the required elements in the "Annotate corpus" body content of the platform, we are able to perform different searches according to the purpose of our research. The three sub-corpora are the following: (1) the linguistics papers hold 80 RAs which amount to 636,620 tokens; (2) the engineering papers comprise 64 RAs and 653,787 tokens; and (3) the medicine papers cover 108 RAs and the total number of tokens is 454,573. The search of additive, contrastive and consecutive logical markers was done in the "Analyse corpus" body content of the platform.

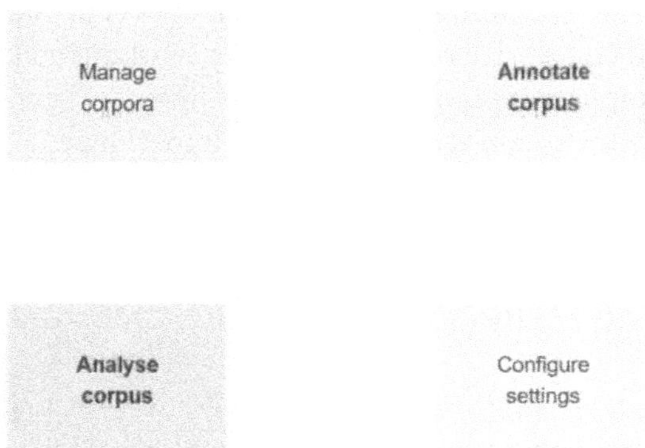

Figure 1. Main layout of the platform

Within the section of "Analyse corpus", we have extracted the statistics of each academic discipline per categories so as to specify the total amount of metadiscourse elements divided into the following markers: boosters, logical markers, code glosses, frame markers, endophoric markers, evidentials, hedges, attitude markers, engagement markers, self-mentions, modality, and epistemic stance. A deeper level of analysis may report on the total number of items per category from any of the three corpora, which the annotator has previously tagged manually in the context where they appear, and has further examined whether it is a metadiscourse marker or not according to its sense.

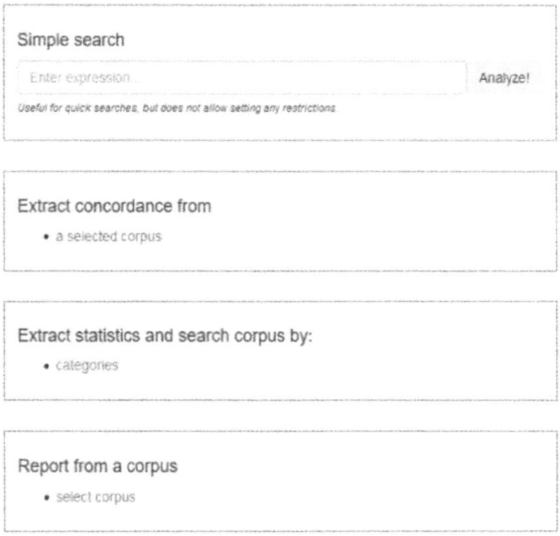

Figure 2. Layout of the "Analyse corpus" section

For example, in the linguistics corpus, the "and" conjunction appears up to 10,219 times but only 3,189 occurrences have been tagged as a metadiscourse marker because it introduces additional information. This additional information joins two propositions, but not two names. Despite the multiple values that the conjunction "and" may possess in a specific genre, only inter-sentential uses of logical markers have been considered as metadiscoursal since they explicitly mark the relationship between the ideas (*Alonso-Almeida, 2008*, p. 172; *Mur-Dueñas, 2009b*, p. 250). In light of this distinction, in the following example there are three occurrences of "and", but only the second is analysed as an additive logical marker; the other two are annotated as "Not Metadiscourse marker" because they link adjectives dependent on the same or different noun phrases.

(1) An alternative (**and** our preferred option) is to treat the agreement class as 'inquorate' **and** label the two nouns as lexical exceptions, with neuter gender in the singular **and** feminine in the plural. (LIN, text 31)

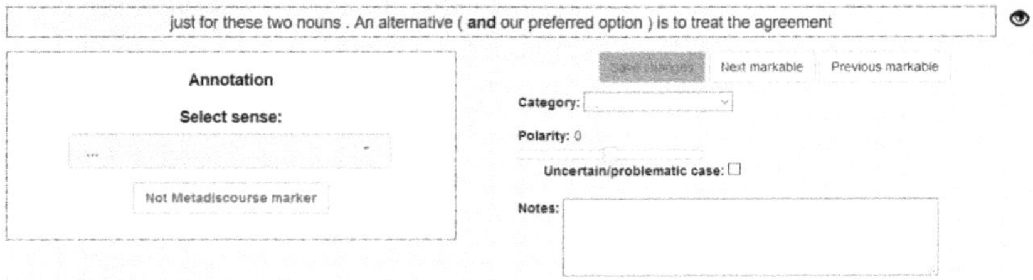

Figure 3. Layout of annotation of "and" in intra-sentential position

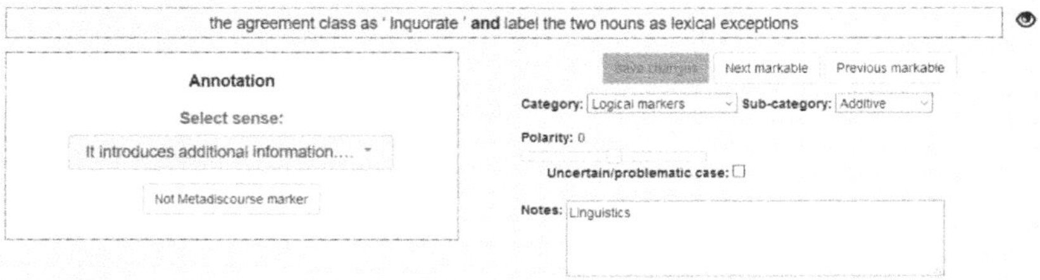

Figure 4. Layout of annotation of "and" in inter-sentential position

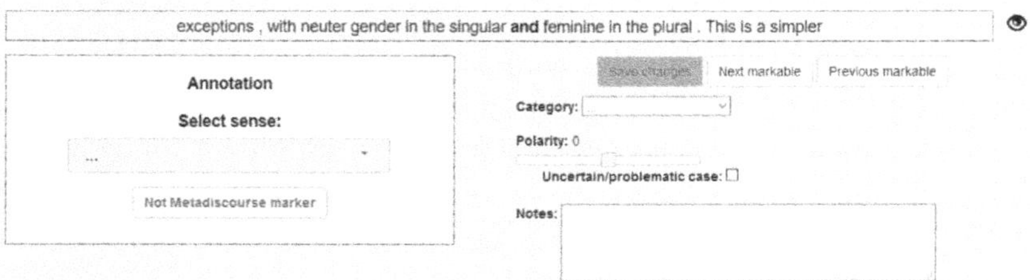

Figure 5. Layout of annotation of "and" in intra-sentential position

This meticulous procedure has been applied to all potential metadiscourse markers, based on restrictions such as the following:

- "Rather": it can express an opposite proposition (Logical marker: contrastive); it can define something by contrast (Code glosses: reformulation); or it can indicate "to a slight degree" (Hedges: hedges-adverbs).

- "So": it summarises what is said (Logical marker: consecutive); or it means "similarly, in the same way" (Logical marker: additive); or it can be the same as "therefore" (Logical marker: consecutive).
- "Then": it can indicate the consequence of an action (Logical marker: consecutive); or it can be defined as "next, after a previous action" (Logical marker: consecutive).
- "Next": it can reflect "a further aspect" (Frame markers: sequencers); or it can refer to the following section (Endophoric marker: cataphoric/ anaphoric); or it can also be interpreted as "in the following step" (Logical markers: consecutive).
- "Following": it can be assessed as "listed or shown next" (Endophoric marker); as "after and act" (Logical marker); or as "using the same method, idea or theory" (Evidential).

The metadiscourse markers have been categorised according to existing models of logical markers such as *Hyland's (2005a)*, *Martin and Rose's (2003)*, and *Mur-Dueñas' (2007*, *2009a*, 2009b, *2011)*, among others.

The METOOL device incorporates some variations in the taxonomy of logical markers, as the following classification shows:

1. Additive: "in addition", "furthermore", "moreover", "similarly", "also", "further", "so", "additionally", "likewise", "and", "thereafter", "as well".
   (2) In Walman, recategorization according to a diminutive/affective classification is widespread, **and** for this there is a set of diminutive gender agreement forms. Note **also** the instances in the Iwaidjan language Mawng (Singer 2010) and in Yawuru (Nyulnyulan family, Hosokawa 1996). (LIN, text 31)
2. Contrastive: "in contrast", "but", "yet", "rather", "nevertheless", "instead", "still", "however", "alternatively", "conversely", "by contrast", "though", "needless to say", "otherwise", "despite the fact".
   (3) The authors considered introducing a monetary cost for each decision; **however**, points in Envision do not correlate with an increase in cost. (ENG, text 1)
3. Consecutive: "thus", "therefore", "as a result", "consequently", "then", "hence", "as such", "accordingly", "so", "next", "following", "for * reason", "in turn", "so that".

(4) We showed that doctors did practice some but not all the relevant ICC skills and that the ICC style of the doctors was mainly biomedically centred. **Hence**, it is unlikely that post-graduate medical trainees will acquire all the required ICC skills merely by modelling their behaviour on the example of their clinical supervisors. (MED, text 25)

4. Analysis of Logical Markers in the Linguistics, Engineering and Medicine Corpora

Bearing in mind the dissimilar length of the RAs in the three corpora, the results which are presented below are normalised per 10,000 words. The aim is to establish the general frequency of the three types of logical markers in the three disciplines and suggest a possible pattern or preference of metadiscoursal categories employed by each one.

Table 1. Frequency of logical markers in the three corpora

	Linguistics corpus		**Engineering corpus**		**Medicine corpus**	
	Total	Per 10,000 words	Total	Per 10,000 words	Total	Per 10,000 words
Additive	4552	71,50	6077	92,92	4398	96,75
Contrastive	2601	40,85	1246	19,05	822	18,08
Consecutive	1131	17,76	1021	15,61	370	8,29
TOTAL	8284	130,11	8344	127,58	5590	123,12

As can be seen in *Table 1*, the additive logical markers are the most numerous in the three disciplines, whereas the contrastive and consecutive ones show a more considerable variation in regard to the discipline in which they are evaluated. In the case of the contrastive logical markers, for instance, the linguistics corpus contains the highest number especially when contrasted with the engineering and medicine corpora, the number of which is practically reduced by half. Conversely, the consecutive logical markers present a similar proportion in the linguistics and engineering corpora, followed by the medicine RAs which reflect around half of the items. In the following subsections, each table portrays the frequency of use of the ten most repeated additive, contrastive and consecutive logical markers in decreasing order.

4.1. Additive Logical Markers

Table 2. Frequency of additive logical markers

Linguistics			**Engineering**			**Medicine**		
	Total	Per 10,000 words		Total	Per 10,000 words		Total	Per 10,000 words
And	3189	50.09	And	4792	73.29	And	3633	79.92
Also	863	13.55	Also	693	10.59	Also	390	8.57
Further	172	2.70	Further	139	2.12	Further	101	2.22
In addition	91	1.42	In addition	120	1.83	In addition	99	2.17
Similarly	76	1.19	Moreover	119	1.82	Additionally	53	1.16
Moreover	67	1.05	Furthermore	84	1.28	Furthermore	47	1.03
Furthermore	40	0.62	Similarly	54	0.82	Moreover	38	0.83
Likewise	27	0.42	Additionally	49	0.74	Similarly	18	0.39
Additionally	14	0.21	Thereafter	11	0.16	Thereafter	9	0.19
So	13	0.20	So	11	0.16	As well	5	0.10

These markers entail a relationship of parallelism and continuation and signal that "what comes next is in the same argumentative lines as the previous discourse unit" (*Mur-Dueñas, 2007,* p. 43). As we can observe, the same conjunctions occupy the first four positions in the three corpora: "and", "also", "further", and "in addition". "And" is the conjunction functioning as the prevalent organising device, especially in the hard pure and applied disciplines, with 4,792 and 3,633 tokens respectively. It is followed by quite a distance by “also”, the use of which is similar in the linguistics and engineering disciplines but less common in the medicine corpus, with only 390 tokens. The lowest positions keep some similarities pertaining to the marker used, though in different corpora. For example, “moreover”, “furthermore” and “similarly” keep a close position which varies between the fifth and seventh places; in contrast, “additionally” also appears in the three types of RAs but is slightly more used in the medicine corpus, in the fifth position. The markers which are prominent in the three last places differ in the corpus where they are located, as in “likewise”, present only in the linguistic RAs; “thereafter”, in the engineering and medicines RAs; “so”, in the engineering and linguistics texts, and “as well”, found only in the medicine corpus with 5 tokens.

There is no indication whatsoever suggesting a higher frequency of additive linkers in the linguistic corpus, which is usually associated with description and the report of results rather with their interpretation (Khansari, 2017, p. 343; *Mur-Dueñas, 2009b*, p. 256). On the contrary, conjunctions like “moreover”, “furthermore”, and “additionally” present a greater occurrence in the Engineering corpus than in the Linguistic one, for example.

4.2. Contrastive Logical Markers

Table 3. Frequency of contrastive logical markers

Linguistics			**Engineering**			**Medicine**		
	Total	Per 10,000 words		Total	Per 10,000 words		Total	Per 10,000 words
But	1114	17.49	However	467	7.14	But	348	7.87
However	583	9.15	But	447	6.83	However	291	6.40
Rather	200	3.14	Rather	55	0.84	Rather	35	0.76
Though	190	2.98	Instead	54	0.82	In contrast	26	0.57

Table 3. *Continued*

Linguistics			Engineering			Medicine		
In contrast	98	1.53	Still	50	0.76	Still	25	0.54
Instead	92	1.44	In contrast	47	0.71	Yet	23	0.50
Yet	69	1.08	Yet	37	0.56	Otherwise	21	0.46
Nevertheless	64	1.00	Though	32	0.48	Instead	15	0.32
Still	52	0.81	Nevertheless	19	0.29	Though	11	0.24
Otherwise	41	0.64	Otherwise	10	0.15	By contrast	10	0.21

These markers establish a relationship of opposition or contrast. In this confrontation, the second idea usually alters the first (*Mur-Dueñas, 2007*, p. 46). In *Table 3*, we can notice that the three top contrastive conjunctions coincide in the three disciplines. "But" is extensively more frequent in the Linguistics texts with 1,114 tokens followed in quite a lower number by the Medicine and Engineering ones (447 tokens in Engineering and 348 tokens in Medicine). "However" is in first position in the engineering RAs (467 tokens), but in the second place in linguistics (583 tokens) and medicine papers (291 tokens). "Rather" is third in all the texts though its use is considerably higher in the linguistic papers (200 tokens as compared with 55 tokens in Engineering and 35 tokens in Medicine). An array of contrastive markers can be then examined in different decreasing places in the three corpora. In general, its use drops considerably after the fifth position though with variations in the total frequency. For example, "instead", and "in contrast" are predominant in central positions. "Still" occupies the ninth position in the Linguistic corpus (52 tokens) but the fifth position in the Engineering and the Medicine ones (50 and 25 tokens respectively). Similarly, "otherwise" is in the last position in the Linguistic and Engineering disciplines (41 and 10 tokens respectively) but in the seventh position in the Medicine RAs (21 tokens). "Though" appears in the fourth position in the linguistics corpus, but it is less employed in engineering and medicine RAs where it ends up relegated to positions eight and nine respectively. "Yet" is less frequent in the three disciplines, alongside "nevertheless", only present in linguistics and engineering texts. Finally, it is worth mentioning "by contrast", only evident in the Medicine corpus with 10 occurrences.

4.3. Consecutive Logical Markers

Table 4. Frequency of consecutive logical markers

Linguistics			**Engineering**			**Medicine**		
	Total	Per 10,000 words		Total	Per 10,000 words		Total	Per 10,000 words
Thus	369	5.79	Therefore	276	4.22	Therefore	134	2.94
Then	243	3.81	Thus	262	4.00	Thus	75	1.64
Therefore	213	3.34	Then	120	1.83	Then	34	0.74
So	93	1.46	Hence	106	1.62	As a result	26	0.57
Hence	75	1.17	As a result	50	0.76	So	21	0.46
As a result	42	0.65	Consequently	42	0.64	Following	21	0.46
In turn	41	0.64	As such	28	0.42	As such	14	0.30
As such	30	0.47	So that	25	0.38	Hence	14	0.30
Accordingly	28	0.43	So	22	0.33	Consequently	12	0.26
Consequently	17	0.26	Accordingly	17	0.26	So that	11	0.24

Through these markers, a relationship of result or consequence is created between two elements of the discourse. As it occurs in the two tables above, the three top consecutive markers are recurrent in the first three positions: "therefore", "thus" and "then". "Hence", "so" and "as a result" are the most common in the fourth and fifth positions. From the sixth place onward the markers show quite a lower frequency in the three disciplines and do not share any positions except for "as such" in both the Engineering and Medicine corpora. Moreover, "as such" and "hence" share the same number of tokens in the Medicine RAs. "So that" with a consecutive meaning is only found in the hard applied and pure linguistics. It is also noticeable the use of "in turn" as a marker only in the Linguistic corpus, and of "following" in the Medicine corpus. In general, the frequency of consecutive connectors in the medicine RAs is less numerous as contrasted with the linguistic and engineering ones, especially from the second marker onwards where the occurrences drop below 100. Although it is beyond the scope of this study, this lesser use of consecutive markers could be related to the fact that the medical research field does not depend so much on the subjective interpretation of research data, as it is the case of the Linguistic discipline (*Dahl, 2004*, p. 1822).

5. Conclusion

After the analysis, we can observe relevant similarities in the use of the three types of logical transition markers, which are said to aid in the interactive relationship between the writers and their readers in the disciplines selected for our study. For example, the additive linkers are the most employed, followed in number by the contrastive and the consecutive ones. Furthermore, the same markers occupy the first three or four positions. In the case of additive logical markers, the most recurrent ones are "and", "also", "further" and "in addition". As for the contrastive logical markers, the results signal the same three predominant linkers: "however", "but" and "rather". Similarly, in the consecutive logical markers, "therefore", "thus" and "then" are the most frequent.

However, their use per discipline is quite varied. Whereas the presence of additive linkers is higher in the Medicine RAs, the occurrence of opposing and consecutive devices is lower than in the Linguistic and Engineering research fields. Although soft pure disciplines like (applied) Linguistics are considered to be more subjective and more dependent on additive markers, as said above, the current research shows that it is not always the case. Indeed, both hard applied and pure disciplines reveal a higher amount of additive conjunctive elements. Conversely, the Linguistic RAs hold twice the quantity of contrastive logical markers in comparison with the Engineering and Medicine corpora. In any case, the variance existing between the incidence of additive linkers on the one side and contrastive and consecutive on the other is considerable, and suggests a heavy necessity of accumulating ideas in the elaboration of arguments.

This being said, the current study has only been applied to academic RAs written in English. A further step in our research is to conduct the same study of logical transition markers in a parallel corpus of Spanish articles belonging to the same three disciplines. After the analysis of both corpora, further results and conclusions will be obtained and some precise differences will be elucidated as to the frequency of the linkers employed. Likewise, this future investigation will provide some insight into the way in which arguments are constructed in both languages.

References

Alonso-Almeida, F. (2008). The pragmatics of and-conjunctives in Middle English medical recipes. *Journal of Historical Pragmatics, 9*(2), 171–199.

Alonso-Almeida, F., & Carrió-Pastor, M. L. (2017). Variation and function of modals in linguistics and engineering research papers in English. In J. I. Marín-Arrese, J. Lavid-López, M. Carretero, E. Domínguez-Romero, M. V. Martín-de-la-Rosa, & M. Pérez-Blanco (Eds.), *Evidentiality and modality in European languages: Discourse-pragmatic perspectives* (pp. 277–309). Bern: Peter Lang.

Álvarez-Gil, F., & Domínguez-Morales, E. (2018). Modal verbs in the abstract genre in the field of tourism. *Revista de Lenguas para Fines Específicos, 24*(2), 27–37.

Becher, T., & Trowler, P. (2001). *Academic tribes and territories: Intellectual enquiry and the cultures of disciplines* (2nd ed.). Philadelphia: Open University Press.

Biber, D., Johansson, S., Leech, G., Conrad, S., & Finegan, E. (1999). *Longman grammar of spoken and written English*. Harlow: Longman.

Cao, F., & Hu, G. (2014). Interactive metadiscourse in research articles: A comparative study of paradigmatic and disciplinary influences. *Journal of Pragmatics, 66*, 15–31.

Crismore, A., Markkanen, R., & Steffensen, M. S. (1993). Metadiscourse in persuasive writing: A study of texts written by American and Finnish university students. *Written Communication, 10*, 39–71.

Dafouz-Milne, E. (2003). Metadiscourse revisited: A contrastive study of persuasive writing in professional discourse. *Estudios Ingleses de la Universidad Complutense, 11*, 29–52.

Dafouz-Milne, E. (2008). The pragmatic role of textual and interpersonal metadiscourse markers in the construction and attainment of persuasion: A cross-linguistic study of newspaper discourse. *Journal of Pragmatics, 40*, 94–113.

Dahl, T. (2004). Textual metadiscourse in research articles: A marker of national culture or of academic discipline. *Journal of Pragmatics, 36*, 1807–1825.

Degaetano-Ortlieb, S. (2015). Evaluative meaning and cohesion: The structuring function of evaluative meaning in scientific writing. *Discours* (Online), *16*. https://journals.openedition.org/discours/9053.

Eggins, S. (2004). *An introduction to systemic functional linguistics* (2nd ed.). London: Continuum.

Halliday, M. A. K., & Hasan, R. (1976). *Cohesion in English*. London: Longman.

Halliday, M. A. K., & Matthiessen, C. (2004). *An introduction to functional grammar* (3rd ed.). London: Hodder Arnold.

Hosokawa, K. (1996). Yawuru grammar. Australian National University.

Hyland, K. (1998). Persuasion and context: The pragmatics of academic metadiscourse. *Journal of Pragmatics, 30*, 437–455.

Hyland, K. (1999). Disciplinary discourses: Writer stance in research articles. In C. N. Candlin & K. Hyland (Eds.), *Writing: Texts, processes and practices* (pp. 99–121). London: Longman.

Hyland, K. (2004). *Disciplinary discourses. Social interaction in academic writing*. Ann Harbor: The University of Michigan Press.

Hyland, K. (2005a). *Metadiscourse: Exploring interaction in writing*. London: Continuum.

Hyland, K. (2005b). Stance and engagement: A model of interaction in academic discourse. *Discourse Studies, 7*(2), 173–192.

Hyland, K. (2008). Persuasion, interaction and the construction of knowledge: Representing self and others in research writing. *International Journal of English Studies, 8*(2), 1–23.

Hyland, K. (2010). Metadiscourse: Mapping interactions in academic writing. *Nordic Journal of English Studies, 9*(2), 125–143.

Hyland, K., & Jiang, F. (Kevin). (2020). Text-organizing metadiscourse. Tracking changes in rhetorical persuasion. *Journal of Historical Pragmatics, 21*(1), 138–165.

Hyland, K., & Tse, P. (2004). Metadiscourse in academic writing: A reappraisal. *Applied Linguistics, 25*(2), 156–177.

Jiang, F. (Kevin), & Ma, X. (2019). Positioning and proximity of reader engagement: Authorial identity in professional and apprentice academic genres. In C. Sancho Guinda (Ed.), *Engagement in professional genres* (pp. 29–46). Amsterdam and Philadelphia: John Benjamins.

Khansari, P. (2017). A discourse analysis of academic writing: The use of additive linkers in academic journal articles. *Journal of Language and Communication, 4*(2), 335–350.

Khedri, M., & Kritsis, K. (2018). Metadiscourse in applied linguistics and chemistry research article introductions. *Journal of Research in Applied Linguistics, 9*(2), 47–74.

Khedri, M., Chan, S. H., & Ebrahimi, S. F. (2013). An exploration of interactive metadiscourse markers in academic research article abstracts in two disciplines. *Discourse Studies, 15*(3), 319–331.

Livnat, Z. (2012). *Dialogue, science and academic writing*. Amsterdam and Philadelphia: John Benjamins.

Lorés-Sanz, R., Mur-Dueñas, P., & Lafuente-Millán, E. (Eds.). (2010). *Constructing interpersonality: Multiple perspectives in written academic genres*. Newcastle upon Tyne: Cambridge Scholars Publishing.

Martin, J. R. (1992). *English text: System and structure*. Amsterdam and Philadelphia: John Benjamins.

Martin, J. R., & Rose, D. (2003). *Working with discourse: Meaning beyond the clause*. London and New York: Continuum.

Mauranen, A. (1993). Contrastive ESP rhetoric: Metatext in Finnish-English economic texts. *English for Specific Purposes, 12*, 3–22.

Mur-Dueñas, P. (2007). Same genre, same discipline; However, there are differences: A cross-cultural analysis of logical markers in academic writing. *ESP Across Cultures, 4*, 37–53.

Mur-Dueñas, P. (2009a). Designing EAP materials based on intercultural corpus analyses: The case of logical markers in research articles. *Revista de Lingüística y Lengua Aplicadas, 4*, 125–135.

Mur-Dueñas, P. (2009b). Logical markers in L1 (Spanish and English) and L2 (English) business research articles. *English Text Construction, 2*(2), 246–264.

Mur-Dueñas, P. (2011). An intercultural analysis of metadiscourse features in research articles written in English and in Spanish. *Journal of Pragmatics, 43*, 3068–3079.

Peacock, M. (2010). Linking adverbials in research articles across eight disciplines. *Ibérica, 20*, 9–33.

Singer, R. (2010). Inflectional and derivational morphology in Mawng: Obligatory versus optional marking. Morphology, 20(2), 333–360. https://doi.org/10.1007/s11525-010-9155-1

Sullivan, D. (1996). Displaying disciplinarity. *Written Communication, 13*(2), 221–250.

Swales, J. (1990). *Genre analysis: English in academic and research settings*. Cambridge: Cambridge University Press.

Swales, J. (1993). Genre and engagement. *Revue Belge de Philologie et Histoire, 71*(3), 689–698.

Thompson, G. (2005). But me some buts: A multidimensional view of conjunction. *Text, 25*(6), 763–791.

Thompson, G. (2013). Picking an argument: Politicians' choice of persuasive strategies. In L. Fontaine, T. Bartlett, & G. O'Grady (Eds.), *Systemic functional linguistics. Exploring choice* (pp. 192–211). Cambridge: Cambridge University Press.

Vande Kopple, W. J. (1985). Some exploratory discourse on metadiscourse. *College Composition and Communication, 36*(1), 82–93.

MARÍA LUISA CARRIÓ-PASTOR / HANNA SKORCZYNSKA
Universitat Politècnica de València / Universitat Politècnica de València

Lexical Diversity and Lexical Density of Metadiscourse Devices in Academic English Papers on Linguistics, Engineering and Medicine

1. Introduction

This paper deals with four topics that have rarely been studied in combination, that is, academic English papers, metadiscourse, lexical diversity and lexical density. The reason for this is that most of the studies on lexical diversity and lexical density focus on the acquisition of second language vocabulary (*To, Fan & Thomas, 2013*). As *Gregori-Signes and Clavel-Arroitia (2015*, p. 546) explained: "Lexical density, lexical diversity or lexical richness (*Daller, van Hout & Treffers-Daller, 2003*) are terms which refer to statistical measures that gauge the lexical richness of texts and may also be used to assess students' overall progress". However, in this chapter we study the lexical density and lexical diversity of the metadiscourse devices used in academic papers in order to establish whether there are any differences in three specific fields of knowledge, namely, engineering, linguistics and medicine. We have chosen these particular areas because we considered they may represent the way papers are written in hard sciences (engineering), soft sciences (linguistics) and in a combination of soft and hard sciences (medicine).

Several researchers (*Hyland & Tse, 2004; Hyland, 2005; Carrió-Pastor, 2016, 2019a, 2019b, 2019c, 2020a*) have studied metadiscourse devices, although focusing mainly on their use and function. In this paper, however, we specifically pay attention to the study of lexical density and lexical diversity of metadiscourse devices in specific fields of knowledge because we are interested in identifying whether they are used in a different way. This finding could provide further information about the use of rhetorical strategies in different fields of knowledge in academic English.

Thus, with the aim of filling this gap, we compare two measures that have seldom been used to study metadiscourse in academic research papers: lexical diversity and lexical density. Lexical diversity is a measure of how many different words are used in a corpus, while lexical density provides a measure of the proportion of lexical items in a corpus (*Vermeer, 2000; Malvern et al., 2004; Johansson, 2008; Jarvis, 2013a*). We believe that the analysis of these two items related to metadiscourse devices could be useful to understand their nature and to know which devices may be more difficult to understand and use than others.

Thus, the objectives of this chapter are, first, to examine whether lexical density and lexical diversity are sensitive to specific fields of knowledge (linguistics, engineering and medicine) and to the different types of rhetorical markers (textual and interpersonal). The second is to study whether the frequencies of use of rhetorical markers in different domains, i.e. textual and interpersonal, could be in line with lexical diversity and lexical density in academic English. And the third is to investigate to what extent lexical diversity and lexical density are correlated and occur with similar frequencies in different domains.

To accomplish these objectives, this chapter is divided into several sections. First, the introduction explains the aims of the chapter. This is then followed by a section that explains the theoretical background of lexical density, lexical diversity, metadiscourse and academic English. After that, we describe the corpus and the method followed in this analysis, and then display and discuss the results in the following section. Our study ends with the conclusions regarding the accomplishment of our objectives.

2. Lexical Density, Lexical Diversity and Metadiscourse in Academic English

Most authors agree that lexical quality is a multidimensional linguistic aspect that can be observed by means of a set of measures, one of which is lexical density (*Malvern et al., 2004*). As *Johansson (2008*, p. 65) explained, "Lexical density is then defined as the total number of words with lexical properties divided by the total number of orthographic words. The result is a percentage for each text in the corpus". The concept of lexical density (*Ure, 1971*) is used to describe the proportion of lexical or content words to the total number of words in language. Later, lexical density was redefined by *Halliday (1985)*, who referred to the term "items" rather than words when it came to lexical density since he considered that it might take more than one word to represent a meaning, as occurs for example in phrasal verbs or idioms.

In relation to lexical density, *Johansson (2008*, p. 65) incorporated the "notion of information packaging; a text with a high proportion of content words contains more information than a text with a high proportion of function words (prepositions, interjections, pronouns, conjunctions and count words)". To understand how to calculate the lexical density of a text, we should know what lexical items and grammatical items are. Lexical items are the carriers of meaning in language, or "content words", and are called "lexical" because they function in lexical sets, such as nouns, verbs, adjectives and adverbs. Conversely, grammatical items are considered to be function words such as articles, pronouns, most prepositions, conjunctions, some classes of adverbs and finite verbs.

Thus, we may assume that texts have different lexical densities and the causes could be, for example, related to the age of the speakers, their language proficiency, the modality of discourse (oral or written), the discursive genre or the specific settings of the discourse, and so forth. The notion of lexical density therefore refers to the informative content of the texts. Some authors measure it by calculating the proportion of content words over the total number of words and others calculate a ratio between the content and function words or closed list words. In either case the index accounts for the informational density of the discourse even though the greater or lesser lexical density is not always clearly noticeable to the listener or reader; it may only be evident in highly specific discourse.

We have considered it significant to study lexical density in metadiscourse as numerous investigations show the relevance of this indicator to distinguish between oral and written discourse (*Ravid, 2006;*

Berman & Nir, 2010), among genres (*Johansson, 2008*, *Berman & Nir, 2010; Berman, Nayditz & Ravid, 2011; Fuentes, Hernández & Salcedo, 2019*) and among specific fields of study (*Gholami, Mosalli & Nikou, 2012*). Very few, however, have focused on the analysis of lexical density in metadiscourse devices used in specific fields of academic English.

The second topic considered in this chapter is lexical diversity, variety or richness. This normally refers to the ability to use different words and avoid repetition in discourse (*Read, 2000*). As *Johansson (2008*, p. 62) indicated, "For a text to be highly lexically diverse, the speaker or writer has to use many different words, with little repetition of the words already used". *Jarvis (2013*, p. 88) added to this concept: "diversity is a condition or quality that arises from the juxtaposition of multiple varied or different, elements within the same domain, such as a field of view. However, it is also more than this because diversity is affected by the specific relationships among the elements in the domain, such as how well they complement one another, as well as by the unique contribution to diversity that each element makes". We also believe that there is variety among different specific fields of knowledge within a genre, and this is why here we study different fields of academic English to identify lexical diversity. It should be taken into account that this calculation has been mainly used in studies on first and second language acquisition, bilingualism, multilingualism and language testing and assessment to study the complexity of vocabulary knowledge and language proficiency of learners (*Jarvis, 2013a*), but in this paper we analyse academic discourse written by native English speakers in linguistics, medicine and engineering.

Lexical diversity is measured through the type-token ratio (TTR), which is the ratio between the different words (types) and the total number of words (tokens) (*Waller, 1993*). Since the TTR can only be applied in texts of equal length, some correction formula, such as STTR or D, is usually employed for working with texts of different lengths (*Malvern & Richards, 1997; Malvern et al., 2004; Duran et al., 2004; Jarvis, 2002, 2013a, 2013b*). In various studies, lexical diversity has been shown to be sensitive to the age or language proficiency factor and discursive genre (*Malvern et al., 2004; Hudson, 2009; Berman & Nir, 2010*). However, it has been criticized for being a measure that cannot properly account for the richness involved in the notion of diversity (*Duran et al., 2004*; *Jarvis, 2013a*), because it would only measure the non-repetition of words and not the compositional complexity involved in this concept. In this chapter we have included the calculation of lexical diversity through STTR because we consider the corpora studied has different length and this measure may add valuable information about the lexical nature of metadiscourse devices.

The last topics taken into account in this research are metadiscourse and English academic papers, which are quite frequently studied in combination. Metadiscourse can be described as a key aspect in discourse that links the interactions between speakers and listeners who often come from the same discourse community with common rhetorical practices (*Hyland, 1998*, *2005;* Gillaerts & de *Velde, 2010; Mur-Dueñas, 2011*). It is usually used to carry out discursive explorations of rhetorical strategies mainly in academic English, but it is also found in other genres. Metadiscourse has been analysed by many researchers such as Mauranen (1993), *Hyland and Tse (2004)*, *Dahl (2004)*, *Hyland (2005*, *2010)*, Ädel (2006), Vande Kopple (2012) and *Carrió-Pastor (2016a*, *2019a, 2019b, 2019c, 2020b)*.

Traditionally, scholars differentiate between two main types of metadiscourse interaction (*Thompson, 2001*). On the one hand, textual (also called interactive) metadiscourse categories involve the management of the flow of information and thus serve to guide readers through the content of the text. On the other hand, interpersonal (also called interactional) metadiscourse categories aim to involve readers in the argument or ethos of the text (*Hyland, 2005*). These categories are divided by Hyland into 10 subcategories, as outlined in the following.

On the one hand, the textual category is divided into:

- Logical markers: This subcategory includes elements that join parts of a sentence or propositions; their function is to produce a "logical" flow of discourse, and include *and*, *but*, *in addition*, *further, however*, etc.
- Code glosses: This subcategory comprises words that are used to provide examples or reformulate propositions in order to clarify ideas; examples include words such as *for example*, *e.g.*, *in other words*, etc.
- Frame markers: They are used to organise the discourse and to provide a sequence in the flow of ideas; for example, *first*, *second*, *finally*, *in brief*, *in sum*, etc.
- Endophoric markers: These refer to previous or subsequent parts of the discourse, linking the different ideas and parts; they include words

such as *as noted earlier, in this paper, above, previously, before, see Table X*, etc.

- Evidentials: They include references to the source of information stated in discourse; for example, *as X stated, this has been pointed out by*, etc.

On the other hand, the interpersonal category is divided into:

- Hedges: Devices used to mitigate, limit the commitment and soften the statements of discourse; academic writers tend to use hedges to seem humble, and they include examples such as *may*, *might*, *could*, *theorize*, *assume*, *speculate*, etc.
- Boosters: These are used to reinforce the beliefs of speakers, highlighting their convictions; some examples are *determine*, *show*, *demonstrate*, *reveal*, *highlight*, *confirm*, *emphasize*, *conclude*, etc.
- Attitude markers: These markers show the writer's evaluation about certain facts; some examples are *important*, *consistent*, *significant*, *critical*, *interesting*, *difficult*, etc.
- Engagement markers: These markers are used to involve readers in the text, including them in discourse to convince them about the ideas of the writer, thereby forming a group. They include words such as *we*, *us*, *see*, *note*, etc.
- Self-mentions: These refer to explicit mentions about the writer of academic discourse; some examples include *we*, *us*, etc. or references to papers written by the authors.

The different subcategories of textual and interpersonal categories of academic English have been studied by several researchers. For example, *Hyland (2005, 2010)* analysed interactive and interactional markers in academic writing, *Mur-Dueñas (2011)* studied the same categories in academic business papers, *Cao and Hu (2014)* analysed the paradigmatic and disciplinary influences on interactive metadiscourse, *Abdollahzadeh (2019)* focused on hedges in academic writers, and *Carrió-Pastor* studied several metadiscourse elements in academic writing, i.e. textual markers (*2013*), modal verbs (*2014*), interactive markers (*2016a*), hedges (*2016b*) and attitude markers (*2019a*). These analyses paid attention to the use of metadiscourse markers by researchers and provided some language patterns with the intention of identifying the rhetorical patterns of academic writing.

In this chapter, academic discourse is studied to identify the lexical density and lexical diversity of metadiscourse markers taking into account different fields of knowledge. This point of view has seldom been taken into consideration by metadiscourse researchers with the exception of just a few, such as *Gholami, Mosalli and Nikou (2012)*, who studied the lexical complexity of metadiscourse markers in soft and hard sciences. Here we go deeper into this concept with the aim of better understanding the nature of metadiscourse devices in specific fields of knowledge.

This study is part of a broader project which aims to identify and analyse metadiscourse strategies in English and Spanish, funded by the Spanish Ministerio de Economía y Competitividad (Reference FFI2016-77941-P). The project aims to analyse metadiscourse strategies used in academic English and Spanish in several disciplines to detect variation in the use of the two languages in linguistics, medicine and engineering. It also seeks to identify whether papers written in English and Spanish use metadiscourse devices in an appropriate way.

3. Material and Method

The corpus was composed of a total of 1,744,980 words, distributed in three subcorpora of medicine, engineering and linguistics research papers in English. The subcorpora consisted of 64 engineering papers, 108 medicine papers and 80 linguistics papers. The papers had been published between 2016 and 2018 by native English speakers (identified by the authors' affiliation and surnames) in reputed journals included in Journal Citation Reports (JCR).

The data of the corpus extracted with *WordSmith* can be seen in *Table 1*:

Table 1. Data of the three subcorpora compiled

Text statistical analysis	Engineering	Medicine	Linguistics
tokens used for word list	653,787	454,573	636,620
types (distinct words)	14,796	15,287	20,765
type/token ratio (TTR)	5.62	4.79	5.32
standardised TTR (STTR)	35.98	34.70	36.99
standardised TTR std. dev.	61.24	63.99	63.48
standardised TTR basis	1,000	1,000	1,000
mean word length (in characters)	5.16	5.25	5.04
word length std. dev.	3.04	3.13	3.00
sentences	11,950	14,568	15,343
mean sentence length (in words)	22.02	21.89	25.42
std. dev.	12.87	16.15	15.45
paragraphs	40	84	46
mean paper length (in words)	6,579.30	3,796.57	8,479.43
std. dev.	2,154.80	1,582.37	3,575.06

The corpus was analysed and the different frequencies of metadiscourse devices in the textual and interpersonal categories were identified. Then the data for lexical diversity and lexical density were calculated. In doing so we took into account *Jarvis' (2013a*, p. 88) definition, "lexical variability, lexical variation, and lexical variety [...] are usually operationalized into measures designed to capture the proportion of words in a language sample that are not repetitions of words already encountered. Lexical diversity is thus often understood as the inverse of the word repetition rate".

Hence, the frequencies that we analysed in this proposal are, on the one hand, the data identified with the help of a tool designed to identify metadiscourse devices considering whether they are textual or interpersonal, *Metool*, and, on the other hand, the data extracted with *WordSmith Tools* and *Adelex Analyser* to detect lexical density and lexical diversity. Additionally, the results were also checked manually. In the case of lexical density and lexical diversity, we classified the tokens of the corpus and the number of different words, that is, the types, with *WordSmith*. Then, following *Halliday (1985)*, we distinguished between lexical items, with meaning and consisting mainly of nouns, adjectives, verbs and adverbs, and functional items, such as prepositions, conjunctions, determiners, pronouns, etc. In the study reported in this chapter, we chose the functional words and elaborated a list to identify the most frequent ones in the three subcorpora. We identified and grouped lemmas instead of considering just words and we also took into account the fact that the three subcorpora had different numbers of types.

In the following step, lexical diversity was calculated, the second by means of the formula (Number of different words/Total number of words) × 100, bearing in mind the information from the analysis and the STTR obtained from *WordSmith*.

Table 2. Types and tokens of the three subcorpora

Data corpus	Engineering	Medicine	Linguistics	Total
Types	14,796	15,287	20,765	50,848
Tokens	653,787	454,573	636,620	1,744,980

Lexical diversity was calculated with *WordSmith*, which identified the STTR, and *Adelex Analyser* was also employed to analyse the text entered by the user, resulting in the following information: type/token ratio; lexical diversity index and frequency list of the text.

We also considered the length of the three subcorpora to identify lexical density and lexical diversity as, in general, the longer the text is, the higher the number of different words will be. Lexical density was calculated with the tool *Analyze my writing* (https://www.analyzemywriting.com/index.html), which is an online text content and readability tool. Lexical density is defined as the number of lexical words (or content words) divided by the total number of words in a corpus. Thus, the tool counts the total number of lexical words and then calculated the percentage of lexical words of the corpus.

It is theoretically possible for a text to have high lexical diversity and a frequent use of metadiscourse devices but low lexical density or vice versa, that is, high lexical density and a frequent use of metadiscourse devices but low lexical diversity. We calculated lexical diversity and lexical density with the aim of providing more information about metadiscourse patterns and their use in specific settings. For the comparison of results, we used the values of normalised data: STTR and normalised frequencies to 10,000 of the percentages of lexical density.

We also focused on the analysis of the metadiscourse strategies used in academic English with the aim of identifying patterns that pinpoint differences in specific fields of knowledge. For this study, we selected the fields of engineering, which belongs to the so-called hard sciences, linguistics, which can be included in the field of soft sciences, and finally medicine, a research area that combines characteristics from both hard and soft sciences. The taxonomy used to identify discourse markers is based on previous studies on metadiscourse by *Thompson (2001)* and *Hyland (2005)*, who identified two categories (textual and interpersonal, see definitions above) and ten subcategories that determined the way writers present their findings to readers. The taxonomy used in this study was explained in detail in the previous section. The textual category was divided into logical markers, code glosses, frame markers, endophoric markers and evidentials, and the interpersonal category was divided into hedges, boosters, attitude markers, engagement markers and self-mentions.

After identifying the different metadiscourse devices, the results were normalised to 1,000 words, as the number of different words varied from one subcorpus to another. Thus, in the results we examined whether lexical density, lexical diversity and the use of metadiscourse markers were sensitive to specific fields of knowledge (linguistics, engineering and medicine) and to the different types of rhetorical markers (textual and interpersonal) and compared the frequencies showing examples. Finally, conclusions were drawn.

4. Results and Discussion

Once all the data had been analysed, we organised the results taking into consideration the analyses carried out and, lastly, discussing the objectives.

4.1. Results of the Metadiscourse Devices in Academic Writing

The analysis of the three subcorpora identified a total of 39,361 textual metadiscourse markers. *Table 3* shows the raw data and the frequencies normalised to 1,000 words (N) of textual markers:

Table 3. Textual markers found in the three corpora

Textual markers	Engineering Occurrences (N)	Medicine Occurrences (N)	Linguistics Occurrences (N)
Logical markers	8,512 (13.01)	5,635 (12.39)	8,578 (13.47)
Code glosses	1,864 (2.85)	808 (1.77)	3,548 (5.57)
Frame markers	888 (1.35)	513 (1.12)	1,697 (2.66)
Endophoric markers	1,026 (1.56)	172 (0.37)	833 (1.30)
Evidentials	1,396 (2.13)	1,186 (2.60)	2,705 (4.24)
Total	13,686 (20.93)	8,314 (18.28)	17,361 (27.27)

If we compare the frequencies of the normalised results of textual markers used by the three specific fields of knowledge, we can observe that logical markers are the most frequently used by academic writers, a fact also noticed by *Hyland (1998)* after comparing soft and hard sciences. The second and third most frequent textual subcategories are code glosses and evidentials, showing that academic writers are aware of the importance of clarifying ideas and providing evidence about their statements. If we focus on the specific fields of knowledge, linguists used more textual markers than engineers and medical researchers. This may be due to the fact that they are aware of the importance of guiding readers but, as *Dahl (2004)* suggested, it may also be because linguists do not have such a long tradition in research, their papers are more argumentative and there is no stable structure accepted by the rest of the researchers that guides readers. This author explained that, "Since medical reporting is so formally organised, the content presented is forced into information categories in a given sequence, and no extra processing effort is needed by the expert reader to orient him or herself within the text. This is also clearly reflected in the absence of words referring to parts of the article" (*Dahl, 2004*, p. 1819). Hence, following this reasoning, this means that engineers and linguists are less formally organised in academic discourse. Thus authors need to use more textual devices to guide the reader, while medical researchers share a long tradition in the way they write their papers as "The text is presented to the reader in the highly structured IMRD format" (*Dhal, 2004*, p. 1819). Another study by *Breivega et al. (2002)* indicated that the aim of medical articles is not to create a high degree of functional connection in the text, although maintaining a distinction between data and their interpretation is preferred.

Now, focusing on interpersonal markers, *Table 4* shows the data extracted from the analysis in occurrences and frequencies normalised to 1,000 words:

Table 4. Interpersonal devices found in the three corpora

Interpersonal markers	**Engineering (N to 1,000 words)**	**Medicine (N)**	**Linguistics (N)**
Hedges	6,908 (10.56)	3,930 (8.64)	10,994 (17.26)
Boosters	2,523 (3.85)	1,965 (4.32)	3,952 (6.20)
Attitude markers	4,537 (6.93)	3,254 (7.15)	5,083 (7.98)
Engagement markers	1,380 (2.11)	399 (0.87)	3,240 (5.08)
Self-mentions	1,424 (2.17)	1,607 (3.53)	2,400 (3.76)
Total	16,772 (25.65)	11,155 (24.53)	25,669 (40.32)

In the table, it can be seen that linguists used more interpersonal markers, but here some results should be commented on. Medical doctors used more attitude markers, boosters and self-mentions than engineers. This could be caused by the nature of medical papers, which basically explain the results obtained by a research team, and very often report on the benefits gained from experiments with new drugs or treatments that should be highlighted (boosters and attitude markers). At the same time, mentions to the team should also be included in the paper.

Some of the results extracted coincide with *Hyland's (1998*, p. 445), where he noticed that "[...] writers used more textual than interpersonal forms in this corpus, and that hedges and connectives were the most frequent devices followed by code glosses and evidentials". In this study, hedges and logical markers (connectives) are more frequently used but they are followed by boosters and attitude markers. These findings could imply that scientific writing has changed and authors are more aware of the use of boosters and attitude markers to present claims with less caution and deference than was the norm thirty years ago. This could entail a change in the concern for expressing arguments explicitly.

4.2. Results of the Analysis of Lexical Density

The lexical density test is a readability test designed to show how easy or difficult a text is to read. Clearly, academic writing should be easy to understand by scholars who share the same specific field of knowledge, that is, it is written to be understood by expert readers. Nevertheless, we thought that the identification of lexical density in engineering, medicine and linguistics could provide some information that indicated disciplinary variability and complemented the frequencies obtained from the analysis of metadiscourse markers. The results by field of knowledge are shown in *Table 5* and in the different figures below.

Table 5. Tokens and lexical density of the corpus

Data corpus	Engineering	Medicine	Linguistics
Tokens	653,787	454,573	636,620
Lexical density	58.36 %	57.62 %	56.08 %
Normalised lexical density	0.88 %	1.23 %	0.87 %

Figure 1 shows the results of Engineering analysis of lexical density.

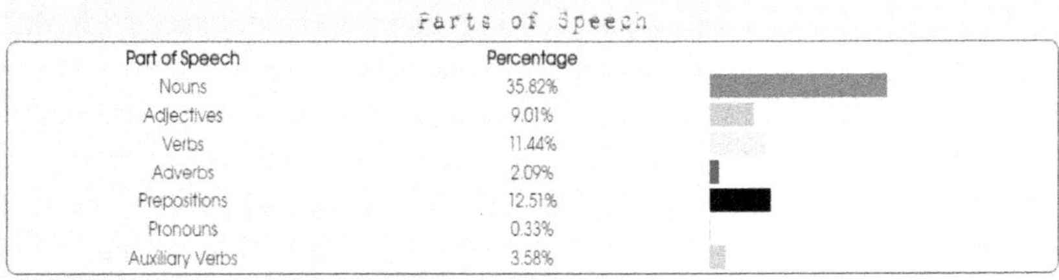

Figure 1. Lexical density, percentage of lexical and grammatical words in engineering

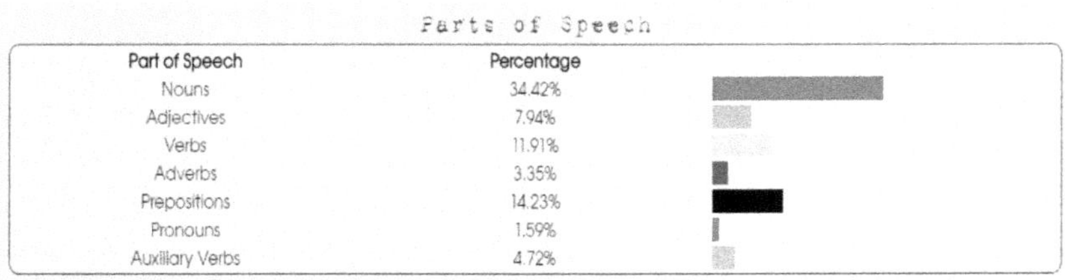

Figure 2. Lexical density, percentage of lexical and grammatical words in medicine

Figure 2 shows the lexical density of medicine in lexical and grammatical items.

Figure 3 shows the lexical density of linguistic academic papers.

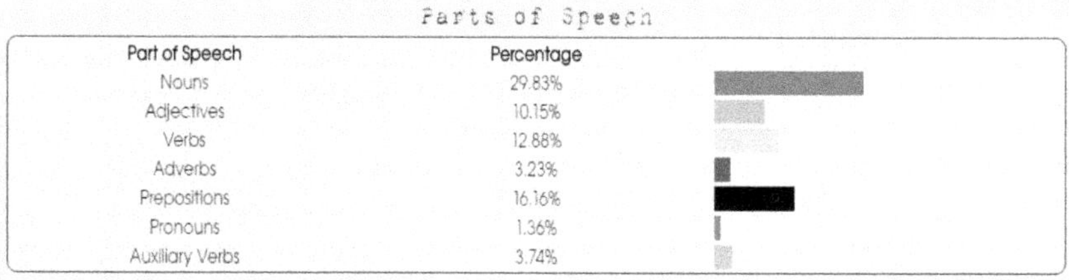

Figure 3. Lexical density, percentage of lexical and grammatical words in linguistics

The lexical density of a text attempts to measure the proportion of the content (lexical) words over the total words. Texts with a lower density are more easily understood, thus it can be seen that in linguistics, texts have a lower density. On the contrary, in medicine, papers include a higher number of lexical items addressed to specialised readers and, thus, they are more complex for the layperson. All the academic papers follow the same pattern, academic writers used more nouns than verbs, adjectives and adverbs.

If we compare these results with those found in metadiscourse markers, we can see that the higher the frequencies of metadiscourse devices used by linguists, engineers and medical researchers are, the lower the frequencies in lexical density will be. This is also connected with the fact that we obtained more occurrences in textual markers, which are grammatical items. In this vein, linguists used more textual markers to guide readers and, thus, fewer lexical items in academic discourse. These findings are in line with *Hyland (1998*, p. 445): "[...] preferred uses of metadiscourse might reflect broad areas of intellectual inquiry, knowledge structures and their associated forms of discourse". In this sense, the preference for textual and interpersonal markers may also indicate a lower degree of lexical density. Writers may pay more attention to metadiscourse devices and less attention to content words.

4.3. Results of Lexical Diversity

Regarding the analysis of lexical diversity that was performed with *Wordsmith tools*, the results of the corpus can be observed in *Table 6*:

Table 6. Data taken into account in the analysis of lexical diversity with *WordSmith tools*

Text statistical analysis	Engineering	Medicine	Linguistics
Types (distinct words)	14,796	15,287	20,765
Type/token ratio (TTR)	5.62	4.79	5.32
Standardised TTR	35.98	34.70	36.99
Mean word length (in characters)	5.16	5.25	5.04
Sentences	11,950	14,568	15,343
Mean sentence length (in words)	22.02	21.89	25.42
Paragraphs	40	84	46
Mean paper length (in words)	6,579.30	3,796.57	8,479.43

The aim of calculating lexical diversity is to analyse the number or variety of words encountered in the three subcorpora. *As Jarvis (2013*, p. 88) explained, "Lexical diversity is thus often understood as the inverse of the word repetition rate". It can be observed that the results of the type/token ratio show that linguists use fewer repeated words, while in the medical subcorpora less lexical diversity was identified. These findings were unexpected if compared with lexical density. The medicine corpus has the lowest lexical diversity but the highest lexical density. In contrast, in the linguistics corpus the highest lexical diversity and lower lexical density were obtained. This therefore means that in linguistics, academic writers use a lower number of words but the words are not repeated so frequently as in engineering and medicine.

Finally, with the aim of comparing the results, the total data extracted from the analysis of the corpus are shown in *Table 7*. The normalised frequencies of the textual markers, the interpersonal markers and the normalised average frequency of metadiscourse, as well as the normalised results of lexical density and lexical diversity can be seen below:

Table 7. Comparison of results of metadiscourse, lexical density and lexical diversity

Total	**Engineering**	**Medicine**	**Linguistics**
Textual markers	20.93	18.28	27.27
Interpersonal markers	25.65	24.53	40.32
N average frequency of metadiscourse markers	66.88	42.81	67.59
Normalised Lexical density	0.88 %	1.23 %	0.87 %
Lexical diversity (standardised TTR)	35.98	34.70	36.99

As can be observed, linguists used metadiscourse markers and distinct words (lexical diversity) more frequently in academic English. On the contrary, medical doctors used fewer metadiscourse markers but more lexical words (lexical density). It can therefore be observed that high or low use of metadiscourse devices in academic writing is not related to lexical density and lexical diversity. Linguists seem to be more aware of the use of rhetorical strategies and of a wider variety of words to explain the introduction, method, results and conclusions. We found similar frequencies in engineering, but all the frequencies were average, that is, they were figures between those of medical doctors and linguists. Medical doctors used fewer metadiscourse markers and, as explained above, this may be due to the long tradition in research which means that the writers do not need to interact with readers or to persuade them. Lexical density is also high, which means that medical researchers used lexical words. Yet, as the fact that lexical diversity is low could mean that many words are repeated because medical research focuses on very specialised research that does not need to be explained or require the use of synonyms.

A graphical comparison of the results can be seen in *Figure 4*:

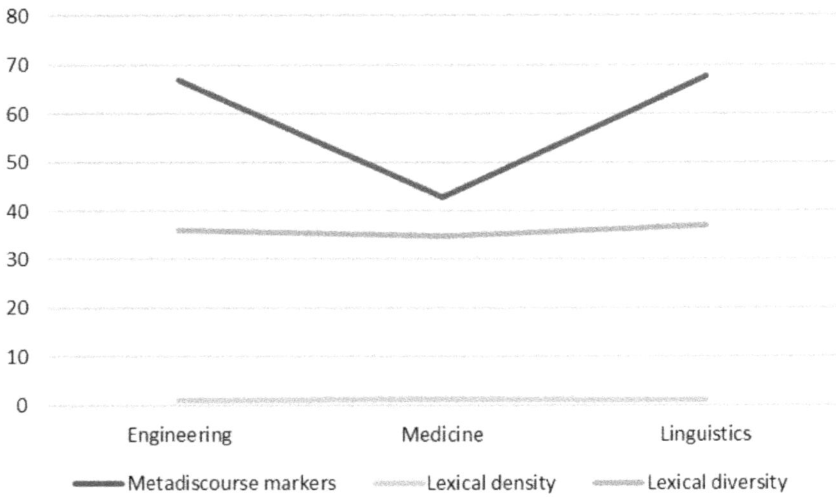

Figure 4. Comparison of metadiscourse devices, lexical density and lexical diversity data

Hence, the results obtained in lexical density and lexical diversity are quite similar. The greatest divergence was found in the use of metadiscourse devices. Some examples from the corpus are shown below to illustrate the differences in the three fields of study analysed. Engineering is shown in example (1), medicine in (2) and linguistics in (3):

1. Engineering: "Since there is a difference in the chemical potentials of the left and right leads, electrons are transferred across the molecular junction in order to maintain equilibrium, as shown in *Figure 2*. However, the electrons must cross an energy barrier to pass from the contact to the molecule [7]."
2. Medicine: "All patients were intended for long term androgen deprivation therapy and started treatment no earlier than 12 weeks before randomisation. There were no age restrictions; patients were required to have no contraindications to radiotherapy and no clinically significant cardiovascular history."
3. Linguistics: "In the three interviews, the participants self-identified each of the eight learning outcomes. *Table 6* charts the participants' self-identified references (in percentage) to each of the learning

> outcomes across the three interviews, and *Table 7* shows selected responses from the interviews. In all cases, the first interview had the highest percentage of student-identified transfer across all the learning outcomes."

Therefore, the analysis of lexical diversity and lexical density combined with the study of the use of metadiscourse suggests that there are in fact differences in the way academic writers construct their image and interact with readers. Linguists should know a wider variety of words than medical doctors or engineers but readers of medical research should be familiar with the structure and specific topic before reading papers, as writers do not guide them and use more lexical words than in the other two domains. Once all the data analysed has been shown and the results discussed, the extent to which our objectives have been met is addressed in the conclusions.

5. Conclusions

After analysing the data to answer the first objective, that is, to examine whether lexical density and lexical diversity are sensitive to different domains, namely linguistics, engineering and medicine, it has been proved that there are in fact differences. Linguists use a greater number of different words than engineers and medical researchers while medical doctors use more lexical words and fewer grammatical words than linguists and engineers (see *Tables 5* and *6*). This was checked manually in the corpus and it was observed that medical journals are very specific and repeat lexical words, while linguists use a wider variety of vocabulary. Engineers behave in a similar way to linguists but with lower frequencies, and these findings are in line with *Dahl (2004*, p. 1819), when she explains that the fact "the medical texts turned out to be very different from the texts in the other two disciplines is not very surprising". Hence, here we have also proved that medical research papers do not have the same structure or follow the same rhetorical patterns as other domains.

The second objective was to study whether the frequencies of use of rhetorical markers in different domains, i.e. textual and interpersonal, could be in line with lexical diversity and lexical density in academic English. The results were not similar, as it was observed that the frequencies in lexical density and lexical diversity were not very different, but we did find differences in the use of metadiscourse devices. Logical markers were frequently used as well as attitude markers and boosters, which implies that writers show their findings in a way that is not as humble as how they used to do it (*Hyland, 1998*). This finding should be corroborated in further diachronic studies that definitely show that there is a difference in the way academic writing is used nowadays to describe experiments and to convince readers about their importance.

Regarding the last objective, to investigate to what extent lexical diversity and lexical density are correlated and occur with similar frequencies in different domains, a variety of data was obtained. In the results (see *Tables 3* and *4*), we observed that academic writers used similar frequencies of metadiscourse devices in engineering and linguistics, but medical researchers used fewer devices. This is in line with the results obtained regarding lexical density and lexical diversity, as the data obtained differ in medical research, showing the specific nature of this type of research. *Dahl (2004)* suggested that this could be due to the long tradition of medical research, but it could also be connected to the high specificity of medical journals, as commented before.

We think that further studies to identify whether there could be any differences in other domains, such as architecture, law and economics will be carried out in future work as we believe that patterns that allow us to understand the way we communicate in academic English need to be identified. Frequency, accuracy and complexity of words can be a line of research that complements the results of lexical density, lexical diversity and metadiscourse in academic writing.

References

Abdollahzadeh, E. (2019). A cross-cultural study of hedging in discussion sections by junior and senior academic writers. *Ibérica, 38*, 177–202.

Adel, A. (2006). Metadiscourse in L1 and L2 English: A corpus-based study of academic writing. Amsterdam: John Benjamins Publishing.

Berman, R., & Nir, B. (2010). The lexicon in writing–speech-differentiation. Developmental perspectives. *Written Language & Literacy, 13*(2), 183–205.

Berman, R., Nayditz, R., & Ravid, D. (2011). Linguistic diagnostics of written texts in two school-age populations. *Written Language & Literacy, 14*(2), 161–187.

Breivega, K., Dahl, T., & Fløttum, K. (2002). Traces of self and others in research articles. A comparative pilot study of English, French and Norwegian research articles in medicine, economics and linguistics. *International Journal of Applied Linguistics, 12*(2), 218–239.

Cao, F., & Hu, G. (2014). Interactive metadiscourse in research articles: A comparative study of paradigmatic and disciplinary influences. *Journal of Pragmatics, 66*, 15–31.

Carrió Pastor, M. L. (2013). A contrastive study of the variation of sentence connectors in academic English. *Journal of English for Academic Purposes, 12*, 192–201.

Carrió-Pastor, M. L. (2014). Cross-cultural variation in the use of modal verbs in academic English. *SKY Journal of Linguistics, 27*, 153–166.

Carrió-Pastor, M. L. (2016a). A contrastive study of interactive metadiscourse in academic papers written in English and in Spanish. In F. Alonso Almeida, L. Cruz García, & V. González Ruiz (Eds.), *Corpus-based studies on language varieties* (pp. 89–114). Bern: Peter Lang.

Carrió-Pastor, M. L. (2016b). Mitigation of claims in medical research papers: A comparative study of English and Spanish writers. *Communication & Medicine, 13*, 249–261.

Carrió-Pastor, M. L. (2019a). Different ways to express personal attitudes in Spanish and English engineering papers: An analysis of metadiscourse devices, affective evaluation and sentiment analysis. *Lodz Papers in Pragmatics, 15*(1), 45–67.

Carrió-Pastor, M. L. (2019b). Do writers express the same attitude in historical genres? In I. Moskowich et al. (Eds.), *Writing history in Late Modern English. Explorations of the Coruña Corpus* (pp. 237–259). Amsterdam: John Benjamins.

Carrió-Pastor, M. L. (2019c). Authorial engagement in business emails. In C. Sancho-Guinda (Ed.), *Engagement in Professional Genres* (pp. 47–66). Amsterdam: John Benjamins.

Carrió-Pastor, M. L. (2020a). Variation in the use of self-mentions in different specific fields of knowledge in academic English. In M. L. Carrió-Pastor (Ed.), *Corpus analysis in different genres: Academic discourse and learner corpora* (pp. 13–32). London: Routledge.

Carrió-Pastor, M. L. (Ed.). (2020b). *Corpus analysis in different genres: Academic discourse and learner corpora*. London: Routledge.

Dahl, T. (2004). Textual metadiscourse in research articles: A marker of national culture or of academic discipline. *Journal of Pragmatics, 36*, 1807–1825.

Daller, H., van Hout, R., & Treffers-Daller, J. (2003). Lexical richness in the spontaneous speech of bilinguals. *Applied Linguistics,* 24(2), 197–222.

Duran, P., Malvern, D., Richards, B., & Chipere, N. (2004). Developmental trends in lexical diversity. *Applied Linguistics, 25*(2), 220–242.

Fuentes, K., Hernández, S., & Salcedo, P. (2019). Descripción de la diversidad y densidad léxicas en noticias escritas por estudiantes de periodismo. *Revista Brasileira de Linguística Aplicada, 19*(3), 499–528.

Gholami, J., Mosalli, Z., & Nikou, S. (2012). Lexical complexity and discourse markers in soft and hard science articles. *World Applied Sciences Journal, 17*(3), 368–374.

Gillaerts, P., & Van de Velde, F. (2010). Interactional metadiscourse in research article abstracts. *Journal of English for Academic Purposes, 9*(2), 128–139.

Gregori-Signes, C., & Clavel-Arroitia, B. (2015). Analysing lexical density and lexical diversity in university students' written discourse. *Procedia-Social and Behavioral Sciences, 198*, 546–556.

Halliday, M. A. K. (1985). *Spoken and written language*. Oxford: Oxford University Press.

Hudson, R. (2009). Measuring maturity. In R. Beard, D. Myhill, J. Riley, & M. Nystrand (Eds.), *The SAGE handbook of writing development* (pp. 349–362). London: SAGE Publications Ltd.

Hyland, K. (1998). Persuasion and context: The pragmatics of academic metadiscourse. *Journal of Pragmatics, 30*, 437–455.

Hyland, K. (2005). *Metadiscourse: Exploring Interaction in Writing*. London: Continuum.

Hyland, K. (2010). Metadiscourse: Mapping interactions in academic writing. *Nordic Journal of English Studies, 9*(2), 125–143.

Hyland, K., & Tse, P. (2004). Metadiscourse in academic writing: A reappraisal. *Applied Linguistics, 25*, 156–177.

Jarvis, S. (2002). Short texts, best-fitting curves and new measures of lexical diversity. *Language Testing, 19*(1), 57–84.

Jarvis, S. (2013a). Capturing the diversity in lexical diversity. *Language Learning, 63*, 87–106.

Jarvis, S. (2013b). Defining and measuring lexical diversity. In S. Jarvis & M. Daller (Eds.), *Vocabulary knowledge: Human ratings and automated measures* (pp. 13–44). Amsterdam: John Benjamins Publishing.

Johansson, V. (2008). Lexical diversity and lexical density in speech and writing: A developmental perspective. *Lund University, Dept. of Linguistics and Phonetics. Working Papers, 5*, 61–79.

Malvern, D., & Richards, B. (1997). A new measure of lexical diversity. In A. Ryan & A. Wray (Eds.), *Evolving models of language: Papers from the annual meeting of the British Association for Applied Linguistics* (pp. 58–71). Clevedon: Multilingual Matters.

Malvern, D., Richards, B., Chipere, N., & Duran, P. (2004). *Lexical diversity and language development: quantification and assessment*. New York: Palgrave Macmillan.

Mauranen, A. (1993). Cultural differences in academic rhetoric: A text-linguistic study. Bern: Peter Lang.

Mur-Dueñas, P. (2011). An intercultural analysis of metadiscourse features in research articles written in English and in Spanish. *Journal of Pragmatics, 43*(12), 3068–3079.

Ravid, D. (2006). Semantic-pragmatic development in textual contexts during the school years: The noun scale. *Journal of Child Language, 33*, 791–821.

Read, J. (2000). *Assessing vocabulary*. Cambridge: Cambridge University Press.

Thompson, G. (2001). Interaction in academic writing: Learning to argue with the reader. *Applied Linguistics, 22*(1), 58–78.

To, V., Fan, S., & Thomas, D. (2013). Lexical density and readability: A case study of English textbooks. *Internet Journal of Language, Culture and Society, 37*, 61–71.

Ure, J. (1971). Lexical density and register differentiation. In G. Perren & J. Trim (Eds.), *Applications of Linguistics* (pp. 443–452). London: Cambridge University Press.

Vande Kopple, W. J. (2012). The importance of studying metadiscourse in academic writing. In K. Hyland & P. Tse (Eds.), Metadiscourse in writing (pp. 93–111). London: Continuum.

Vermeer, A. (2000). Coming to grips with lexical richness in spontaneous speech data. *Language Testing, 17*, 65–83.

Waller, T. (1993). Characteristics of near-native proficiency in writing. In H. Ringbom (Ed.), *Near-native proficiency in English* (pp. 183–293). Åbo, Finland: English Department, Åbo Akademi University.

CARME BACH / MARIA DOLORS CAÑADA PUJOLS

Universitat Pompeu Fabra / Universitat Pompeu Fabra

Interactive Metadiscourse Markers in Abstracts Written by Undergraduate Students[1]

1. Introduction

The *abstract* is a specialized type of academic discourse, like a lecture, literature review or research article, and therefore related to the expression and transmission of knowledge. The scientific literature offers numerous studies on the abstract as an academic genre based on corpora created by researchers who are themselves experts in their respective disciplines (*Cavalieri, 2014;* Dos *Santos, 1996; Lorés & Bondi, 2014; Saeeaw & Tangkiengsirisin, 2014*). Nonetheless, there exist relatively few studies which analyse how student writers acquire mastery over this genre (*Aktas & Cortes, 2008; Díez Prados, 2018*). As a contribution to filling this gap in the research, in the present study we will examine a corpus of abstracts written by undergraduates, focusing in particular on their use of interactive metadiscourse markers and the relationship between such markers and the rhetorical structure of the texts.

1 This work was supported by the *Assessment of Discourse Competence in Adult Plurilingual Learners: Detecting Learners' Needs and Instructions for Autonomous Learning* project (EDU2016-75874-P) under the *Plan Nacional de Investigación Científica, Desarrollo e Innovación Tecnológica 2016* of the Spanish Ministry of Economy, Industry and Competitiveness and co-financed by the Spanish State Research Agency (AEI) and the European Union's Regional Development Fund (FEDER). The authors of this article belong to the Gr@el research group (*Grup de recerca sobre aprenentatge i ensenyament de llengües* 'Language Learning and Teaching Research Group'), which is funded by a Catalan government AGAUR 2017–2019 grant (ref. 2017 SGR 915).

Within the Spanish context, the study of these textual products assumed special importance following the enactment of a law in October 2007 regarding the regulation of university educational practices, which stipulated that all undergraduate or master's degree programmes had to include a final thesis project in their curriculum. In other words, the requirement to prepare such a final thesis project was no longer the prerogative of individual Spanish universities but rather mandated for all by the state. This meant that the writing of abstracts by university undergraduates has become a universal academic practice throughout Spain. The student-authored abstract is therefore, in our view, a genre very much deserving of the sort of detailed description and analysis that we propose to undertake in the present study.

1.1. The Abstract as a Discourse Genre

An abstract is a type of summary that precedes an academic or scientific article and is typically positioned on the first page immediately after the title. Its function is to concisely provide information about the article's contents so that potential readers can obtain very quickly a general idea of what the article offers in order to decide whether it worth reading in full or not. Formally, it synthesizes the key elements contained in the article, namely the topic that is covered, the methodology applied and, above all, the results obtained.

The abstract belongs to the family of academic genres which includes both oral texts such as lectures or oral presentations and written texts like essays, personal commentaries or literature reviews. It is also characterized by broad variation across disciplines (*Venegas, Zamora & Galdames, 2016*).

The *final thesis project* (henceforth TFG, from Spanish *Trabajo de Fin de Grado*)[2] is an academic genre that is evaluative in nature (*Venegas et al., 2016*) since the student is awarded a grade or mark on their

2 This is the official term used in Spain and therefore what we will use here, though elsewhere such a text may be referred to as an *undergraduate dissertation*, *undergraduate thesis*, *undergraduate research project*, *undergraduate final year project* or *final year research project*.

TFG by academic instructors, something which is not true of other scientific texts. As with any scientific or academic article, the TFG is preceded by an abstract, which is likewise the object of assessment. According to *Venegas et al. (2016)*, abstracts may be descriptive, structured or informative. A descriptive abstract is one which very briefly (in around 100 words) reports the work carried out and is more commonly seen in conference programs than in scientific journals. Structured abstracts are characterized by a list of sections corresponding to aim, study design, location and context, participants (or other objects of study), interventions, outcome measures and main results and conclusions. Finally, informative abstracts are the most common in scientific contexts such as journals or conference proceedings and academic contexts like master's theses, doctoral dissertations and so on. They are typically between 150 and 200 words in length and act as "substitutes" for the full document in question.

Neither the rhetorical organization of abstracts nor their other discourse features can be understood without first describing the functions associated with the genre. First of all, such features make it possible to index the text in various databases, either at the local level, as in a university electronic repository, or at the international level, in reference listings such as *Linguistics and Language Behavior Abstracts* or *Web of Science*. Second, they orient the reader in terms of the essential contents of the full text by succinctly describing the aim, methodology, results and so on. Finally, they have a clearly persuasive function, since one of their chief purposes is to convince the reader to go on and read the text in its entirety. In the words of *Jiang and Hyland (2017*, p. 1), "Research article abstracts have become an important genre in all knowledge fields, playing a crucial role in persuading readers and reviewers, to take the time to go further into the paper itself. This promotional aspect of abstracts is well known [...] ."

1.2. The Rhetorical Structure of Abstracts

The structure of the abstracts of academic or scientific articles as well as the articles themselves have been the object of considerable scrutiny in the literature. In the present study, following the work of *Swales (1990)* and *Bhatia (1993)*, we understand *rhetorical move* as referring to each particular fragment of a text that has a specific communicative goal. Thus, as we have noted, an abstract must follow the macrostructure of the original text, with the result that the structure and content of the two texts must perforce be very similar. An academic text is made up, in da Cunha's words, of "prototypical contents in a particular order, such as the reason for the study, its aim, the current state of knowledge on the issue, the theoretical framework, methodology, analysis, results and conclusions. Thus, the summary of this textual genre must also reflect the main contents of the work, albeit concisely, and in the same order (our translation)" (*2016*, p. 108).

Along the same lines, *Sancho (2014)* indicates in his guidelines for students and instructors that every abstract must include an introduction (I), methods (M), results (R) and discussion (D). In prescribing this, Sancho is stressing that the abstract must follow the IMRD structure typical of many research articles, as already pointed out by *Swales (1990)*. The IMRD acronym reflects the *Introduction, Methodology, Results, Discussion* and *Conclusion* rhetorical moves which Swales identified in these texts, similar to the structure described for such articles by *Bhatia (1993)*, who in the first of these moves also includes the *aims* of the research.

In his study on the abstracts of specialized articles in the area of applied languages, Dos *Santos (1996)* notes the presence of a fifth move not previously identified, which appears sequentially first in the abstract and serves to contextualize the research by describing the current state of knowledge, citing prior studies or posing a particular problem. In the present article we will adopt Dos *Santos's (1996)* proposal, which in addition to incorporating the earlier concepts is situated in the same discipline as that focused on here, namely applied languages. The emergence like this of a rhetorical move not previously detected in work on a particular discourse genre led *Venegas, Núñez, Zamora and Santana (2015)* to coin the term *emerging movement*. Though we instead use the label *emerging move*, this concept will prove useful when instances of this very phenomenon arise in our own data, as we will see below.

1.3. Metadiscourse Markers

Metadiscourse markers are defined by *Hyland and Tse (2004)* and *Hyland (2005)* as a category through which to analyse a text either in terms of the interaction between the writer and his/her text (what could be called the *textual-interactive* function of the text) or between the writer and his/her readers (the *interactional* function of the text). In the present article, we will analyse only those metadiscourse elements present in our corpus that serve a textual-interactive function, in other words, those intended to construct a text that is coherent for the reader. As Hyland puts it, "The use of resources in this category therefore addresses ways of organizing discourse, rather than experience, and reveals the extent to which the text is constructed with the reader's needs in mind" (*2005*, p. 49).

According to *Hyland (2005)*, there exist five types of interactive metadiscourse markers, to wit, *transition markers*, *frame markers, endophoric markers, evidentials* and *code glosses*, which we will call *definitional contexts* in this paper, following *Alarcón, Bach and Sierra (2007)* and *Alarcón, Sierra, Aguilar and Bach (2008)*. Within the category of frame markers we will also include *metadiscursive nouns*, which Jiang and Hyland regard as a neglected feature of metadiscourse elements: "We set out here to correct this oversight and attempt to map what we call metadiscursive nouns onto *Hyland's (2005)* metadiscourse model, showing how these nouns promote interactions between writers and readers in academic writing" (*2018*, p. 509). In fact, these nouns can make a significant contribution to creating cohesion in an abstract, since they allow the recovery (whether anaphoric or cataphoric) of discursive fragments. In addition, as pointed out by Jiang and Hyland, they play a key role in the construction of textual coherence. In their words, "In the interactive dimension, metadiscourse nouns also help to create logical coherence from discoursal cohesion, shaping texts to what readers will find most familiar, plausible and persuasive" (*2018*, p. 520). These metadiscursive nouns have been discussed previously by *Vendler (1968)*, *Halliday and Hassan (1976)*, who call them *general nouns*, and *Francis (1986)*, who prefers the term *anaphoric nouns*. For his part, *Schmid (2000* and *2018*) refers to them as *shell nouns*.

After briefly describing our methodology in Section 2, we will explore in greater depth all of these textual metadiscourse resources in Section 3, illustrating them with examples from our own data.

2. Methodology

The corpus under study here was made up of thirty-five abstracts in L2 English written by undergraduate students doing a degree in Applied Languages at a Spanish university and comprised a total of 6,441 words. Prior to writing, the students received general instructions about how to prepare a TFG but were not given specific details about how the write the thesis as a whole or the abstract in particular. The length of the abstracts they produced varied considerably, ranging from a minimum of 78 words to a maximum of 286, the average being 184.

In order to analyse the macrotextual and microtextual features of the abstracts we used the ATLAS.ti software, which permits the researcher to conduct qualitative data analysis by labelling text as a function of the categories which emerge in it, which in turn makes it a simple task to measure the frequency with which the phenomena under study occur. In this study, we used the software to label two elements in our corpus of student-written abstracts: first, at the macrotextual level, we labelled the rhetorical moves, whether they were categories suggested by the literature or emerging moves not previously anticipated (see above); and second, at the microtextual level, we identified the various metadiscourse categories, which we labelled following *Hyland and Tse (2004)* and *Hyland (2005)*, but also including the abovementioned metadiscursive nouns, in line with Jiang and Hyland (2017) and Jiang and Hyland (2018). Finally, we looked for relationships among categories across the two dimensions. Analysis of the full corpus was conducted independently by the two authors, and results were then compared. The few instances where there were discrepancies in labelling were discussed until a common position was reached. This process ensured total reliability of categorization.

3. Analysis of the Data

3.1. Macrotextual Features of the Corpus

Our macrotextual analysis of the abstracts yielded a total of seven moves: *introduction*, *aims*, *methodology*, *results*, *conclusions*, *structure* and *limitations*. The first five match the prototype for research paper abstracts set forth in *Dos Santos (1996)*, while *structure* and *limitations* constitute emerging moves. Though we are cognizant that the location of a move within a text is an important issue (see da *Cunha, 2016*), we will not deal with this parameter here.

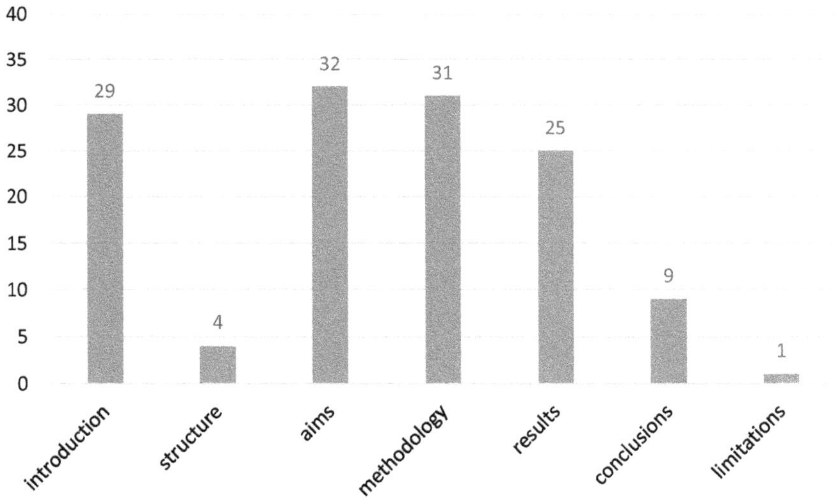

Figure 1. Frequency of occurrence of rhetorical moves in the abstracts

As can be observed in *Figure 1*, the most frequent moves are those that present *aims*, *methodology* or *introduction*, in that order. It is worth noting that the number of moves in a given text in the corpus was variable. Seventy-four per cent of the texts had between four and five moves, whereas others had two or three, and yet others had only one (which was either *introduction* or *aims*). In addition, several of the student writers included elements from a particular move, whether the *introduction* (three students), *aims* (five students) or *methodology* (five students), in two separate blocks rather than as a single unit – an approach that yielded a reiterative structure hardly appropriate for a brief summary, it might be noted. We will now analyse in detail each of the moves identified.

First, the *introduction*, one of the more frequent rhetorical moves, as noted, was fairly variable in length. The main function of this move is to situate the reader and attract his/her attention, "to sell the research being offered," to quote Dos *Santos (1996*, p. 485). In his own corpus of research paper abstracts, Dos Santos identified four possible submoves within the introduction, namely *stating current knowledge*, *citing previous research*, *expanding on previous research* and *stating a problem*, with the first and last of these being the most common according to his study.

In the abstracts in our dataset, the *introduction* always appears as the initial move. In general, the student writers begin by setting out the topic and then introduce the reason or justification for their TFG, that is, they present the gap in knowledge that their work is intended to fill. This is illustrated in the excerpt in (1) below, where the student first introduces the topic (terminology used in the bottled water industry in Catalonia) and then explains the need for further linguistic research in this area, specifically relating written genres with the colloquial oral register, which will constitute the primary aim of his/her TFG.

(1) This paper deals with the terminology used during the process of industrialization of water in the bottling plants of Catalonia. The water sector offers many jobs throughout the territory, and Catalan is the vehicular language of many of the people who work at the bottling plants. We can find terminology in all areas and for this reason, it is necessary and essential to have a terminological vocabulary about this sector. This vocabulary is an opportunity for linguistic normalization and for all specialists since it can facilitate the work they do and reduce the ambiguities that may arise while working. EN_04

In our view, the *introduction* move reveals in many instances the identity of the writer as more student than researcher, given that it fails to concisely situate the area of knowledge which frames the research but instead extensively showcases the writer's own knowledge, presumably with a view to positive evaluation on the part of a professor. In the *introduction* in (2), though the writer successfully situates her work within the field of discourse analysis, in this case the discourse of Spanish social media "influencers", she does so at such length that she fails to include her *aims*, *methodology* and *results*, moves which are indispensable to the abstract genre.

(2) This paper analyses two creative influencers that are associated with the company Tantanfan and these are La Vecina Rubia and La Moderna de Pueblo two creatives that make language the core of the product and that, in addition, make use of emotional marketing to attract the maximum number of public and, in this way, they built their identity. Hence language is the way to attract followers and, therefore to do business. In this paper we also observe how irony and sarcasm can have a positive effect on receivers and, in this way, can be included in emotional marketing and, consequently, in positive marketing. EN_28

Nonetheless, she is exceptional in omitting the *aims* move, given that nearly all (91.4%) the student writers refer to them, with thirty-two occurrences out of thirty-five abstracts. In general, the *aims* move is kept very brief, being limited to one or two sentences, as exemplified in (3).

(3) The purpose of this study is to analyze the interferences that can be found in the colloquial Catalan lexicon of Barcelona. EN_22

A presentation of the *methodology* also appears in most of the abstracts (88.6%), with only four failing to do so. Often, this information about the methodology employed suffers from an excess of detail that is not in keeping with a summarizing genre. This can be seen in (4), where the student writer goes into great detail about how the experiment was carried out and what statistical analyses were applied to the data.

(4) An experimental methodology has been followed: thirty women were asked to take part in two voice recognition parades: one containing voices of other women, and the other one containing voices of men. Afterwards, success recognition percentages were computed and compared taking into account the sociolinguistic variables of the participants. The exact same test was repeated in order to obtain more reliable results and reduce the degree of affectation of data. EN_31

In a similar vein, (5) is unnecessarily detailed with regard to the design of the questionnaire.

(5) Nineteen students participated voluntarily in the present study by completing an online questionnaire designed ad hoc. This questionnaire is composed of a total of 26 questions (11 closed and 15 open); it was structured in 3 big blocks: origin, motivation and uses and learning styles. EN_20

The *results* move, whose purpose is to briefly summarize the main findings of the research, occurs somewhat less often in the corpus, appearing in twenty-five out of thirty-five abstracts. A typical example is shown in (6).

(6) Once we analyzed the subjects' point of view, the results showed that, in the present, university students have prejudices in relation to the non-native teachers, but to a lesser extent compared to what former studies had stated. EN_13

Finally, the *conclusions* move appears in only nine abstracts, which suggests that a proportion of Spanish university students graduate without having fully developed their cognitive reasoning skills and with a poor mastery of the abstract genre. To put it a different way, the student writers have difficulty discerning the higher-level implications of the results that they have obtained through their research. The *conclusions* always appear at the close of the abstract and provide explanatory information derived from the *results* move, as we see exemplified in (7).

(7) In conclusion, idioms reflect part of the identity of the people that use them. Therefore, the idioms should not be based on nonnative suggestions, but on the necessities of each person. EN_07

To conclude our macrotextual analysis of the rhetorical structure of the abstracts in the corpus, we will mention two emerging moves not previously noted in the literature whose presence in this dataset are surely due to the fact that the writers are students and not expert researchers. These emerging moves refer to the *structure* of the TFG and its *limitations*. While these moves show a relatively low frequency (11.4%), they are worth mentioning because they help us to characterize the discursive competence of the writers.

The first emerging move we will label *structure*, as exemplified by (8). Though it is not the case here, in some instances this move even makes references to the TFG's appendixes.

(8) Firstly, we will present and compare the most common approaches used in sentiment analysis. Secondly, we will investigate the resources available for sentiment analysis in Spanish. Then, we will explain the structure and operation of

the program we have created. Finally, we will mention possible future lines of research. EN_35

The existence of this move can be explained by confusion about the difference between the discourse features of an abstract and those of the introduction to an article. Although we identified only four cases of this move in the corpus, such confusion may reflect an widespread tendency among student writers, and not only in Spain, given the fact that student writing guidelines published by the University of Melbourne state that "Although it is placed at the beginning of your paper, immediately following the title page, the abstract should be the last thing that you write, once you are sure of the conclusions you will reach,"[3] to cite just one example. Note that in (8) this incomplete understanding of the genre's situational parameters has a clear impact on the abstract at the textual level: first, it affects the use of verb tenses, since triggers a use of the future, a tense not appropriate to this discourse genre; and second, it requires the use of structural markers in a type of text in which they should not be needed and which in addition have the effect of adding length to the abstract at the expense of more important content.

We interpret this deficiency in the rhetorical structure as evidence of difficulty on the part of the student writer in interpreting the enunciative context, and this also occurs with the *limitations* move. In fact, only one student recognizes in his/her abstract the limitations implicit in his/her work, but in doing so he/she detracts from the promotional function that is characteristic of this genre and to which we referred above. We see in (9) the excerpt in question.

(9) We must say that the aim of the study is not focused on establishing linguistic results that can be applied to all the linguistic reality in the Catalan language [...]. EN_22

3.2. Microtextual Features of the Corpus

As noted above, the corpus was analysed at the microtextual level by detecting the presence in it of interactive metadiscourse markers, that is,

3 This may be accessed at https://services.unimelb.edu.au/__data/assets/pdf_file/0007/471274/Writing_an_ Abstract_Update_051112.pdf.

those markers that guide a reader through a text. We will apply *Hyland's (2005)* classification of these markers into transition markers, frame markers, evidentials and definitional contexts, to which we will add, as forewarned above, metadiscursive nouns. Hyland's classification also includes endophoric markers, no examples of which were identified in this corpus, though this is unsurprising given the concise nature of the abstract genre.

3.2.1. Transition Markers

A transition marker is a discourse marker that "expresses relations between main clauses" (*Hyland, 2005*, p. 49). We have therefore only selected the discourse markers that are parenthetical connectives, that is, those which are "syntactically peripheral items indicating basic logico-argumentative meaning" (*Cuenca, 2013*, p. 193). Such markers appear a total of fifty-seven times in the corpus, in some instances only once ("because", "furthermore", "in spite of", "inasmuch as", "nonetheless", "particularly", "recently", "singularly", "ultimately"), in others multiple times, as shown in *Table 1* below (items in the table subsume variants such as "in addition to" or "though"). Most (66.7%) of these forms occurred at the beginning of sentences, the remainder appearing medially.

Table 1. Frequency of occurrence of transition markers

however	**6**	**thus**	**3**
but	5	although	2
in this way	5	consequently	2
therefore	5	even though	2
despite (of) [sic]	4	hence	2
in addition	4	likewise	2
moreover	4	nevertheless	2

To further analyse these transition markers, we determined the fundamental relationship conveyed by each marker type, adopting for this purpose *Cuenca's (2013*, p. 193) classification. Though Cuenca stipulates four basic semantic relationships, in the present study we will make use of only three of them, namely *addition* (the utterances thus joined must be regarded as a sum of meanings), *contrast* (which implies the addition of content that diverges relative to the preceding content) and *consequence* (which conveys a cause-and-effect relationship among statements). We will not concern ourselves with Cuenca's fourth type of relationship, which she labels *disjunction* (alternative formulations of the same content) since markers of this sort always introduce definitional contexts, which we will treat them separately in Section 3.2.4 below. This keeps us consistent with Hyland and Tse, who indicate that transition markers "comprise the rich set of internal devices used to mark additive, contrastive and consequential steps in the discourse, as opposed to the external world" (*2004*, p. 168).

Almost half of the transition markers present in the corpus indicate contrast (43%), the rest showing consequence (37.8%) or addition (18.8%).[4] An example of the use of the most common type, a contrastive transition marker (in boldface), can be seen in (10).

(10) Research regarding sign languages has become more and more widespread and it allows us to have new visions of these Languages. *Nonetheless* there are a lot of fields that have yet to be analyzed in these languages. EN_06

The second most common type of transition marker observed in the corpus is of the consequence type, exemplified in (11). Here the student presents the object of study ("new texts and new forms of expression"), then uses the marker ("hence") to justify why this issue merits study.

(11) With the emergence of new technologies, new texts and new forms of expression have appeared. *Hence*, there is a necessity of having more information about these texts, knowing how they are composed and what resources they use. EN_16

Finally, occurring much less frequently, additive transition markers add new information along the same lines as that already provided. In (12), the student presents the results of his TFG, and then, by means of the additive marker "in addition", adds a final complementary element to this move.

4 Excerpts are reproduced verbatim from the original TFG texts, regardless of their grammaticality or quality.

(12) It is observed that first-generation immigrant students in Catalonia achieve better results than the rest of Autonomous Regions and the OECD average, as well as differences in performance once the discount of the ESCS index has been applied. *In addition*, the results have also shown that the difference in the performance of students of foreign origin between Catalonia and Quebec is linked to the socioeconomic background at home. EN_03

With regard to the distribution of sequencing discourse markers among the various rhetorical moves identified, it can be seen in *Figure 2* that most appear in the *introduction* or *results* moves. In the former case, given the relative length of this move in these student abstracts, transition markers serve to ensure text cohesion and also make it easier for the writer to transition from the presentation of the topic to the justification for his/her study.

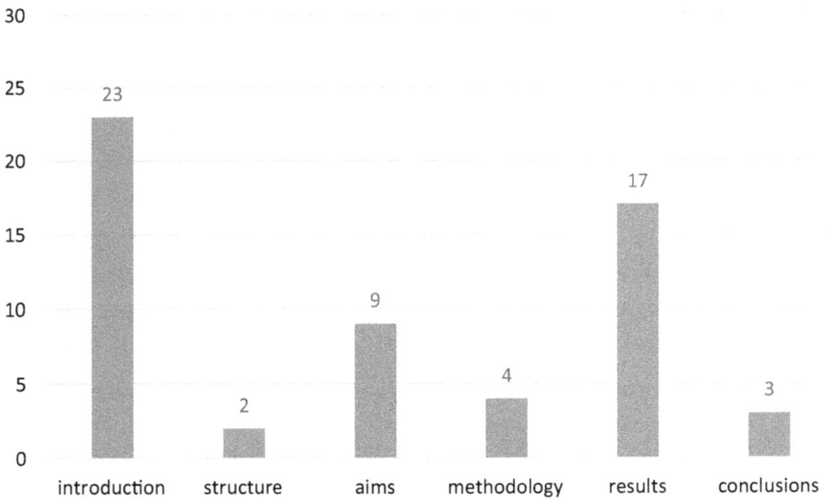

Figure 2. Distribution of sequencing discourse markers across rhetorical moves

3.2.2. Frame Markers

Within the category of frame markers, we find elements that make reference to and signpost the structure of the text. As we noted above, this group of markers comprises two subgroups, namely sequencing discourse markers, which give shape to the overall organization of the text (see Section 3.2.2.1), and metadiscursive nouns, which create links between different parts of the text (see Section 3.2.2.2).

3.2.2.1. Sequencing Discourse Markers

Sequencing discourse markers – what Hyland and Tse refer to simply as "frame markers" – serve as "references to text boundaries or elements of schematic text structure" (*2004*, p. 168). We identified a total of eighteen such sequencing discourse markers in the corpus. Those which appear more than once are shown in *Table 2* below. In addition, we found one occurrence each of "afterwards", "in conclusion", "lastly" and "then".

Table 2. Frequency of occurrence of sequencing discourse markers

Finally	10
Firstly	2
On the one hand	2
On the other hand	2
Secondly	2

It should be noted that these forms were detected in only fourteen of the thirty-five abstracts in the corpus, and even in these fourteen their distribution was uneven. Nine abstracts included only one such marker, whereas thirteen markers were concentrated in just five texts – a rather high density for this genre. An example of this high density can be seen in (13), which reproduces the entire abstract.

(13) The aim of this project is the creation of a lexicon-based sentiment analysis program for tweets in Spanish that can serve as a base for future experiments and improvements. *Firstly*, we will present and compare the most common approaches used in sentiment analysis. *Secondly*, we will investigate the resources available for sentiment analysis in Spanish. *Then*, we will explain the structure and operation of the program we have created. *Finally*, we will mention possible future lines of research. EN_35

Regarding the distribution of sequencing discourse markers across rhetorical moves, they occurred most often in the *results* move (30.5%), where the marker functioned to organize the findings or introduce the last sentence, regardless of whether this involved drawing a conclusion or not.

3.2.2.2. Metadiscursive Nouns

The use of metadiscursive nouns is particularly useful in the writing of abstracts, given that these texts are so short that the presence of other frame markers would hardly be appropriate. Jiang and Hyland describe metadiscursive nouns "as those which refer to the organization of the discourse or the readers' understanding of it. They are a subset of abstract nouns and distinguished from them by their unspecific semantic meaning" (*2018*, p. 510). In our corpus, metadiscursive nouns are basically used to signpost the different processes or phases of the research carried out and may express either anaphoric or cataphoric relationships. An example of a noun ("factors") used anaphorically can be seen in (14), and in (15) we see another noun ("field") making cataphoric reference to an antecedent.

(14) There are seven *factors* that influence, positively or negatively, the acquisition and transmission of the language: 1) reverse intergenerational language transmission – when the daughters pass on the language or languages to their parents, 2) the relationship with the family in Morocco, 3) early schooling, 4) the input and output in Moroccan Arabic, 5) the immigrant generation, 6) the traditional role of mothers, and 7) the hierarchy among the siblings. EN_05

(15) It has been shown that vocabulary is one of the hardest but also most crucial aspects when learning a foreign language. Although its importance, it has not been until the last decades that experts have started analysing this *field*. EN_23

Altogether we identified ninety-two metadiscursive nouns in the corpus. The frequency of occurrence of those that appeared more than once are shown in *Table 3*. Quite a few more appeared only once: they were "approach", "basis", "characteristics", "criteria", "data", "difficulty", "evaluation", "focus", "function", "goal", "idea", "limitations", "novelties", "object", "obstacles", "problem", "procedures", "proposal", "questions", "research", "sample", "solution", "sources", "suggestions", "techniques", "tests", "theme" and "topic". One of the features of our corpus is thus the wide variety of metadiscursive nouns it contains.

Table 3. Frequency of occurrence of metadiscursive nouns

Results	18	elements	2
Aims	7	field	2
Methodology	5	findings	2
Objective	5	hypothesis	2
Factor(s)	4	phase(s)	2
Analysis	3	purpose	2
Aspect(s)	3		
Study	3		
Fact	3		

As can be seen, the most frequent metadiscursive nouns in the corpus are "aims" and "results". In fact, if we examine the distribution of these nouns across the various rhetorical moves (see *Figure 3*), we will see that they are precisely (and unsurprisingly) most frequent in the *aims* and *results* moves. Though other linguistic procedures may open the moves, the use of the metadiscursive nouns "aims" and "results" reveals the important role played by these elements in the discursive construction of the TFG abstracts.

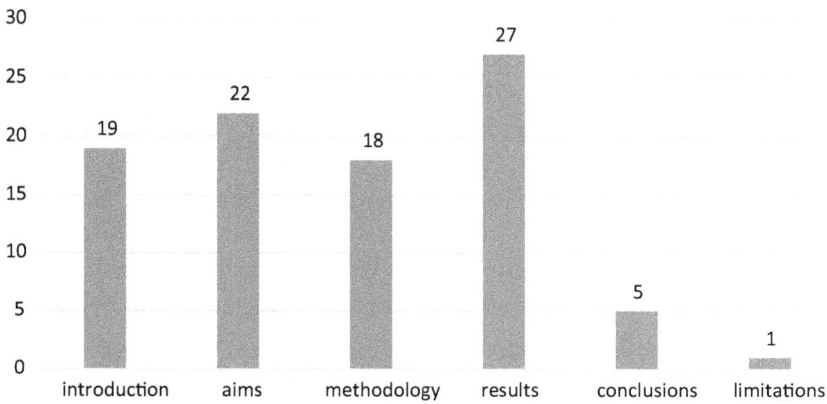

Figure 3. Distribution of metadiscursive nouns across rhetorical moves

3.2.4. Definitional Contexts

Although *Hyland (2005)* uses the term *code glosses* to refer exclusively to reformulative discourse makers, in the present study we prefer, in line with other previous work (*Alarcón et al. 2007, 2008*), to analyse in our corpus the definitional contexts in which such markers appear. Thus, we have marked those excerpts which in one way or another explain a term that appears in the abstract, including the reformulation discourse marker itself and the new formulation proposed. In the examples below we indicate in boldface the reformulative resource.

We regard definitional context as yet one more interactive metadiscourse element given that it comprises a helping hand that the writer offers the reader, based on his/her assessment of how much knowledge the reader is likely to have available. This sort of helping hand can take the form of reformulations, explanations, definitions or clarifications. In our corpus we found a total of twenty occurrences of this sort of metadiscursive procedure. Half adopted the form of a reformulation through the use of parentheses, dashes or commas. In these instances the preceding term is stipulated ("integrated approach", "kinds", etc.) or defined, as in (16), where the writer infers that many readers are unlikely to understand what "fictitious languages" refers to.

(16) Within the world of artificial languages are the fictitious languages, *that is*, those designed for an unreal situation, which are often used in literary and audiovisual contexts. EN_32

In this dataset, acronyms occur frequently in definitional contexts, nearly always preceding the definition, as in "Escola Oficial d'ldiomes (EOI)" or "Televisió d'Eivissa i Formentera (TEF)", though sometimes following it, as in "TAFL (teaching of Arabic as a foreign language)". Another form found in the corpus consists of reformulation using the markers "in other words" or "that is", as in (16) above. Finally, the use of a colon to connect the term with its gloss allows the writer to introduce an enumeration of from two to four elements, as we see in (17).

(17) In this way, through a methodological triangulation of four different sources: observations, qualitative interviews, focus group and analysis of didactic materials, we have been able to verify the impact that an appropriate curriculum planning can have on the teaching of foreign languages. EN_25

With regard to the distribution of definitional contexts across rhetorical moves (see *Figure 4*), we note that they occur most frequently in the *introduction* (18.4%) or *methodology* (18%), appearing only sporadically in the other moves. In the *introduction* move, the writer seeks to ensure that the readier will understand the concepts or terminology employed, while in the *methodology* move, definitional contexts are used to provide details of the instruments used or the characteristics of informants.

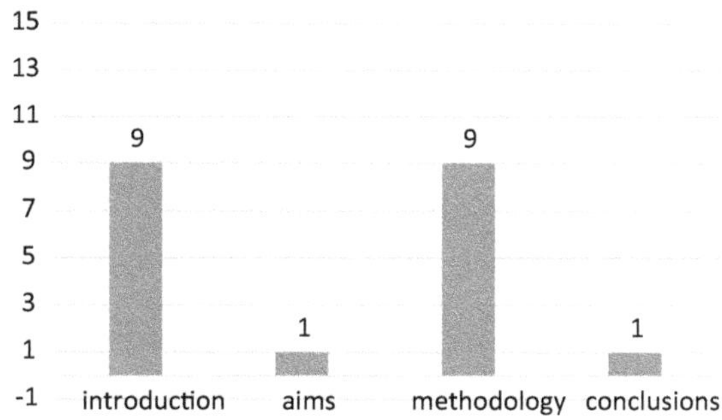

Figure 4. Distribution of definitional contexts across rhetorical moves

Finally, it is important to point out that all the occurrences of definitional contexts in the corpus were concentrated in only eleven of the thirty-five abstracts. Seven of these contained only one instance of a definitional context, whereas two included two and two others contained four or five.

We conclude this section by underlining the predominance of frame markers in these student-authored abstracts. In fact, as can be seen in *Figure 5*, more than half the discourse markers used in the texts corresponded to the frame marker category, whether metadiscursive nouns (49.2%) or sequencing discourse markers (9.6%).

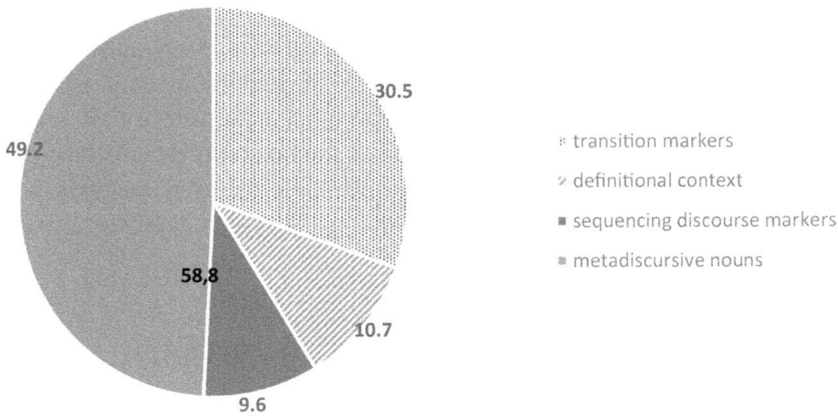

Figure 5. Percentages of use of the various categories of markers

4. Conclusions

From the analysis we have carried out it is clear that these abstracts written by last year Spanish university undergraduates are essentially hybrid texts situated on a continuum between a kind of student academic discourse written with one eye on evaluation and a specialized discourse produced by and directed at expert readers. The problems we have detected in the writing of these texts leads us to conclude that, for students, the TFG abstract genre is an *occluded genre*, in *Swales' (1996)* terminology, that is, a text genre whose characteristics are not, for one reason or another, properly understood by those who must produce it. Hence, the hybrid nature of the result is manifested in a kind of double identity for the author, with some features deriving from his/her situation as a student and others more fitting to a novice researcher.

The identity of the apprentice writer can be seen at two levels. At the macrotextual level, it is betrayed by the presence of the two emerging moves – *structure* and *limitations* – that we have noted. At the microtextual level, the student writer is apparent through the heavy use of sequencing discourse markers with contrastive meaning in the *results* move, thereby placing limits on the scope of the results themselves and also through the use of definitional contexts, basically within the *introduction* and *methodology* moves.

With regard to the novice researcher identity, this is made evident through the obvious presence of the classic abstract moves, namely *introduction*, *aims*, *methodology*, *results* and, to a lesser degree, *conclusions*. Likewise noteworthy is the use of frame markers, mostly metadiscursive nouns intended to ensure text cohesion – a feature also typical of abstracts written by the expert researcher, as we have noted.

Being discourse competent in a particular genre implies having internalized the features of that genre at not only the linguistic level but also the sociocultural and pragmatic levels, that is, in direct relation to the context in which the genre is produced and received. The research described here reveals certain gaps in the degree of discourse competence exhibited by these student writers with regard to the abstract genre. We believe it is of utmost importance that student writers should be made aware of what they need to know in order to achieve full mastery of any genre. It is hoped that the analysis of student work provided in this study will contribute to that goal with regard to the writing of academic or scientific abstracts.

References

Aktas, R. N., & Cortes, V. (2008). Shell nouns as cohesive devices in published and ESL student writing. *Journal of English for Academic Purposes, 7*, 3–14.

Alarcón, R., Bach, C., & Sierra, G. (2007). Extracción de contextos definitorios en corpus especializados: hacia la elaboración de una herramienta de ayuda terminográfica. [Extraction of definitional contexts in specialised corpora: Towards the Elaboration of a Support Tool for Terminography]. *Revista Española de Lingüística, 37*, 247–278.

Alarcón, R., Sierra, G., Aguilar, C., & Bach, C. (2008). Definitional verbal patterns for semantic relation extraction. *Terminology, 14*(1), 74–98.

Bhatia, V. K. (1993). *Analysing genre: Language use in professional settings*. London: Longman.

Cavalieri, S. (2014). Variation across disciplines. The case of applied linguistics and medicine. In M. Bondi & R. Lorés (Eds.), *Abstracts in academic discourse: Variation and change* (pp. 161–174). Berne, Switzerland: Peter Lang.

Cuenca, M. J. (2013). The fuzzy boundaries between discourse marking and modal marking. In L. Degand, B. Cornil, & P. Pietrandrea (Eds.), *Discourse markers and modal particles: categorization and description* (pp. 191–216). Amsterdam-Philadelphia: John Benjamins.

da Cunha, I. (2016). *El trabajo de fin de grado y de máster. Redacción, defensa y publicación* [The final-year Undergraduate and Master Dissertations. Drafting, Oral Presentation and Publication]. Barcelona, Spain: Universitat Oberta de Catalunya.

Díez Prados, M. (2018). Abstract nouns as metadiscursive shells in academic discourse. *Caplletra, 64*, 153–178.

dos Santos, M. B. (1996). The textual organization of research paper abstracts in applied linguistics. *Text, 16*(4), 481–499.

Francis, G. (1986). *Anaphoric nouns* [Discourse analysis monographs II]. Birmingham, UK: English Language Research, University of Birmingham.

Halliday, M. A. K., & Hasan, R. (1976). *Cohesion in English*. London: Longman.

Hyland, K. (2005). *Metadiscourse*. London: Continuum.

Hyland, K., & Tse, P. (2004). Metadiscourse in academic writing: A reappraisal. *Applied Linguistics, 25*(2), 156–177.

Jiang, F., & Hyland, K. (2017). Metadiscursive nouns: Interaction and cohesion in abstract moves. *English for Specific Purposes, 46*, 1–14.

Jiang, F., & Hyland, K. (2018). Nouns and academic interactions: A neglected feature of metadiscourse. *Applied Linguistics, 39*(4), 508–531.

Lorés, R., & Bondi, M. (2014). Introduction. In R. Lorés & M. Bondi (Eds.), *Abstracts in academic discourse: Variation and change* (pp. 9–17). Berne, Switzerland: Peter Lang.

Saeeaw, S., & Tangkiengsirisin, S. (2014). Rhetorical variation across research article abstracts in environmental science and applied linguistics. *English Language Teaching, 7*(8), 81–93.

Sancho, J. (2014). *Com escriure i presentar el millor treball acadèmic: guia pràctica per a estudiants i professors* [How to write and present the best pieces of academic work: Practical guide for students and teachers]. Vic, Spain: Eumo.

Schmid, H.-J. (2000). *English abstract nouns as conceptual shells: From corpus to cognition*. Berlin: Mouton de Gruyter.

Schmid, H.-J. (2018). Shell nouns in English: A personal roundup. *Caplletra, 64*, 109–128.

Swales, J. (1990). *Genre analysis: English in academic and research settings*. Cambridge, UK: Cambridge University Press.

Swales, J. (1996). Occluded genres in the academy: The case of the submission letter. In E. Ventola & A. Mauranen (Eds.), *Academic writing: Intercultural and textual issues* (pp. 45–58). Amsterdam: John Benjamins.

Venegas, R., Núñez, M. T., Zamora, S., & Santana, A. (2015). *Escribir desde la pedagogía del género. Guías para escribir el trabajo final de grado en licenciatura* [Writing from pedagogy of Genre. Guides to writing final-year Undergraduate Dissertations]. Valparaíso, Chile: Ediciones Universitarias de Valparaíso, Pontificia Universidad Católica de Valparaíso.

Venegas, R., Zamora, S., & Galdames, A. (2016). Hacia un modelo retórico-discursivo del macrogénero trabajo final de grado en Licenciatura [Towards a rhetorical-discursive model of the undergraduate final-year dissertation macro-genre]. *Signos, 49*(1), 247–279.

Vendler, Z. (1968). *Adjectives and nominalizations*. The Hague: Mouton.

LUCÍA BELLÉS-CALVERA

Universitat de València

Metadiscourse in Classroom Discourse: An Analysis of Interactive Markers in CLIL Seminars

1. Introduction

Over the last decades the educational dimension has undergone an internationalization process where programmes have been tailored to face new multilingual realities. This communicative environment has shaped a number of measures and initiatives around the globe that seek to provide future generations with social and professional skills. In this regard, the European Union has enhanced the learning of at least two foreign languages by embracing the proliferation of bilingual and multilingual practices at all educational levels, particularly at tertiary education (*Jover, Fleta & González, 2016*; *European Commission, 2015*; *Stavans & Hoffmann, 2015; Lasagabaster, 2012; Airey, 2011; Dalton-Puffer, 2011; Hazelkorn, 2011*).

This need for internationalization and communication has responded to the marketization and Englishisation processes of the academic world (*Engwall, 2016*; *Hultgren, 2014*). Such phenomena have laid the foundations of new pedagogical approaches where English is the preferred means of communication in multilingual contexts (*Graddol, 1999*). In this regard, the global status of English as a lingua franca has shaped the linguistic landscape of the academic world (*McIntyre, 2009*; *Crystal, 2003*). Not only does English work as a contact language in journal publications, conferences, evaluation and university rankings (*Curry & Lillis, 2018*; *Hamel, 2013*), but as a language of instruction in a broad range of disciplinary subjects.

Major trends in foreign language teaching involve Canadian immersion programmes, English for Academic Purposes (EAP), English for Specific Purposes (ESP), Task-Based Instruction (TBI), Content-Based Instruction (CBI), English as a Medium of Instruction (EMI) or Content and Language Integrated Learning (CLIL). All of them represent different approaches to foreign language teaching and learning may differ to a great extent, but it is the CLIL approach the one that will be explored in this chapter.

The primary aim of CLIL courses is to help learners acquire content taught by using an additional language as the means of communication (*Coyle, Hood & Marsh, 2010*; *Lorenzo, Casal & Moore, 2010*). Not only will participants learn subject-related content, but they will also develop their communicative competence in the target language. Therefore, unlike other approaches previously mentioned, CLIL instructors have the challenging task of simultaneously developing students' cognitive and linguistic skills by exposing them to comprehensible input so that they become familiar with the academic discourse of a given discipline. In so doing, effective CLIL practices can be observed.

Nonetheless, the implementation of this model has brought challenges to policymakers, stakeholders, educators and students. Issues such as language planning and policies, teacher training, language proficiency and assessment have become a priority in higher education institutions. Previous research on academic discourse has focused on the use of metadiscoursal elements in academic texts of a range of disciplines, whether written or spoken (*Carrió Pastor, 2018*; *Bellés-Fortuño, 2018*; *Lee & Subtirelu, 2015*; *Bu, 2014*). Considerable attention has been devoted to lectures, which have proven to be the main instructional genre (*Flowerdew, 1994*). In fact, it is through discourse that university members interact and adapt the sociocultural norms that help construct our identity (*Mauranen, 1993*). Other university events that have been examined include students' written productions, research articles, textbooks and communications delivered in conferences (*Charles, 2013*).

While research on interpersonal discourse has been valuable in describing the set of metadiscoursal strategies employed by faculty members, particularly in written academic texts (*Hyland, 2010*; *Bellés-Fortuño & Querol Julián, 2010*), little research has looked at students' discourse in seminar sessions. The communication patterns that occur during students' speech need to be further explored to support best practices in CLIL classrooms, especially when dealing with disciplines belonging to different fields of expertise, such as Humanities and Health Sciences. Such comparisons can provide a useful insight for CLIL instruction in the sense that CLIL teachers can reflect about effectiveness of their teaching practices. Understanding the role of discourse markers and the relationship between different parts of the text is fundamental for the comprehension of their students' needs with regard to content acquisition and communicative competence.

So far, the incorporation of digital resources in educational settings has reshaped academic discourse with the emergence of mixed modes of communication (*Breuer & Archer, 2016*; *Ädel, 2010*). The integration of such tools in CLIL programmes has had an impact on the use of English as an academic language. It has been argued that multimodal practices help the audience construct meaning through the use of verbal and non-verbal elements (*Kuteeva & Mauranen, 2018*; *Morell, 2015*). Evidence may be found in the use of PowerPoint presentations where discourse is reinforced with visual aids, particularly when instruction occurs in a language other than students' L1. Unfortunately, it may also entail some drawbacks in terms of organisation and interaction (*D'Angelo, 2018*). Teachers' and students' command of the language may result in the use of a number of strategies, including rephrasing utterances or the use of participants' mother tongue to enhance socialization and negotiation of meaning.

The current study is part of a larger research project that investigates the implementation of CLIL modules at a university level in six degrees belonging to the field of Humanities and Health Sciences, the focus being on interpersonal strategies used by undergraduate students. Previous analyses on CLIL discourse have been approached as regards written and oral performance in primary and secondary education (*Llinares, Morton & Whittaker, 2012*; *Lasagabaster, 2011*; *Ruiz de Zarobe, Sierra & Gallardo, 2011*; *Gallardo del Puerto, Gómez Lacabex & García Lecumberri, 2009*). At tertiary education, research has especially examined EMI programmes rather than modular-CLIL programmes, where partial instruction in a foreign language is included in the course syllabus (*Bentley, 2010*).

This chapter explores the discourse strategies deployed by first-year History undergraduate students and third-year Medicine undergraduate students to organize their speech and engage the audience in project-based seminars. This paper aims at describing the use of interpersonal metadiscourse within and across two disciplinary domains. In so doing, it is necessary to examine the extent to which these interactive features differ in each area of expertise when presenting disciplinary topics. Following Hyland's model of metadiscourse (*2017*, *2005a*), the analysis focuses on multimodal classroom practices held in project-based seminars where English is the language of instruction. Hence, CLIL discourse, more specifically interactive devices (e.g. transitions, code glosses, frame markers, endophoric references and evidentials), has been supported with visual aids. What makes this contribution valuable is that this contrastive analysis is based on authentic recorded seminars offered in the areas of Humanities and Health Sciences at a higher education institution. The collaboration of CLIL lecturers and students at a Spanish university was decisive to gather a small corpus of project-based seminars and hence present the results and the discussion of this study. Overall, this article sheds light on the development of successful CLIL programmes. The description of real CLIL multimodal practices can boost the development of scaffolding strategies that address the cognitive and communicative demands of the academic world.

2. Metadiscourse in the Classroom

The exploration of academic discourse patterns in the content classroom has contributed to the design of effective teaching practices. The use of discourse markers has proven to play a significant role in the organization and comprehension of academic events. It is evident that educators need to provide students with comprehensible input so that they can internalize new concepts, but it is the analysis of students' discourse which can help faculty members identify and meet their learning needs. Contrary to lectures, students' participation occurs primarily in seminar sessions as they seek to negotiate meaning and discuss different points of view (*Soter et al., 2008*).

Within this instructional practice, topics related to the subject matter are discussed in smaller groups so that learners can develop their critical thinking skills (*Curzon, 2003*). In this regard, the structure of seminar sessions may differ depending on the use of internal elements. These learning practices can thus be implemented as group discussions, research talks and project-based seminars (*Young, 1994*). Group discussions are conceived as academic events where students discuss content-related topics. Secondly, research talks are similar to lectures in that they are given by specialists in the field. Finally, project-based seminars are devoted to foster students' academic progress by means of written and spoken projects.

It is evident that interaction is pivotal in the learning process. The sub-field of discourse analysis committed to the examination of these markers has been regarded as metadiscourse. This umbrella term, also known as metatalk or metatext, has been defined as an umbrella term for the linguistic devices that have to do with text organization, evaluation and interaction processes (*Hyland, 2005a, 2005b*).

Preliminary studies at a tertiary education level have been concerned with university lectures. The aspects of metadiscourse that have received most attention involve text structure, display questions, referential and evaluative asides (*Morell, 2020; Molino, 2017; Bellés-Fortuño, 2016; Llinares & Dalton-Puffer, 2015*; *Crawford Camiciottoli, 2005*; *Thompson, 2003*). However, there seems to be a lack of research in the language learning context. Some studies have considered learners' speech based on Hyland's macro-functions of language, namely ideational (*Llinares & Morton, 2010*; *Whittaker & Llinares, 2009*), interpersonal (*Martin & White, 2005*) and textual (*Whittaker, Llinares & McCabe, 2011*). Classroom discourse has also been examined interaction from sociocultural perspectives (*Kraker, 2000*) and other features of the learning context, such as competitiveness and content comprehension (*O'Boyle, 2015*; *Hultgren, 2014*).

Despite the relevance of metadiscourse in academic events, little is known about CLIL learners' language use and the challenges they may face to explain content and signal shifts in academic discourse. These features play a significant role in the content classroom, especially in seminar sessions devoted to the presentation and discussion of group projects. In this sense, spoken discourse can be somehow prepared by following scripts and rehearsing at home, but as their performance and audience interaction take place in real time, it is possible to identify the learning areas that need to be reinforced.

This chapter seeks to explore the use of metadiscoursal features in two CLIL project-based seminars where English is the vehicular language. Based on Hyland's interpersonal model of metadiscourse (*2005a*), the focus of this study is on the examination of interactive markers in CLIL discourse. Thus, this project departs from the following research questions:

1. What types of interactive metadiscourse are employed in CLIL pedagogical practices at the interpersonal level?
2. Do interactive forms of interpersonal metadiscourse differ in type and frequency between project-based seminars offered in the fields Humanities and Health Sciences?

The compilation of a small corpus has thus been crucial to describe the structure of academic discourse, either in terms of text organization and teacher-student interaction. As for pedagogical implications, the analysis of the findings suggests that the implementation of scaffolding techniques may be necessary to meet the linguistic and cognitive needs of CLIL participants. The next section gives an account of the methodological procedures employed to gather and analyse the data of this study.

2. Methodology

This section includes a detailed description of the methodological approach with regard to the participants, the procedure and the research instruments that were necessary for the collection and examination of metadiscoursal strategies in CLIL settings.

2.1. Context

This study has been conducted at a Spanish university where CLIL instruction is granted in all degrees given that at least 5% of the credits need to be taught in English. Given that this higher education institution offers CLIL-modular programmes, interaction in English is mainly held in seminar sessions rather than in lectures. The modules examined in this research project correspond to *History of the Classical World* and *Epidemiology and Public Health*, which are offered within the degrees of *History and Heritage* and *Medicine* respectively. These project-based workshops students were devoted to students' group performance with an average of five-minute and ten-minute presentations.

2.2. Participants

The subjects taking part in this study are enrolled in CLIL modules offered within the disciplines of Humanities and Health Sciences. The selection process of CLIL modules was determined by short interviews scheduled with CLIL lecturers, where they were informed about this research project. Their implication involved their consent to attend and audiotape those seminars following a CLIL approach. The anonymity of all the subjects was granted by means of an informed consent.

The analysis includes two CLIL teachers and fifty-two undergraduate students coursing first-year and third-year modules in the degrees of *History and Heritage* and *Medicine* respectively. Both CLIL lecturers are bilingual speakers of Spanish and Catalan. Most undergraduate students are also bilingual or multilingual speakers, some of them having an extended linguistic repertoire (9.6%).

2.2.1. History and Heritage

As to History and Heritage, thirty out of forty learners attended the module of *History of the Classical World* regularly. The group consisted of twenty-seven males and thirteen females with students of all ages, from eighteen to sixty years old. Therefore, it should come as no surprise that their linguistic background differs to a certain extent due to factors such as age and exposure to the target language. Most of them were bilingual speakers of Spanish and Catalan, but their command of the English language was quite heterogeneous. The linguistic background of some of these participants also included Romanian, Arabic, French and Portuguese.

Theoretical instruction was entirely delivered in Spanish except for the practical component of the module. Four CLIL seminars were allocated, but only two of them have been considered for the analysis of the current study. These seminars were devoted to group presentations dealing with ancient Rome. The topics could deal with (a) elements of Roman culture, art and religion (e.g. architecture, sculpture, food, entertainment, etc.). The one selected by the group should be used to boost its popularity in today's society; (b) research about a day in the life of a member of Roman society (e.g. Patrician, Plebeian, soldier, gladiator, vestal virgin, etc.)

2.2.2. Medicine

A total of twenty-two third-year undergraduate students participated in the seminars organized for the compulsory module of *Epidemiology and Public Health.* The group comprised eleven males and eleven females aged between twenty and twenty-two years old who came from all over the Spanish territory.

As in *History of the Classical World,* a CLIL workshop was designed to foster the use of the target language by means of oral presentations. Within these communicative events, students had to devise a research protocol on a topic of their choice as the basis of future research projects in the field of Medicine.

2.3. Procedure

As previously mentioned, attendance to these sessions was possible thanks to CLIL lecturers' collaboration, which was discussed in scheduled interviews at earlier stages of this study. Attendance to pre-selected seminars in English where students' performance would be audio-taped made it necessary to design consent forms and observation rubrics to keep a record of relevant details taking place during the session. In so doing, a short talk was given to students about the main aspects of the research project so that they could make a final decision about their participation. Fortunately, all the informants were eager to collaborate in this project and a consent form was distributed to report their approval. Hence, the recording of these seminars allowed for the transcription and creation of a small corpus contrasting two areas of expertise.

2.4. The Corpus

The corpus for this study contains two communicative events that have been recorded at a Spanish university with a small mp3 gadget (i.e. *Olympus digital voice recorder WS-831*). The sample that addresses issues related to *History of the Classical World* equal 5,116 words and is 110 minutes long as opposed to the second seminar which deals with *Epidemiology and Public Health.* The latter consists of longer contributions registered in 119 minutes that amount to 12,390 words. The two CLIL seminars included in this study are part of a larger study dealing with CLIL classroom discourse. The larger corpus consists of ten CLIL seminars delivered in six different courses and rises up to a total number of 62,253 words. As this is a comparative study, three of them were delivered in the degrees of History and Heritage, Humanities: Intercultural Studies and Tourism, whereas the remaining seminars belong to the areas of Medicine, Nursing and Psychology.

Table 1 illustrates the CLIL seminars that make up the corpus, providing information about the disciplinary fields, the modules where CLIL sessions were delivered, the discourse function, the sub-genre, the number of words per session and the minutes that were tape-recorded.

Table 1. Seminar sessions for analysis

Field	Module	Discourse function	Genre	Number of words	Duration
History and Heritage	History of the Classical World	Monologic and interactive	Project-based seminar	5,116	110 min.
Medicine	Epidemiology and Public Heatlh	Monologic and interactive	Project-based seminar	12,390	119 min.
Total				**17,506**	**229 min.**

CLIL seminars were selected as a genre for analysis for several reasons. First of all, they were the only pedagogical practices of the module in which a language other than Spanish was used as the means of communication. Therefore, at the time of data collection there were more opportunities to keep a record of students' participation. Indeed, seminars have proven to be highly interactive practices meant to negotiate meaning and share a wide range of perspectives on a given topic. For this study, only project-based seminars were considered given that similarities can be found in terms of genre structure.

Other criteria that are have favoured the comparability of the two samples have to do with teacher-student interaction and the use of English as the means of communication in the classroom. Classroom discourse is characterized by higher levels of students' participation and their contributions may include higher levels of metadiscoursal features in contrast to other forms of seminars. Nevertheless, the two sets of samples may differ in terms of size and domains.

Additional research instruments that allowed for the analysis of the larger research project involve interviews, observation rubrics, online questionnaires and placement tests.

2.4.1. Analytical Framework

This study is based on the interpersonal model of metadiscourse proposed by *Hyland (2005a)*, which encompasses the description of interactive and interactional linguistic features (*Thompson, 2001*). Thus, the interpersonal macrofunction comprise markers that are necessary in terms of audience interaction, text organization and evaluation. The interactive category is meant to structure written and spoken productions through transitions, frame markers, endophoric references, evidentials and code glosses, thereby guiding listeners through the text. These resources serve a number of functions, including the addition and contrast of ideas, reference to other parts of the text or to other sources, the reformulation of utterances and the exemplification of ideas (*Table 2*).

Table 2. Hyland's interpersonal model (*2005a, p. 49*): Interactive elements

Category	Examples
Transitions	In addition, also, and, likewise, in contrast, but, however, rather, thus, therefore, hence...
Frame markers	Firstly, next, overall, in conclusion, aim to, seek to, show, with regard to, concerning, in terms of...
Endophoric references	Above, earlier, previously, below, later, following...
Evidentials	According to, As X argued..., past research, previously
Code glosses	That is, in other words, such as, for example, for instance, as in

Drawing on *Hyland's (2005a)* interpersonal model, only interactive metadiscoursal items have been considered for study in the present chapter. All the instances have been manually retrieved and counted to determine not only their distribution patterns but also the frequency of metadiscourse in each field of study. A detailed analysis of these results is provided in the following section.

3. Results and Discussion

This section shows the main features of interpersonal metadiscourse observed in both learning contexts. The type, form and distribution patterns of interactive and interactional devices have been analysed and compared for the purpose of this research.

The findings from the analysis of twenty-two oral presentations have revealed that interactive metadiscourse is used to a large extent in project-based seminars. *Table 3* below indicates that the most frequent elements in classroom discourse correspond to transitions (73%). The remaining interactive categories are also present in these teaching practices, but their distribution patterns may differ to a certain extent between both fields. From these results it could be observed that Medicine students made a greater use of interactive metadiscoursal markers than History learners, especially because the formers had more opportunities to take long turns. A closer look at the frequency of interactive markers suggests that participants draw heavily on the organization of spoken discourse as it enhances comprehension.

Table 3. Interactive metadiscoursal markers

Category	Humanities	Health Sciences	Total
Transitions	70 %	73 %	72 %
Frame markers	18 %	13 %	14 %
Endophoric references	7 %	6 %	7 %
Evidentials	0 %	2 %	1 %
Code glosses	5 %	6 %	6 %

3.1. Transitions

Compared to other forms of seminar practices, project-based seminars consist of a high number of transitions, the most common ones being *and, but, also* and *so*. These interactive resources have been widely used to make speech coherent and cohesive and thus help the audience, particularly the teacher who assesses their performance, process academic content effectively.

Undergraduate students structure their spoken contributions through the introduction of additive, contrastive and consecutive ideas. In the field of History, the contributions of the subjects are characterized by an extensive use of additive markers (e.g. *and, also* and *apart from*).

(1) [...] Colosseum is a place in the centre city ***and*** in there realize a different games.

(2) The Roman theatre is a copy of the Greek theater. But everything wasn't a Greek copy. The theatres ***also*** had parts that were Roman.

(3) ***Apart from that***, what is the most striking thing – the most unexpected or surprising thing that you have learnt about weddings or divorces?

The occurrence of *and* seems to be repetitive at certain moments. In fact, the presence of this coordinate conjunction is occasionally followed by a short pause. Such a break gives students some time to articulate a new utterance.

(4) ***And*. . .*and*,** generally the funerals divide in five parts.

The only contrastive marker identified in this CLIL seminar has to do with *but*, which amounts to 21 cases. As for the number of consecutive markers, it is slightly higher (36) recognizing items such as *so, therefore* and *then*.

(5) Another point of the combat is to throw the other man on the floor, **so** he can defend himself ***but*** also it's easy to keep him.

Unlike the field of History, there is an extended use of transition markers in medical research projects. The additive items that were distinguished involve *and, in addition, furthermore, moreover, also* and *apart from*.

(6) ***In addition,*** it will generate a high social cost and very big medical problems.
(7) ***Furthermore,*** we analyse data collection and analysis.

An extensive use of contrastive markers has been observed in medical spoken discourse includes *but, however, yet, nevertheless, instead* and *still*. Evidence of consecutive markers may be found in *so, then, therefore,* and *consequently*. The examples below were noted during group performance and discussion.

(8) [. . .] it's an important source of caffeine **so** it has a stimulating effect and detects error systems in the humans. ***However,*** we don't know much about it [. . .]
(9) Why is sex a co-variant ***instead of*** a main variable?

The large occurrence of these logical markers reveals the need to signal different sections and ideas when presenting disciplinary content. Participants' linguistic awareness can also be noted thanks to the variety of resources observed in spoken discourse. An identification of the features can give an account of students' linguistic repertoire and help teachers to provide corrective feedback to those who need to enrich their transition markers in the target language.

3.2. Frame Markers

As regards frame markers, it is evident that their use allows for the connection of different parts and sections of the communicative event as they are the second most popular metadiscoursal features in CLIL seminars.

Statistically speaking, a large number of frame markers was found in the module of History rather than in Medicine (18%). As can be seen below, instances such as *first, second* and *after this* served to introduce the different parts of the Roman theatre as well as to keep on talking about Roman wedding ceremonies.

(10) [...] I'm going to talk about the Roman theatre. ***First,*** I will explain the, its origin and its parts [...] ***In second place,*** I'm going to talk about the Importance of the theatre for the Romans.

(11) ***After this,*** what they start is the ceremony in which the capitulations wear it and they, the authorization for the dowry that the father of the bride received here reflected in the tabulae nuptial.

On the other hand, even though there is a lower frequency of frame markers in the field of Medicine (13%), their academic performance is based on a rich number of interactive resources. Apart from sequencing ideas, they make use of frame markers to announce the objectives of their research protocols and change the topic, namely *the purpose of, finally, turning into* and *regarding*, among others.

(12) ***Finally,*** I will summarize the presentation talking about the relevance of the proposal and the applicability that it has in both medical practice and the visual health.

(13) ***The purpose of our project*** is to see the influence of aerobic exercise in patients aged 60 to 75 with heart failure over a year of evolution.

(14) ***So now, turning into*** the first part that I'm going to explain you, let's consider our hypothesis.

(15) ***Regarding*** the study limitations difficulties, one of the main limitations in the study has been to minimise the patient follow-up losses and to continue to guarantee data collection at the time of performing echocardiograms to see the LVEF.

The appropriate use of these cues can help students convey meaning and boost their participation in the content classroom.

3.3. Endophoric References

Endophoric devices stand for a set of linguistic expressions that refer to preceding and following ideas or parts within a given text, namely anaphora and cataphora respectively. Even though the frequency of endophoric references is slightly higher in historical discourse (18%), no significant differences were found between both learning contexts. Regarding historical discourse, the presence of cataphoric elements outnumbers anaphoric elements, which is limited to one case.

(16) Like the, the gladiators, ***like I said,*** they trained, their lives is not easy and they trained in public places like the arena and they trained so hard to be in good form.
(17) Now ***we are going to talk*** about the diet of the gladiator.

As to anaphoric references in the medical area, they were primarily used to comment on sections or information that had been previously mentioned. As can be seen in the examples that follow, Medicine students would refer to health institutions and objectives of the study.

(18) Eh we chose the [Name of a health department within a hospital] because, ***as I said,*** because it's a department that all of us know and is more, it's not difficult to contact with the GP and explain our project and it's a department that have all the requirements that we need.
(19) [...] And however, apart from the ***objectives*** that I just ***mentioned***, we also want to consider the need to control myopia among young medical students and to avoid further cases of low vision in a future.

Given that after each group performance there were a few minutes for discussion, teachers' contributions were also considered. As can be seen below, the expert on epidemiological issues made use of anaphoric references. More specifically, she pointed out sections that should be modified to improve their research projects.

(20) For example, what we commented in the ***previous presentations*** is that it's very well that you focus on the introduction in some key articles and this is good.

On the other hand, cataphoric elements were used to briefly introduce sections or information that would be later discussed.

(21) We can see in ***the following table*** the moderate consumption in men is less than a seventeen per week, but in woman is less than eleven per week.
(22) And well, the specific objectives are ***the following ones***, which are: Does drinking decaffeinated coffee have the same effect as drinking it with caffeine?

Overall, the presence of endophorics is similarly represented in both fields of expertise. Because these are multimodal oral presentations, these elements may be explicitly stressed through pictures and nonverbal communication, including iconic, metaphoric, beat or deictic gestures, among others (*McNeill, 1992*).

(23) We can see in the **pyramid** that the, the Mediterranean diet include a moderate a moderation consumption of wine.

(24) [. . .] **In this box** are people and who eh, people have more, more money [. . .]

As noted above, endophoric references are included in participants' speech to signal tables, sections, pictures and figures displayed in their multimedia presentations. These features are generally distinguished in written academic texts (*Hyland, 2005a*), but the fact that medical research protocols are based on a larger written project may explain the incorporation of these elements.

3.4. Evidentials

The use of evidentials has been widely acknowledged in academic texts as they are employed to specify information sources. As expected, Medicine students included these interactive resources to give an account of the literature used as the basis of their research protocol. In so doing, they highlighted key scholars and recent research that has contributed to disseminate knowledge on the selected topic.

References to external sources are quite common in academic presentations, as in lectures (*Lee & Subtirelu, 2015; Biber, 2006*). Personal evidentials, which comprise original research from scholars, are the most frequent sub-category observed in this study. This is clearly illustrated by the excerpts that follow:

(25) ***A publication in BMC ophthalmology journal*** announces that genetic factors play a role in the development of myopia.

(26) ***A group of research from the American Society from Nutrition*** show in a study that when you intake high levels of coffee eh you will reduce the risk of colon cancer.

(27) [. . .] the relation between cardiovascular disease and the wine drink was studied for the first time ***by Doctor Liam***.

(28) For searching the information in our project we have found a lot of very interesting eh articles or investigations. But this article of the eh ***Melanoma***

Characteristics at Diagnosis From The Spanish National Cutaneous Melanoma Registry: 15 Years of Experience that was created by the ***Spanish Academy of Dermatology and Venereology*** was very important to us.

(29) We just took this study from the Internet by the ***NIH-AARP Diet and Health Study, by Loffield and his colleagues*** about coffee intake based on non-Hispanic white men and women during 10 years.

Due to the fact that speech is supported by visual aids, sources may sometimes be omitted within classroom interaction (*Lee & Subtirelu, 2015*). In fact, original research was listed in students' slideshows.

(30) ***There is another study*** which compares the prevalence of myopia eh between Asia, Europe and India, and it says that in Asia the, the prevalence is about eh seventy to ninety per cent and India about forty-five. But about Europe it doesn't say any figure, but it says that the prevalence is higher than in India but less than in Asia.

(31) ***Many studies in humans show*** that eh coffee has eh several cognitive effects such as memory, moves, general commute, and etc. [. . .]

(32) [. . .] during the last years, ***according to the recent data***, have increased the multiple pregnancy risk in Spain.

(33) Though it may paradoxical, ***most** eh **studies claim*** that the increase of maternal age is not only associated to a decrease of fertility.

(34) ***Then we have the bibliography***, it's here.

However, it has been observed that such use of evidentials was not common in the domain of History. Not being familiar with research instruments may be one of the reasons that explain the absence of these resources.

3.5. Code Glosses

As in academic lectures, the use of code glosses in project-based is pivotal to handle disciplinary knowledge (*Flowerdew, 1992; Hyland, 2009*). The elaboration of ideas takes place through reformulations and exemplification markers. On average, the distribution patterns of these features correspond to nearly 7% in both fields of expertise.

CLIL discourse consisted of a reformulated utterance articulated by the Medicine teacher when providing feedback on a research protocol. However, no instances could be distinguished in the area of History.

(35) And, and the variables, eh eh, they were specified, but they should be classified. Classified in the sense which is your outcomes variables, ***that is***, your results.

With regard to exemplifications, no significant differences could be observed in the two learning settings. The most typical markers were *for example, for instance, such as* and *like*. Students mostly used such expressions. Samples of spoken discourse in History-related seminars include:

(36) The diet was based on cereals, ***such as*** garlic, wheat, legumes or other grains.
(37) In the theatre two types of works were represented ***like*** comedies and tragedies.

At some points, it can be noted that some students struggle to articulate speech and may need to reinforce their communicative skills in the target language. In fact, the excerpt below shows that the speaker fails to elaborate the utterance at organizational and linguistic levels. A negative transfer from the student's L1 can be noted in terms of discourse structure and lexical items that do not exist in the English language. This is the case of *desgasted*, which should have been replaced by a most suitable lexical item such as *eroded*.

(38) ***For example***, battles in a, navals battles eh in the Colosseum eh ***uff.*** The Colosseum was also with things are flood, food and water. And the problem is this, the, is in the infrastructure of the Colosseum are ***desgasted*** and destroyed because amm this game is celebrated.

However, medical discourse consisted of more code glosses than historical discourse, namely *for example, such as* and *like*. These served to illustrate summaries, results of past studies, co-variants of their research protocols.

(39) Data adjusted for avoid eh confusing factors, ***for example***, ultraviolet radiation, age, sex and consumption of alcohol, smoking, etc.
(40) And we have this, the co-variants, ***for example***, socio-demographic variables **like** eh **like** eh age, sex, country of origin, anthropometric variables [...].

4. Conclusions

This chapter has explored interpersonal metadiscourse in CLIL programmes offered within the fields of Humanities and Medicine at a Spanish university. The purpose of the study was to describe the main interactive markers employed in each discipline, paying special attention to group performance. This comparative analysis of CLIL seminars shows that use of metadiscourse in the classroom is linked to the context and content of teaching and learning. The findings revealed that transitions are the most frequent interactive feature in the two pedagogical practices under study, followed by frame markers. It seems that there is a greater need to establish explicit relationships between different discourse units, especially when it comes to the different sections of research protocols and daily life of Roman society members. In addition, the use of frame markers has proven to help speakers structure their arguments into different parts. This item is more common in the domain of History, but on the whole it can be noted that both Medicine and History learners find it necessary to sequence and connect their ideas not only to convey meaning but also to enhance comprehension. The frequency of other features, such as endophoric references and code glosses is similar in the content classroom. However, evidentials could only be recognized in medical discourse, probably because the pedagogical focus differed across and within these learning environments. As discussed throughout the chapter, medical discourse was shaped by a rich variety of metalinguistic expressions. Factors such as timing, pedagogical approaches and proficiency in the English language may have had an impact on participants' academic performance. In this sense, Medicine students had more opportunities to organize their speech and engage their audience.

As to pedagogical implications, this study can give an account of the most typical interactive resources in higher education practices where English is the vehicular language. Teachers have the opportunity to review students' discourse preferences and identify the areas that need attention in two disciplinary courses. Action can be taken with regard to text organization, which seems to be the priority of project-based seminars. In other words, learning opportunities can be incorporated in CLIL lessons by giving prompts on content and language structure and offering students academically-oriented materials that contribute to improve their communicative competence in the target language. CLIL instructors may also benefit in the sense that the selection of interpersonal markers is made to facilitate comprehension.

Notwithstanding, limitations in this study should also be acknowledged. First of all, the size of the corpus is small as it does not aim at exploring all the CLIL programmes offered at this Spanish university. Secondly, the number of participants does not correspond to the whole learning community coursing the module due to the arrangement of parallel seminars in different days. Future research in classroom discourse could deal with the use of interpersonal metadiscourse in disciplinary fields other than Humanities and Health Sciences. Other studies could also consider other forms of seminar sessions and students' opinions towards these practices in order to provide a detailed insight into the landscape of higher education learning.

References

Ädel, A. (2010). Just to give you kind of a map of where we are going: A taxonomy of metadiscourse in spoken and written academic English. *Nordic Journal of English Studies, 9*(2), 69–97.

Airey, J. (2011). Talking about teaching in English: Swedish university lecturers' experiences of changing teaching language. *Ibérica: Revista de la Asociación Europea de Lenguas para Fines Específicos (AELFE), 22*, 35–54.

Bellés-Fortuño, B. (2016). Academic discourse markers: A contrastive analysis of the discourse marker then in English and Spanish lectures. *Verbeia, 1*, 57–78.

Bellés-Fortuño, B. (2018). Evaluative language in medical discourse: A contrastive study between English and Spanish university lectures. *Languages in Contrast, 18*(2), 155–174.

Bellés-Fortuño, B., & Querol-Julián, M. (2010). Evaluation in research article abstracts: A cross-cultural study between Spanish and English medical discourse. In R. Lorés-Sanz, P. Mur-Dueñas, & E. Lafuente-Millán (Eds.), *Constructing interpersonality. Multiple perspectives on written academic genres* (pp. 83–98). Newcastle Upon Tyne: Cambridge Scholars Publishing.

Bentley, K. (2010). *The TKT Course CLIL Module*. Cambridge: CUP.

Biber, D. (2006). University language: A corpus-based study of spoken and written registers. John Benjamins.

Breuer, E., & Archer, A. (Eds.). (2016). *Multimodality in higher education*. Leiden: Brill.

Bu, J. (2014). Towards a pragmatic analysis of metadiscourse in academic lectures: From relevance to adaptation. *Discourse Studies, 16*(4), 449–472.

Carrió-Pastor, M. L. (2018). How do we express mitigation in academic language? A corpus driven analysis of metadiscourse devices in English and Spanish. In *International conference: Multidisciplinary and multicultural discourses: Research and profession*. Castellón, Spain: Universitat Jaume I.

Charles, M. (2013). English for academic purposes. In B. Paltridge & S. Starfield (Eds.), *The handbook of English for specific purposes* (pp. 137–153). Malden, MA: Wiley-Blackwell.

Coyle, D., Hood, P., & Marsh, D. (2010). *CLIL: Content and language integrated learning*. Cambridge: Cambridge University Press.

Crawford-Camiciottoli, B. (2005). Adjusting a business lecture for an international audience: A case study. *English for Specific Purposes, 24*(2), 183–199.

Crystal, D. (2003). *English as a global language* (2nd ed.). Cambridge, UK: Cambridge University Press.

Curry, M. J., & Lillis, T. (2018). *Global academic publishing: Policies, perspectives, and pedagogies*. Clevedon, UK: Multilingual Matters.

Curzon, L. B. (2003). *Teaching in further education: An outline of principles and practice* (6th ed.). London and New York: Continuum.

Dalton-Puffer, C. (2011). Content-and-language integrated learning: From practice to principles? *Annual Review of Applied Linguistics, 31*, 182–204.

D'Angelo, L. (2018). Power Point presentations in the classroom: Re-evaluating the genre. *Language Value, 10*(1), 29–46.

Engwall, L. (2016). The internationalisation of higher Education. *European Review, 24*(2), 221–231.

European Commission. (2015). Language teaching and learning in multilingual classrooms. *Education and Training*. Retrieved from https://ec.europa.eu/assets/eac/languages/library/studies/multilingual-classroom_en.pdf

Flowerdew, J. (1992). Definitions in science lectures. Applied Linguistics, 13(2), 202–221. https://doi.org/10.1093/applin/13.2.202

Flowerdew, J. (1994). Research of relevance to second language lecture comprehension: An overview. In J. Flowerdew (Ed.), *Academic listening: Research perspectives* (pp. 7–29). Cambridge: Cambridge University Press.

Gallardo del Puerto, F., Gómez-Lacabex, E., & García-Lecumberri, M. L. (2009). Testing the effectiveness of content and language integrated learning in foreign language contexts: The assessment of English pronunciation. In Y. Ruiz de Zarobe & R. M. Jiménez Catalán (Eds.), *Content and language integrated learning: Evidence from research in Europe* (pp. 63–80). Bristol, UK: Multilingual Matters.

Graddol, D. (1999). The decline of the native speaker. *The AILA Review, 13*, 57–6.

Hamel, R. E. (2013). El campo de las ciencias y la educación superior entre el monopolio del inglés y el plurilingüismo: Elementos para una política del lenguaje en América Latina. *Trabalhos em Linguística Aplicada, 52*(2), 321–384.

Hazelkorn, E. (2011). Measuring world-class excellence and the global obsession with rankings. In R. King, S. Marginson, & R. Naidoo (Eds.), *Handbook on globalization and higher education* (pp. 431–448). Cheltenham: Edward Elgar Publishing.

Hultgren, A. (2014). English language use at the internationalised universities of Northern Europe: Is there a correlation between Englishisation and world rank? *Multilingua, 33*(3–4), 389–411.

Hyland, K. (2005a). *Metadiscourse.* London and New York: Continuum.

Hyland, K. (2005b). Stance and engagement: A model of interaction in academic discourse. *Discourse Studies, 7*(2), 173–191. https://doi.org/10.1177/1461445605050365.Search in Google Scholar

Hyland, K. (2009). *Academic discourse: English in a global context.* London: Continuum.

Hyland, K. (2010). Metadiscourse: Mapping interactions in academic writing. *Nordic Journal of English Studies, 9*(2), 125–143. https://doi.org/10.35360/njes.218

Hyland, K. (2017). Metadiscourse: What is it and where is it going? *Journal of Pragmatics, 113*, 16–29.

Jover, G., Fleta, T., & Gonzalez, R. (2016). Pre-service education of primary school teachers in the context of foreign language bilingual teaching. *Bordon-Revista De Pedagogia, 68*(2), 121–135.

Kraker, M. J. (2000). Classroom discourse: Teaching, learning, and learning disabilities. *Teaching and Teacher Education, 16*(3), 295–313.

Kuteeva, M., & Mauranen, A. (2018). Digital academic discourse: Texts and contexts: Introduction. *Discourse, Context & Media, 24*, 1–7.

Lasagabaster, D. (2011). English achievement and student motivation in CLIL and EFL settings. *Innovation in Language Learning and Teaching, 5*(1), 3–18.

Lasagabaster, D. (2012). El papel del inglés en el fomento del multilingüismo en la universidad. *ELIA. Estudios de Lingüística Inglesa Aplicada, 12*, 13–44.

Lee, J. J., & Subtirelu, N. C. (2015). Metadiscourse in the classroom: A comparative analysis of EAP lessons and university lectures. *English for Specific Purposes, 37*, 52–62.

Llinares, A., & Dalton-Puffer, C. (2015). The role of different tasks in CLIL students' use of evaluative language. *System, 54*, 69–79.

Llinares, A., & Morton, T. (2010). Historical explanations as situated practice in content and language integrated learning. *Classroom Discourse, 1*(1), 46–65.

Llinares, A., Morton, T., & Whittaker, R. (2012). *The Role of Language in CLIL*. Cambridge: Cambridge University Press.

Lorenzo, F., Casal, S., & Moore, P. (2010). The effects of content and language integrated learning in European education: Key findings from the Andalusian bilingual sections evaluation project. *Applied Linguistics, 31*(3), 418–442.

Martin, J. R., & White, P. R. R. (2005). *The evaluation of language: Appraisal in English*. Hampshire: Palgrave Macmillan.

Mauranen, A. (1993). Contrastive ESP rhetoric: Metatext in Finnish-English economic texts. *English for Specific Purposes, 12*, 3–22.

McIntyre, D. (2009). *History of English: A resource book for students*. London: Routledge.

McNeill, D. (1992). Hand and mind: What gestures reveal about thought. Chicago: University of Chicago Press.

Molino, A. (2017). Repetition and rephrasing in physical sciences and engineering English-medium lectures in Italy. In C. Boggio & A. Molino (Eds.), *English in Italy: Linguistic, educational and professional challenges* (pp. 182–202). Milano, Italy: FrancoAngeli.

Morell, T. (2015). International paper conference presentations: A multimodal analysis to determine effectiveness. *English for Specific Purposes, 37*, 137–150.

Morell, T. (2020). EMI teacher training with a multimodal and interactive approach: A new horizon for LSP specialists. *Language Value, 12*(1), 56–87. Castellón, Spain: Jaume I University ePress.

O'Boyle, N. (2015). The risks of 'university speak': Relationship management and identity negotiation by mature students off campus. *International Studies in Sociology of Education, 25*(2), 93–111.

Ruiz de Zarobe, Y., Sierra, J. M., & Gallardo del Puerto, F. (Eds.). (2011). *Content and foreign language integrated learning: Contributions to multilingualism in European contexts*. Bern, Switzerland: Peter Lang.

Stavans, A., & Hoffmann, C. (2015). *Multilingualism*. Cambridge: Cambridge University Press.

Soter, A. O., Wilkinson, I. A., Murphy, P. K., Rudge, L., Reninger, K., & Edwards, M. (2008). What the discourse tells us: Talk and indicators of high-level comprehension. *International Journal of Educational Research, 47*(6), 372–391.

Thompson, G. (2001). Interaction in academic writing: Learning to argue with the reader. *Applied Linguistics, 22*, 58–78.

Thompson, S. (2003). Text-structuring metadiscourse, intonation and the signaling of organization in academic lectures. *Journal of English for Academic Purposes, 2*, 5–20.

Whittaker, R., Llinares, A., & McCabe, A. (2011). Written discourse development in CLIL at secondary school. *Language Teaching Research, 15*(3), 343–362.

Whittaker, R., & Llinares, A. (2009). CLIL in social science classrooms: Analysis of spoken and written productions. In Y. Ruiz de Zarobe & R. M. Catalán (Eds.), *Content and language integrated learning. Evidence from research in Europe* (pp. 215–234). Bristol: Multilingual Matters.

Young, L. (1994). University lectures: Macro-structure and micro-features. In J. Flowerdew (Ed.), *Academic listening: Research perspectives* (pp. 159–176). Cambridge: Cambridge University Press.

IVALLA ORTEGA-BARRERA / ELENA QUINTANA-TOLEDO

Universidad de Las Palmas de Gran Canaria / Universidad de Las Palmas de Gran Canaria

Engagement Markers in Medical Recipes: Evidence from G.U.L. MS Hunter 93 (T.4.10)

1. Introduction

The study of reflexivity, understood as the capacity of natural language to be used to refer to itself (*Hockett, 1960*; *Lyons, 1977*, p. 5), pervades much of recent scholarly research in discourse analysis, applied linguistics and pragmatics in the form of metadiscourse. Ever since *Harris (1959*, p. 944) first introduced the term to describe units of information "which talk about the main material", the notion has variously undergone definitions, categorisations and revisions, starting in the eighties thanks to *Williams (1981)*, *Vande Kopple (1985)* and *Crismore (1989)*. The analysis of metadiscourse markers in academic discourse has become, in fact, one of the most fruitful areas of research in the last three decades, both cross-disciplinary (*Hyland and Jiang, 2018*; *Hu & Cao, 2015*; *Cao & Hu, 2014*; *Hyland 2005a*, *1998a*, *1998b*, *1998c*) and cross-culturally (*Alonso-Almeida, 2015a*, *2015b*; *Carrió-Pastor, 2014*; *Mur-Dueñas, 2011*, *2010*; *Neff-van Aertselaer & Dafouz-Milne, 2008*).

Taken at face value, metadiscourse is a functional category which can shed light on the strategic use of language as it makes manifest how discourse participants, i.e. both text producers and receivers, and text themselves are related to each other. The concept is built upon the "view of writing as social engagement" (*Hyland, 2005a*, p. ix), placing the emphasis on aspects such as authorial presence, audience awareness and discourse organising features which aim at ensuring effective communication. Engagement, in particular, is seen as "an alignment dimension where writers acknowledge and connect to others, recognizing the presence of their readers" (Hyland, *2005b*, p. 176) and, together with stance, contribute to a better understanding of the dialogic and/or interactional character of different types of discourse. Attitude and engagement are also closely related in the Appraisal framework, where the "valuation of emotions, people's behaviour and the aesthetic quality of things constitute the expression of attitude" and engagement is "the dialogic space afforded for the negotiation of these values" (*Mei, 2007*, p. 257). With special reference to those linguistic items which signal reader engagement, *Hyland (2005a*, p. 53; *1999*, p. 8) regards them as "devices that explicitly address readers, either to focus their attention or include them as discourse participants".

The role of metadiscourse in scientific communication has been also addressed in some diachronic studies. Referring to metadiscursive comments in early English medical writing, *Taavitsainen (2000*, p. 191) implicitly draws attention to the role of engagement by positing that "[e]vidence of the sender adjusting the text according to the addressee or the target group is important here, and audience response may be anticipated and taken into account". *Taavitsainen and Hiltunen (2012*, p. 179), on their part, point that "in the late medieval period, medical texts representing different traditions employ different metadiscourse devices, and styles of writing vary according to intended audiences". Engagement markers, then, seem to be specially interesting to look at as they can provide us with valuable insight into the reader-oriented discursive functions of scientific writing in earlier periods of English. Drawing on the broad approach to metadiscourse (*Hyland, 2005a, 2005b*), our aim in this paper is precisely to explore the occurrence of engagement markers in John de Feckenham's *Booke of Soueraigne Medicines*, a sixteenth century medical manuscript housed in Glasgow University Library and edited by *Ortega-Barrera (2014)*. This research is intended to complement others such as *Taavitsainen (2000, 2001a)*, *Quintana-Toledo (2009)*, *Alonso-Almeida (2012)* or *Álvarez-Gil (2018)*.

Taavitsainen (2000, 2001a) finds out that metadiscursive comments with a clear interpersonal function started being commonplace in medical writing in the transition from the late medieval to the early modern period. Authorial stance and reader involvement were codified through several resources such as (im)personal expressions, evidentials and modal verbs, which not only brought about changes in the rhetoric of science but also reflected the shift that was underway in scientific thought-styles. *Quintana-Toledo (2009)* analyses a corpus of Middle English medical recipes drawing on *Hyland's (2005)* metadiscourse model. Her findings reveal that engagement markers are one of the most frequent resources, specifically, personal pronouns, which, depending on the context, can mark solidarity and membership in the same community or social differentiation. In a later period, i.e. eighteenth century, *Alonso-Almeida (2012*, p. 218) observes an increasing tendency in the use of hedges in astronomy texts which again evinces "a changing attitude of writers both in society and in their understanding of the academic representation of knowledge and scientific novelties". Recently, *Álvarez-Gil (2018*, p. 94) has shown that adverbial metadiscourse devices work as perspectivisers "in the elaboration of historical knowledge".

This said, the paper is structured as follows: the next section deals with the concept of metadiscourse, the broad and the narrow approaches which can be adopted in its study and the presentation of *Hyland's (2005a, 2005b*) taxonomy. The third and fourth sections focus on the description of the corpus and the analysis of the engagement markers found in it respectively. The last section summarises the conclusions derived from this study.

2. Metadiscourse and Engagement

Virtually all scholars engaged in analysing metadiscourse in different genres and languages would agree without reservation that it remains conceptually elusive. For example, *Hyland and Tse (2004*, p. 156) point to its being "under-theorized and empirically vague" as the reason for the difficulties encountered when operationalising the concept in analyses of real texts. A key issue here is the identification and classification of those linguistic units which have the potential to count as metadiscursive, and this is heavily influenced by the perspective researchers endorse. On the whole, there are two main trends in metadiscourse studies: integrative and non-integrative (*Mauranen, 1993*), or broad and narrow (*Ädel, 2006*), or interactive and reflexive (*Ädel, 2010*). These pairs of labels are fairly equivalent from a theoretical standpoint, but *Ädel's (2006)* terminology will be preferred in this discussion.

The broad approach deals with metadiscourse in relation to those linguistic features which signal (i) the authors' presence in their texts by commenting on the text itself or its structural organisation as well as (ii) the authors' attitudes towards the information presented and the potential readers themselves. *Vande Kopple (1985)*, *Crismore, Markkanen and Steffensen (1993)* and *Hyland (1998b)* embody the broad approach and put forward classifications which are structured around two main axes, namely, textual metadiscourse and interpersonal metadiscourse. Even though there is some variation in the terms these authors use, the (sub)categories which can be found in their schemes of metadiscourse have similar functions in general, for instance, all of them include connectives and code glosses (explanations of text material) under textual metadiscourse. Whether or not sequencers (indicators of order or stages in the text), reminders (references to other parts of the text) and topicalisers (indicators of a shift in the topic) are considered to be a category in their own right or a subcategory within connectives varies from author to author, i.e. *Crismore, Markkanen and Steffensen (1993)* and *Hyland (1998b)* see them as separate categories. Additionally, while *Vande Kopple (1985)* and *Hyland (1998b)* take indicators of the source of information, i.e. narrators and evidentials respectively, to be more textually-oriented, *Crismore, Markkanen and Steffensen (1993)* group them in interpersonal metadiscourse as attributors. Another important feature in metadiscourse models is epistemicity, which is clearly related to authorial attitudes and, hence, to the interpersonal dimension in *Crismore, Markkanen and Steffensen (1993)* and *Hyland (1998b)*. *Vande Kopple (1985)* regards it as textual, though. Other interpersonal features listed in these pioneering metadiscourse systems have to do with (i) explicit references to the writer, i.e. person markers, (ii) the expression of the writer's attitude to the information presented, i.e. attitude markers, and (iii) devices aimed at establishing bonds between the writer and the reader, i.e. commentaries or relational markers.

Schiffrin (1980) and, above all, *Mauranen (1993)* paved the way for the narrow approach to metadiscourse, which is mainly concerned with the functions of text-organising elements. *Schiffrin (1980*, p. 231) characterises "metatalk" as self-referential comments which are made as the discourse unfolds to "bracket the discourse organisation and the expressive implications of what is being said". *Mauranen (1993*, p. 152), for whom "reflexivity" is a text-internal feature, defines it as "an explicit expression of the writer's awareness of the current discourse as text, that is, with his or her awareness that he/she is dealing with discourse, with linguistic expressions which are putting across a message". In *Mauranen's (1993*, pp. 173–186) framework, overt authorial presence can be assigned different degrees of explicitness, ranging from high to low explicit reflexivity. Elaborating *Mauranen's (1993)* contribution, *Ädel (2006*, p. 180) presents a reflexive model of metadiscourse which aims to be "a middle ground" between the broad and the narrow approaches. It has two general categories, namely, (i) metatext and (ii) writer-reader interaction. Metatext may be (i) impersonal, i.e. text-code oriented, or (ii) personal, i.e. participant-oriented (e.g. *as we have seen*), writer-oriented (e.g. *as I have shown*) and reader-oriented (e.g. *as you have seen*). Writer-reader interaction can only be personal, but it can be participant-oriented (e.g. *I know you think that*) or reader-oriented (e.g. *dear reader*).

As shown above, polarity has naturally characterised views on metadiscourse, if only because of the terminology used to refer to them. *Hyland (2017)* has recently reassessed them observing that taking these conceptions as opposing one another does not seem to be really adequate since it prevents us from getting a more complete picture than is possibly attainable by considering them as two complementary frameworks by definition. All the subtleties of the metadiscourse phenomenon could be "more usefully seen as contributing different aspects to our understanding of discourse and as occupying different points on a cline rather than two opposed positions" (*Hyland, 2017*, p. 19). Notwithstanding, the truth is that the role of stance is more prominent in the so-called broad perspective (*Ädel, 2006*, pp. 38–39).

Biber and Zhang (2018, p. 104) use the terms "stance" and "evaluation" to technically refer to "attitudinal or epistemic assessments expressed overtly through lexico-grammatical devices", and "attitudinal or epistemic assessments that are less explicit, expressed lexically or otherwise integrated in the discourse". This stands in sharp contrast with *Alonso-Almeida (2015c*, p. 1), where "stance" and "evaluation" are equated and used to represent attitudes not only towards "people, objects, and ideas", but also towards the self. In this sense, *Du Bois (2007)* puts forward "the stance triangle", an analytical tool aimed at enhancing the understanding of "stance acts" in relation to the agents and the processes involved in stancetaking. The role of social interaction is salient here because stancetaking entails subjects' being set in a dialogical configuration where "the stancetaker (1) evaluates an object, (2) positions a subject (usually the self), and (3) aligns with others" (Du Bois, 2007, p. 163).

Mur-Dueñas (2011, p. 3069) notes that *Hyland and Tse (2004)* and *Hyland (2005a)* accommodate social interaction into their model of metadiscourse by slightly modifying the terminology used in *Hyland (1998b)* to refer to the textual and interpersonal dimensions of metadiscourse. They opt for calling them interactive and interactional instead. In their more recent works, the interactive dimension of metadiscourse comprises resources which help writers organise their discourse. Their choice is determined by what they know of their readers beforehand and by their assumptions regarding their readers' "need for interpretative guidance" (*Hyland, 2005a*, p. 50). Their role goes beyond the mere text-organising function; they are indicators of audience awareness and, as a result, of the interplay between writers and readers. The resources contained in the interactive dimension are (i) transition markers, (ii) frame markers, (iii) endophoric markers, (iv) evidentials, and (v) code glosses. The interactional dimension, on its part, concerns resources which foreground writers' positioning with respect to the informational content and to readers themselves "by intruding and commenting on their message" (*Hyland, 2005a*, p. 49). Interactional strategies evince reader involvement by "expressing solidarity, anticipating objections and responding to an imagined dialogue with others" (*Hyland, 2005a*, pp. 49–50). Resources in the interactional dimension are (i) hedges, (ii) boosters, (iii) attitude markers, (iv) self-mention, and (v) engagement markers.

As commented on earlier in this paper, "[f]eatures of discourse are always relative to a particular audience and social purpose and the effectiveness of writers' attempts to communicate depends on their success in analysing and accommodating the needs of readers" (*Hyland, 1999*,

p. 5). This is most blatantly true in the case of engagement markers, which have been variously referred to as "commentaries" (*Vande Kopple, 1985*; *Dafouz-Milne, 2003*), "commentary" (Crismore, Markkanen & Steffensen, 1983), or "relational markers" (*Hyland, 1999*). *Mur-Dueñas (2008*, p. 197) defines them as "those features by means of which writers bring the readers into the text, involving them in the negotiation of meaning". *For Hyland (2005b*, p. 182), engagement markers include reader pronouns, personal asides, appeals to shared knowledge, directives and questions, whose functions may range from signalling membership to the same discourse community to acknowledging the possibility that their readers may hold conflicting views.

3. Corpus Description

The *Booke of Soueraigne Medicines*, written by John de Feckenham, is a compilation of a total amount of 739 recipes. These recipes are contained in Glasgow University Library, MS Hunter 93 (T.4.10), a manuscript edited by *Ortega-Barrera (2014)*. This manuscript (henceforth H93) is attributed to the medical tradition since it comprises a set of instructions to prepare medicines in order to restore health offered in the traditional *de-capite-ad-pedem*. Written in the second half of the sixteenth century, a period in which most people were illiterate because they could not read and write in Latin, and in which the processes of standardization and vernacularisation were taking place in England, English is the main language used in it, although some Latin and French expressions can be found.

All the texts analysed are indexed in a tabula offered at the beginning of the book that serves as a quick reference in the search of precise information or remedy to restore the health. Although eleven different scribes have contributed to the creation of this volume, this study will only centre on those recipes written by Feckenham, the main scribe, found in folios 1 to 257 which have been assigned to him by paleographic means. This comprises a total number of 709 recipes which represent the recipe genre.

Recipes belonging to the medical register are often found here and there in scientific texts all over the medieval period and even later. These recipes can be classified according to certain parameters, being two of them their origin or associated tradition of writing, on the one hand, and their target audience, on the other (*Taavitsainen, 1994*, pp. 329–330). As regards underlying traditions, recipes may belong either to the learned tradition, where academic treatises and other specialized texts are included, or to remedies and *materia medica* (*Taavitsainen, Pahta & Mäkinen (2006*, p. 86), following *Voigts (1986)*). In relation to their target audience, recipes in the learned tradition seem to have been addressed to a specialist audience, mainly surgeons and physicians, whereas those in the remedybook tradition "were for a large and heterogenous group including village leeches and lay people" (*Taavitsainen, 1994*, p. 330). It would be safe to assume, then, that the writing style in remedybooks could have responded to the heterogeneity of their potential readers. In this light, the profile of the audience of remedybooks as codified through the use of engagement markers can certainly be more appealing to look into than that of recipes in academic texts. This is the reason why we have decided to analyse H93.

The concepts of genre and text type have been used indistinctively by different researchers (*Biber, 1988*; *Görlach, 1992*; *Taavitsainen, 2001b*; *Carroll, 2003*), so the recipe is often categorised as a genre and as a text type. However, as *Ortega-Barrera (2009*, pp. 49–40) notes,

> *Devitt (1993* and 2000), *Bex (1996)*, and *Moessner (2001)* coincide in the fact that the definition of genre is based on external criteria and in that genres are cultural constructs identified by their function and communicative purpose, whereas text types are defined according to internal linguistic features (*Biber, 1988* and *Yw Lee, 2001*).

Martin (1984, p. 25) offers one of the most certain definitions of genre: "a staged, goal oriented, purposeful activity in which speakers engage as members of our culture", and, *Alonso-Almeida (2008)*, following *Martin (1984)*, includes the definition of text type in which this author distinguishes genre and text type: "genre is differentiated from text type in the sense that genre is externally defined, whereas text type is characterised according to internal linguistic criteria" (*Alonso-Almeida, 2008*, p. 10), adding that "[genre] represents the context of culture and how this is manifested in a particular genre in the form of goal oriented stages" (*Alonso-Almeida, 2008*, p. 17), and also highlighting the importance of the cultural context to establish the stages that can be found in a genre.

The recipes under study present a definite generic structure with clearly differentiated sections, all of which have a set of linguistic characteristics, including specific vocabulary. Following *Werlich's (1976)* taxonomy, the text type used is the instructive one. All the possible sections found in this compilation of recipes are: title, ingredients, preparation, application, storage and efficacy, although the order of some of the sections can vary. These sections represent the diagrammatic representation of the generic structure potential, which is: (Title) ^ (Ingredients) * (Preparation) * (Application) * (Storage) * (Efficacy). According to *Alonso-Almeida and Ortega-Barrera (2014*, p. 150), "the circumflex symbol in this diagrammatic representation indicated that one stage compulsorily follows the other, whereas the asterisk is used to show that the order of the stages may vary".

The title is used to signal the beginning of the recipe and it shows what the recipe is good for. The ingredients section contains the list of the different elements or materials needed to do the recipe. The preparation guides the reader to combine the ingredients in order to obtain a plaster, a water, or any other product. The application shows how to administer the product to the sick person. The efficacy section reveals the expected remedy results. All these stages present the following linguistic features: use of noun phrases, use of *and* conjunctions to show temporal and result meaning, use of medical terms (*headach, toothach*), herbs (*saffron, cinquefoyle*), culinary terms (*peel*, *boil*), measures (*ounces*), verbs related to application (*eat*, *drink*) and cooking verbs (*frye, stirr*); use of the second person singular pronoun (*you*), use of imperatives (*take*, *apply*), and use of time expressions (*when*, *first*). An example to show these stages included in a recipe is the following in which the name of each section appears in square brackets:

> [Title] Ffor the emrodes: [Ingredients] Take the broad memsayne leaves com*m*only called cane leaves, which grow in waters. [Preparation] Wash them cleane and putt them in a paper. And drye them in the imbers. [Application] And applye them as hott as may bee suffred; or make this in powder and cast it into the face. [Efficacy] And it helpeth.

The recipes analysed have been punctuated by using the conventions of Present-Day English in an attempt to make the text readable for the current reader so all the examples from H93 offered in this article show a Present-Day English punctuation. For this, the model established by *Alonso-Almeida (2001* and 2003) has been followed since this author combines the analysis not only of the structure but also of the rhetoric as the main bases to modernise the punctuation of the former texts, that is, of manuscripts. Thus, the expansion of abbreviations is shown by using italics. In the following section, we will examine the different engagement markers used in the recipe collection analysed.

4. Engagement Markers and Reader Involvement in H93

According to *Hyland (2004*, p. 14), the concept of reader involvement means "the ways writers explicitly orient to their readers", differentiating between stance and engagement. On the one hand, stance has to do with the

> ways that writers intrude into the discourse to stamp their personal authority onto their arguments or step back from their discourse and disguise their involvement. These features are sometimes called Appraisal (*Martin, 2000*), and refer to the ways writers present themselves and convey their judgement, opinion, and commitments to what they say (*Hyland, 2004*, pp. 15–16).

Engagement, on the other, is related to the presence of the readers into the text, "pulling them along with their argument, focusing their attention, recognizing their uncertainties, including them as discourse participants, and guiding them to interpretations" (*Hyland, 2004*, p. 16). In this article, we will analyse the use of engagement markers as an interactional strategy used by the author of H93, following *Hyland's (2005a, 2005b*) taxonomy. The first stage has consisted in finding and classifying the different types of engagement markers used in H93. Then, a qualitative analysis has been carried out manually.

Considering that H93 is an instructive text, directives are used as the most overt strategy in this recipe collection. *Hyland (2002*, p. 216) posits that "a directive utterance is one expressing an obligation on the reader either to do or not to do something", taking into account the illocutionary acts proposed by *Searle (1976)*. Directives are realised in different ways: "They consist mainly of imperatives (like *consider*, *note* and *imagine*) and obligation modals (such as *must*, *should* and *ought*), and we can see them as directing readers to engage in three main kinds of activity: textual, physical and cognitive" (*Hyland, 2004*, p. 22, based on *Hyland, 2002*). Textual acts "refer readers to another part of the text or to another text" (*Hyland, 2004*, p. 23); physical acts "instruct readers how to carry out research processes or to perform some action in the real-world" (*Hyland, 2004*, p. 23); and cognitive acts "guide readers through a line of reasoning, or get them to understand a point in a certain way" (*Hyland, 2004*, p. 23). These directives will be analysed in the following subsections.

4.1. Imperative Clauses

In his account of text types, *Werlich (1976)* brings to the foreground the role of the specific contextual factors underlying a given communicative situation as crucial to assigning texts to specific text types. When dealing with the instructive text type in particular, which is the one we are concerned with as it applies to recipes, the most prominent contextual focus is "the formation of future behaviour" (*Hatim, 2001*, p. 264). The majority of the actions (if not all) predicated in recipe texts are unmistakably future oriented, since in the context of medical recipes "a future time reference is presupposed" (*Quintana-Toledo, 2019*, p. 118). Additionally, there is a set of "action-demanding sentence[s]" (*Werlich, 1976*, p. 41) in the form of imperatives, whose target is the reader, and which provide him/her with the sequential order of the actions to be taken. These actions, in the end, stand for the steps which have to be followed so that the reader achieves some useful outcome. As *Skaffari (2009*, p. 39) notes, imperatives are an example of "explicit instruction" which makes obvious the existence of an "instructor" who provides "guidance" to someone who does not have the necessary knowledge. In this sense, the directions given are supposed to be observed by virtue of the writer's expertise on how to combine the ingredients and apply them effectively. In short, imperatives mark social distance between addressor, i.e. authoritative voice, and addressee.

The use of these directions is also related to one of the main kinds of activity, what *Hyland (2004)* denominates physical acts as imperatives are used in H93 to instruct readers to make the remedy, explaining them the whole process, from the ingredient collection to the preparation or elaboration of the recipe, and the application of the same, referring to empirical actions given that they are performed in the real world (*Hyland, 2008*, p. 10). Imperative clauses have an implied subject; they address directly to the reader to guide him or her. Examples of the use of imperatives in the different sections found in H93 are the following:

(1) Ffor a bruyse and to gett colour againe: Take wheat bread and crum*m* it into faire spring water. And sett it on the fire. And stirr it well till it bee thick plaster-wise. And lay it to the sore. And it will heale and gett colour shortly.
(2) Ffor boyles, ffelons and vncomes: Take wheat fflower, boares greace, may butter and sage. And stampe it all together. And make a plaster thereof. And lay it to the boyle and ffelon. And it will both ripe it and drawe it. And if it bee fryed, it worketh the better.
(3) A medicine for a weake back: Take the pyth that goeth through the back of an oxe or bullock. And stampe it in a morter putting bread and oatmeale therevnto. And make a pudding of the same. And soe eat it fasting and abstaine one houre after.
(4) A speciall pultesse to avoyd paine: Take iij handfulls of mallowes and a great handfull of vyoletts. And chopp them small. Then take the broth that a pullett is sodd in, and seeth the hearbes in it. And to thick it, take the fflower of barly and putt therein two yelk*es* of eggs. And make a plaster thereof. And apply it to the sore.

In all the examples (1), (2), (3), and (4) the presence of imperatives is evident. In all the recipes examined, the ingredients section starts with the imperative *take*. In the case of (4), the verb *take* is used twice because there is an explanation of the preparation after the presentation of the ingredients and then the reader has to add another one (*Then take the broth that a pullett is sodd in, and seeth the hearbes in it*). This use of the imperative *take* is an example of the way in which the writer is addressing directly to the reader to do the action.

The same happens with the preparation section in which the presence of imperatives is also a characteristic feature: in example (1) *crumm*, *sett* and *stirr*; in examples (2) and (3) *stampe* and *make*; and in (4) *chopp*, *seeth*, *thick*, *putt* and *make*. In the application stage, the imperative is used to explain the reader how to apply the remedy, using *lay* in (1) and (2); *eat* and *abstaine* in number (3); and *apply* in number (4). The use of these imperatives reflects the physical act to which *Hyland (2004)* refers to in order to make the remedy that will restore the health of the sick person.

The high presence of imperatives is a main characteristic of the genre studied, as Rissanen claims: "The only writings in which directives (imperatives) are likely to occur in abundance are works containing instructions and directions, such as medical recipe collections, cookery books, rules, etc." (*1999*, pp. 277–278). Apart from the use of the imperatives, the writer also tries to give the reader the security of getting the expected results by doing the remedy. In this sense, the efficacy sentence is used in some recipes: *and it will heale and gett colour shortly* (example (1)), and *and it will both ripe it and drawe it* (example (2)). These examples of efficacy sentence show the way in which the writer addresses directly to the reader since the author affirms that the physical act made by the reader will end in a remedy that is effective, reinforcing the fact that performing an act in the real world will be productive.

4.2. Obligation Modals

Modal verbs are a category of verbs widely studied because of their particularities and peculiarities. If Alonso-Almeida and Álvarez-*Gil (2020)*, through a solid study about modals and modality, define modality as "the expression of a speaker's evaluation of an event in terms of such notions as probability, possibility, obligation, permission and necessity" (*2020*, pp. 62–63), (cf. also Alonso-Almeida et al., 2019), Lyons (1977) and *Palmer (1986)* establish that modality can be divided into epistemic and deontic. Following other researchers, epistemic is "concerned with matters of knowledge or believe on which basis speakers express their judgements about state of affairs, events or actions" (Hoye, 1997, p. 42), whereas deontic modals refer to the "necessity of acts in terms of which the speaker gives permission or lays an obligation for the performance of actions at some time in the future" (Hoye, 1997, p. 43).

According to *Hyland (2004*, p. 82) engagement markers as directives such as *must*, *have to*, *need* and *should* are used "to align the goals and desires of the writer with those of the reader". In the same vein, he establishes that "these obligation modals express the belief that something should be done, while rhetorically presupposing that the reader will concur" (*Hyland, 2004*, p. 82). In this sense, the main goal of the writer of H93 is to show the reader the way to make some recipes in order to cure sick people.

Alonso-Almeida and Álvarez-*Gil (2020*, pp. 72, 74), in their study on modal verbs found in recipes, conclude that deontic modal verbs (*will*, *shall*, *must*, *may*, *should*, and *can*) are those with a significant score in recipes, establishing that "deontic modal verbs are used to indicate procedure" (*2020*, p. 72). Thus, these authors consider that *should* and *must* are deontic modals that mean advisability since they "are a means to frame some therapeutic recommendations" (*2020*, p. 74).

This is what happens in recipes, in which the writer uses modal verbs as *must* and *ought to* presupposing that the reader is going to follow the directions given in the remedy. In this sense, it can be inferred that most of modal verbs that will be found in our corpus are deontic modals since "the speaker lays an obligation for the performance of actions" (*Hoye, 2013*, p. 43). In this case the goals and desires of the writer are being associated to those of the reader.

Following the abovementioned authors, in H93 there are different examples of the use of deontic modal verbs that *Hyland (2002)* denominated obligation modals. In H93 the obligation modal verbs found are *must* and *ought to*. The modal verb *must* shows 51 occurrences in H93, the modal verb *ought to* is used only once and the verb *should* never appears. The use of *must* and *ought to* appears to be advisory, but they infer an obligation for the reader to get the like effect of the remedy presented.

(5) And when thou will occupie it, you must warme it.
(6) This must bee dronke iij seu*er*all tymes, the patient going to bedd, and clothes enough layd vpon him.
(7) If you bee bound and not soluble, you must vse suppositaries made with hony and salt.
(8) You must wash the place, being broken, with white wyne eu*er*y dressing.
(9) You must dissolue the labdanus with mihree and virgin wax.

(10) A medicine for the measles: Hee that will heale the measles ought first to labour and bestow his endeavo*ur* that they first come all forth.

Examples (5), (6), (7), (8), and (9) illustrate the use of the modal verb *must*, and instance (10) offers the only appearance of the modal verb *ought to*. In (5) the verb *must* implies that the reader will have to heat the product to get the intended result; in number (6), the verb *must* conveys the obligation of taking the remedy the times advised by the writer. It is said that the reader is forced to drink the remedy the times advised following the information given (*the patient going to bedd, and clothes enough layd vpon him*).

In (7) the author, by using the verb *must*, explicitly arguments that the use of suppositories made with honey and salt are the only remedy to improve the patient's health; in (8) the verb *must* suggests that the reader has to wash the place to get the like effect of the remedy. Example (9) shows the verb *must* as an advice since probably the reader cannot take the remedy if the ingredients are not dissolved. In (10), the verb *ought to* also implies an obligation if the person who is sick (*hee*) wants to recover from a disease, in this case, from measles.

All these examples show an implicit obligation because in the case the ill person does not follow the remedy given, he or she will not be able to improve his or her health and, at the same time, they show a procedure and also, as Alonso-Almeida and Álvarez-*Gil (2020)* establish, frame some therapeutic recommendations. It is an unequivocal commitment if the reader wants to be healthy or wants to cure someone. Thus, it is obvious that if the reader changes the modal verbs used in the examples by an imperative form, the meaning will remain the same. In instance number (5) *And when thou will occupie it, you must warme it*, the modal verb *must* can be changed by the imperative form: *and when thou will occupie it, warme it*. The same can be observed in (6) *this must bee dronke iij seuerall tymes, the patient going to bedd, and clothes enough layd vpon him*, that would change into: *drinke this iij seuerall tymes, the patient going to bedd, and clothes enough layd vpon him*. This said, the same can be applied to all the cases in which *must* is used in H93. Moreover, these examples show the implied authority of the writer since through the use of the verb *must*, which denotes obligation and can be interchanged with an imperative form, the author reflects a procedure that has to be followed by the reader, considering the instructions given.

4.3. Person Markers

Person markers are also used to set up a direct relationship between the writer and the reader. Thus, the writer uses different pronouns in H93. The pronoun, that is the most frequently used, is the second-person singular. It is utilised to address directly to the reader. According to *Mele-Marrero and Alonso-Almeida (2011)* this second person singular pronoun is used in directives to make them be stronger since the author is "convinced of the action to be taken" (*2011*, p. 175). Different forms of this pronoun can be found: *you*, its possessive form *your* and their previous forms *thou* and *thy*. The presence of the second-person singular pronoun *you* and *thou* and its possessive forms *your* and *thy* is shown in the following table, in which the number of cases in which they appear are included:

Table 1. Pronouns

Pronoun	Number of cases
You	324
Thou	55
Your	238
Thy	58

As shown in the table, the second-person singular pronoun *you* is present 324 times, whereas its previous form *thou* appears in 55 sentences. It must be taken into account that the use of imperative forms indicates the presence of the second-person singular pronoun, although it is not present in the sentence. The possessive form of this pronoun (*your*) is present in 238 sentences and *thy* is not used so many times as it only appears 55 times in the whole recipe book. The present day second-person singular pronoun (*you*) coexist with its predecessor (*thou*) as its possessive form (*your*) coexists with (*thy*) showing the evolution of the language at that time and spreading the use of the present-day varieties. Some examples of the use of the second person pronoun *you* are:

(11) And drinke a good quantitie in the morning before you rise out of your bed.
(12) And if you can gett noe winter savory, take tyme and more of the hopp.
(13) And vse this dredge fasting as oft*en* as you have need. And you shall fynd ease therein.

Examples in which the second person pronoun *thou* is used are the following:

(14) And putt it in another glasse till thou have need thereof.
(15) And take asmuch of sage as thou hast of the other hearbes by waight.
(16) And if thou make them in may, take hearbe water instead of pimpnell.

In all the previous examples, from (11) to (16) the second-person singular pronoun is used. From (11) to (13), *you* variation is used whereas from (14) to (16) the use of *thou* is shown. Both varieties can be interchangeable since they mean exactly the same. All these examples reveal the mode in which the author addresses directly to the reader in an attempt to make the directive stronger so that the "instructor is convinced of the action to be taken" (*Mele-Marrero & Alonso-Almeida, 2011*, p. 175). It has to be considered that the reader is the person who will prepare the recipe to be applied in order to heal someone affected by the illness intended to be cured, or even the reader will prepare the recipe to heal himself or herself. In this sense, the discourse participants (*Bondi, 2007*, p. 70) can be more than one, and at the same time, there is no information of number and of social status (*Wales, 1996*, p. 73), so there is not an exact reference to the reader. *You* and *thou* "help writers to characterise the interpersonal distance they want to make manifest in their texts to achieve either affectiveness, reader's involvement or even depersonalisation in scientific discourse" (*Mele-Marrero & Alonso-Almeida, 2011*, p. 170).

Another pronoun used in H93 is the first-person singular pronoun *I*, only used once to refer to the writer as shown in the sample to refer to something said by the author (*As I said before*). It establishes a relationship between the writer and the reader since the writer refers to something that has been said previously that the reader is aware of. This also indicates "authorial presence and power position with respect to the audience" (*Mele-Marrero & Alonso-Almeida, 2011*, p. 170).

The third-person singular pronoun (*hee*), that determines a relationship between the writer and the reader, also appears in the recipe book. This pronoun (*hee*) is used in H93 to refer to the patient to whom the remedy will be applied, so it could refer indirectly to the reader himself or herself since the reader could be the ill person. "The use of the third person adds more interpersonal distance" (*Mele-Marrero & Alonso-Almeida, 2011*, p. 175), in this case, between the writer and the patient, since it implies that the reader will follow the instructions given by the writer to cure the sick person or the patient. In the following examples, the use of *hee* can be appreciated:

(17) And annoynt the wound without when hee hath dronke the said potion.
(18) And as warme as hee may suffer it, lay it to.
(19) After that, hee beginneth to sweat.
(20) And then hee shall bee cleane by Gods grace thereof.

It is evident, that the pronoun *hee* in these instances refers to someone to whom the remedy has to be applied, showing the interpersonal distance that exists between the writer and that person.

At the same time, other forms of the third person singular pronoun are also present in H93: the possessive pronoun (*his*) and the object pronoun (*him*) to refer to the patient. These pronouns can be observed in the following instances:

(21) And as hott as the patient may suffer it, lett him take a spoonefull thereof into his mouth.
(22) Ffor him that spitteth blood
(23) And when it is broken and cleansed therewith, heale him with other plasters requisite as of other vlcers
(24) To make a man have appetite to his meate
(25) And lett the sick, when hee is drye in his ague, drinke thereof 3 or 4 tymes
(26) And after that, the matter is mollified and within his body

In all these instances, the pronoun *hee* (75 times) has been used to refer to the person to whom the remedy will be applied, as the possessive one (*his*) (60 appearances) and the object pronoun *him*, used 16 times. Another way to the refer to the third-person, in this case the ill person, is expressed with the words *patient, sick* and even *person*, showing 99, 29 and 5 cases respectively in H93, as it is shown in the following examples:

(27) & then bathe the patient with the liquour as hott as may bee suffered.
(28) Give the patient these 4 waters mixt together in equall quantitie blood warme.
(29) And give it to the sick to drinke at morne iij dayes and every day, iij spoonefulls.
(30) And lett the sick drinke it morning and evening viij dayes.
(31) And lay it to the navell plasterwise of the person that is diseased.
(32) And cause the sick person to drinke thereof warme evening and morning.

As it can be inferred from these examples, the words *patient, sick* and *person* appear mainly in the application section. As abovementioned, this reference to the patient or the sick person could also refer to the reader, or the person who wants to recover his or her healthy condition, although at the same time they are examples of a greater interpersonal distance between the writer and that person.

5. Conclusion

In this paper we have attempted to offer some evidence concerning the use of engagement markers as an interactional strategy in *The Booke of Soueraigne Medicines*, a compilation of Early Modern English medical recipes. The use of the engagement markers in this genre shows the presence of directives and reader pronouns. In the case of directives, the imperatives and the obligation modals are the main strategies found in H93. In the case of imperatives, they appear because the main purpose of a recipe is to instruct readers to make the remedy offered in order to restore health. The use of obligation modals, mainly deontic ones, shows that something should be done and that the reader will follow the procedure to obtain the result. For this, the verbs *must* and *ought to* are those with more occurrences in H93.

In the case of pronouns, the most used one is the second-person singular pronoun *you* and its counterpart *thou*, which address directly to the reader in an effort to make him or her follow a set of instructions or procedures to obtain a medicine that will serve to cure sick people. Thus, other pronouns as the first-person singular pronoun (*I*) and the third-person singular pronoun (*hee*) are also employed in order to signal interpersonal distance. The intention of the use of all these pronouns is to express authorial presence and reader involvement since the author wants to control the situation, that is, the making of the recipe.

This research is a first step in the study of metadiscursive elements in medical recipes. Further studies will evaluate the presence of these or any other engagement markers in medical recipes belonging to the same period and even to those belonging to any other period in order to compare the presence of these markers.

References

Ädel, A. (2010). Just to give you kind of a map of where we are going: A taxonomy of metadiscourse in spoken and written academic English. *Nordic Journal of English Studies, 9*(2), 69–97.

Ädel, A. (2006). *Metadiscourse in L1 and L2 English*. Amsterdam and Philadelphia: John Benjamins Publishing Company.

Alonso-Almeida, F. (2012). An analysis of hedging in eighteenth century English astronomy texts. In I. Moskowich & B. Crespo (Eds.), *Astronomy "playne and simple": The writing of science between 1700 and 1900* (pp. 199–220). Amsterdam and Philadelphia: John Benjamins.

Alonso-Almeida, F. (2015c). Introduction to stance language. *Research in Corpus Linguistics, 3*, 1–5.

Alonso-Almeida, F. (2015a). On the mitigating function of modality and evidentiality: Evidence from English and Spanish medical research papers. *Intercultural Pragmatics, 12*(1), 33–57.

Alonso-Almeida, F. (2001). Punctuation practice in a late medieval English medical remedybook. *Folia Linguistica Historica, 21*(1–2), 207–232.

Alonso-Almeida, F. (2015b). Sentential epistemic and evidential devices in Spanish and English texts on computing. In J. R. Zamorano-Mansilla, C. Maíz, E. Domínguez, & M. V. Martín de la Rosa (Eds.), *Thinking modally: English and contrastive studies on modality* (pp. 383–408). Newcastle upon Tyne: Cambridge Scholars Publishing.

Alonso-Almeida, F. (2008). The middle english medical charm: register, genre and text type variables. *Neuphilologische Mitteilungen, 109*(1), 9–38.

Alonso-Almeida, F., & Álvarez Gil, F. J. (2020). So that it may reach to the Jugular. Modal verbs in Early Modern English recipes. *Studia Neofilologiczne, XVI*, 61–88.

Alonso-Almeida, F., & Ortega-Barrera, I. (2014). Sixteenth century punctuation in the "Booke of soueraigne medicines". *Onomázein, 30*, 146–168.

Alonso-Almeida, F., Álvarez Gil, F. J., & Marrero Morales, M. S. (2019). Shall and will in the corpus of history English texts. *Revista Canaria de Estudios Ingleses, 79*, 181–191.

Álvarez-Gil, F. J. (2018). *Adverbs ending in -ly in late Modern English. Evidence from the Coruña Corpus of history English texts (Estudios de Lingüística Aplicada, Núm. 4)*. Valencia: Editorial Universitat Politècnica de València.

Bex, T. (1996). *Variety in written English*. London: Routledge.

Biber, D., & Zhang, M. (2018). Expressing evaluation without grammatical stance: Informational persuasion on the Web. *Corpora, 13*(1), 97–123.

Biber, D. (1988). *Variation across speech and writing*. Cambridge: Cambridge University Press.

Bondi, M. (2007). Authority and expert voices in the discourse of history. In K. Fløttum (Ed.), *Language and discipline perspectives on academic discourse* (pp. 66–88). Cambridge: Cambridge Scholars Publishing.

Cao, F., & Hu, G. (2014). Interactive metadiscourse in research articles: A comparative study of paradigmatic and disciplinary influences. *Journal of Pragmatics, 66*, 15–31.

Carrió-Pastor, M. L. (2014). Cross-cultural variation in the use of modal verbs in academic English. *SKY Journal of Linguistics, 27*(1), 153–166.

Carroll, R. (2003). Recipes for laces: An example of middle english discourse colony. In R. Hiltunen & J. Skaffari (Eds.), *Discourse perspectives on English: Medieval to modern* (pp. 137–165). Amsterdam and Philadelphia: John Benjamins.

Crismore, A., Markkanen, R., & Steffensen, M. S. (1993). Metadiscourse in persuasive writing: A study of texts written by American and Finnish university students. *Written Communication, 10*, 39–71.

Crismore, A. (1989). *Talking with readers: Metadiscourse as rhetorical art*. New York, Bern, Frankfurt and Paris: Peter Lang.

Dafouz-Milne, E. (2003). Metadiscourse revisited: A contrastive study of persuasive writing in professional discourse. *Estudios Ingleses de la Universidad Complutense, 11*, 29–52.

Devitt, A. J. (1993). Generalizing about genre: New conceptions of an old concept. *College Composition and Communication, 44*(4), 573–586.

Devitt, A. J. (2000). Integrating rhetorical and literary theories of genre. *College English, 62*(6), 696–718.

Du Bois, J. W. (2007). The stance triangle. In R. Englebretson (Ed.), *Stancetaking in discourse. subjectivity, evaluation, interaction* (pp. 139–182). Amsterdam and Philadelphia: John Benjamins.

Görlach, M. (1992). Text-types and language history: The cookery recipe. In M. Rissanen, O. Ihalainen, T. Nevalainen, & I. Taavitsainen (Eds.), *History of Englishes – New methods and interpretations in historical linguistics* (pp. 736–761). Berlin: De Gruyter.

Harris, Z. S. (1959). Linguistic transformations for information retrieval. In *Proceedings of the international conference on scientific information. Washington D.C. November 16–2, 1958 (Volume two. Areas 5–7)* (pp. 937–950). United States of America: National Academy of Sciences.

Hatim, B. (2001). Text linguistics and translation. In M. Baker (Ed.), *Routledge encyclopedia of translation studies* (pp. 262–265). USA and Canada: Routledge.

Hockett, C. (1960). Logical considerations in the study of animal communication. In W. E. Lanyon & W. N. Tavolga (Eds.), *Animal sounds and communication. Proceedings* (pp. 392–430). Washington D.C.: American Institute of Biological Sciences.

Hoye, L. (1997). Adverbs and modality in English. London: Longman.

Hoye, L. (2013). *Adverbs and modality in English*. London and New York: Routledge.

Hu, G., & Cao, F. (2015). Disciplinary and paradigmatic influences on interactional metadiscourse in research articles. *English for Specific Purposes, 39*, 12–25.

Hyland, K. (1998c). Boosting, hedging and the negotiation of academic knowledge. *Text & Talk, 18*(3), 349–382.

Hyland, K. (2002). Directives: Argument and engagement in academic writing. *Applied Linguistics, 23*(2), 215–239.

Hyland, K. (2004). Engagement and disciplinarity: The other side of evaluation. In G. Del Lungo Camiciotti & E. Tognini Bonelli (Eds.), *Academic discourse: New insights into evaluation* (pp. 13–30). Amsterdam: Peter Lang.

Hyland, K. (2008). Persuasion, interaction and the construction of knowledge: Representing self and others in research writing. *International Journal of English Studies, 8*(2), 1–23.

Hyland, K. (2017). Metadiscourse: What is it and where is it going? *Journal of Pragmatics, 113*, 16–29.

Hyland, K. (1998b). Persuasion and context: The pragmatics of academic metadiscourse. *Journal of Pragmatics, 30*, 437–455.

Hyland, K. (2005b). Stance and engagement: A model of interaction in academic discourse. *Discourse Studies, 7*(2), 173–192.

Hyland, K. (1999). Talking to students: Metadiscourse in introductory coursebooks. *English for Specific Purposes, 18*(1), 3–26.

Hyland, K., & Jiang, F. (K.) (2018). In this paper we suggest: Changing patterns of disciplinary metadiscourse. *English for Specific Purposes, 51*, 18–30.

Hyland, K., & Tse, P. (2004). Metadiscourse in academic writing: A reappraisal. *Applied Linguistics, 25*(2), 156–177.

Hyland, K. (1998a). *Hedging in scientific research articles*. Amsterdam and Philadelphia: John Benjamins.

Hyland, K. (2005a). *Metadiscourse. Exploring interaction in writing*. London: Continuum.

Lyons, A. (1977). *Semantics (Volume I)*. Cambridge: Cambridge University Press.

Martin, J. R. (2000). Beyond exchange: Appraisal systems in English. In S. Hunston & G. Thompson (Eds.), *Evaluation in text. Authorial stance and the construction of discourse* (pp. 142–175). Oxford: Oxford University Press.

Martin, J. R. (1984). Language, genre and register. In F. Christie (Ed.), *Language studies: Children's writing: Reader* (pp. 21–29). Geelong: Deakin University Press.

Mauranen, A. (1993). *Cultural differences in academic rhetoric: A textlinguistic study*. Frankfurt am Main: Peter Lang.

Mei, W. S. (2007). The use of engagement resources in high- and low-rated undergraduate geography essays. *Journal of English for Academic Purposes, 6*, 254–271.

Mele-Marrero, M., & Alonso-Almeida, F. (2011). The role of the pronouns he and she in seventeenth-century obstetric directives. *Studia Neophilologica, 83*(2), 169–181.

Moessner, L. (2001). Genre, text type, style, register: A terminological maze? *European Journal of English Studies, 5*(2), 131–138.

Mur-Dueñas, P. (2011). An intercultural analysis of metadiscourse features in research articles written in English and Spanish. *Journal of Pragmatics, 43*, 3068–3079.

Mur-Dueñas, P. (2008). Analysing engagement markers cross-culturally: The case of English and Spanish business management research articles. In S. Burguess & P. Martín-Martín (Eds.), *English as an additional language in research publication and communication (Linguistic insights series)* (pp. 197–214). Bern: Peter Lang.

Mur-Dueñas, P. (2010). Attitude markers in business management research articles: A cross-cultural corpus-driven approach. *International Journal of Applied Linguistics, 20*, 50–72.

Neff-van Aertselaer, J., & Dafouz-Milne, E. (2008). Argumentation patterns in different languages: An analysis of metadiscourse markers in English and Spanish texts. In M. Pütz & J. Neff-van Aertselaer (Eds.), *Developing contrastive pragmatics: Interlanguage and cross-cultural perspectives* (pp. 87–102). Berlin: De Gruyter Mouton.

Ortega-Barrera, I. (2009). The advice genre (1400–1599). Genre and text type conventions. *Studia Anglica Posnaniensia, 45*(2), 39–58.

Ortega-Barrera, I. (2014). *Un Recetario Inédito del s.XVI en la Biblioteca Hunteriana de Glasgow: Edición y Estudio*. Editorial Académica Española.

Palmer, F. R. (1986). *Mood and modality*. Cambridge: Cambridge University Press.

Quintana-Toledo, E. (2009). Middle English medical recipes: A metadiscursive approach. *Studia Anglica Posnaniensia, 45*(2), 21–38.

Quintana-Toledo, E. (2019). *In short tyme it wil heale the sore: A relevance perspective of promising in medical utilitarian texts of the*

Early Modern English period. Valencia: Universitat Politècnica de Valencia.

Rissanen, M. (1999). Syntax. In R. Lass (Ed.), *Cambridge history of the English language III: 1476–1776* (pp. 277–278). Cambridge: Cambridge University Press.

Schiffrin, D. (1980). Metatalk: Organizational and evaluative bracket in discourse. *Sociological Inquiry: Language and Social Interaction, 50*, 199–236.

Searle, J. R. (1976). A classification of illocutionary acts. *Language in Society, 5*(1), 1–23.

Skaffari, J. (2009). The WOMANual: Ancrene Wisse on instruction. In M. Peikola, J. Skaffari, & S.-K. Tanskanen (Eds.), *Instructional writing in English. Studies in Honour of Risto Hiltunen* (pp. 35–53). Amsterdam and Philadelphia: John Benjamins.

Taavitsainen, I. (2001b). Changing conventions of writing: The dynamics of genres, text types, and text traditions. *European Journal of English Studies, 5*(2), 139–150.

Taavitsainen, I. (2001a). Evidentiality and scientific thought-styles: English medical writing in late middle English and Early Modern English. In M. Gotti & M. Dossena (Eds.), *Modality in specialized texts. Selected papers of the first CERLIS conference* (pp. 21–52). Bern: Peter Lang.

Taavitsainen, I. (2000). Metadiscursive practices and the evolution of Early English Medical writing 1375–1550. In J. M. Kirk (Ed.), *Corpora galore: Analyses and techniques in describing English: Papers from the nineteenth international conference on English language research on computerised corpora (ICOME 19-98)* (pp. 191–208). Amsterdam and Atlanta: Rodopi.

Taavitsainen, I. (1994). On the evolution of scientific writings from 1375 to 1675: Repertoire of emotive features. In F. Moreno Fernández, M. Fuster, & J. J. Calvo (Eds.), *Papers from the seventh international conference of english historical linguistics, Valencia, September 1992* (pp. 329–342). Amsterdam and Philadelphia: John Benjamins.

Taavitsainen, I., & Hiltunen, T. (2012). Now as a text deictic feature in late medieval and Early Modern English Medical writing. In U. Busse & A. Hübler (Eds.), *Investigations into the metacommunicative lexicon of English: A contribution to historical pragmatics* (pp. 179–206). Amsterdam and Philadelphia: John Benjamins.

Taavitsainen, I., Pahta, P., & Mäkinen, M. (2006). Towards a corpus-based history of specialized languages: Middle English medical texts. In R. Facchinetti & M. Rissanen (Eds.), *Corpus-based Studies of Diachronic English* (pp. 79–93). Bern: Peter Lang.

Vande Kopple, W. J. (1985). Some exploratory discourse on metadiscourse. *College Composition and Communication, 36*(1), 82–93.

Voigts, L. E. (1986). Medical prose. In A. S. G. Edwards (Ed.), *Middle English prose: A critical guide to major authors and genres* (pp. 315–335). New Brunswick, N. J.: Rutgers University Press.

Wales, K. (1996). *Personal pronouns in present-day English*. Cambridge: Cambridge University Press.

Werlich, E. (1976). *A text grammar of English*. Heidelberg: Quelle & Meyer.

Williams, J. M. (1981). *Style: Ten lessons on clarity and grace*. Glenview, Illinois: Scott, Foresman and Company.

Yw Lee, D. (2001). Genres, registers, text types, domains, and styles: Clarifying the concepts of navigating a path through the BNC jungle. *Language Learning and Technology, 5*(3), 37–72.

ARTHUR MCNEILL

Hong Kong University of Science and Technology

Customizing Vocabulary Software to Reflect Local and Institutional English Wordlists

1. Introduction

The frequency of occurrence of a word in a language is often regarded as an indicator of a word's difficulty level. For many second language (L2) learners, vocabulary acquisition is expected to reflect a progression from high to low-frequency items. Corpora of the English language typically provide users with information about the frequency level of the individual words in the corpus. It is generally assumed that high-frequency words are easy for second language learners to acquire because they occur frequently in everyday use, while low-frequency vocabulary is more difficult to learn because L2 learners receive little exposure to it. In practice, however, L2 learners acquire their vocabulary under different conditions. For example, those who study a second language at school or university may follow a syllabus that has been designed to suit their specific situation, including the selection of vocabulary content that is judged to be relevant to their academic and social needs. Such syllabi are more likely to include, in addition to high-frequency vocabulary, selected mid- to low-frequency words if these are considered important for students' academic development (*Koirala, 2015*; *Masrai & Milton, 2018*). Moreover, since English is a global language with its own distinct varieties, its role and use within different communities may reflect local as well as international communication practices. As a result, the selection of lexical items for a local English curriculum may not be entirely governed by the frequency of occurrence of words in the language in general. This chapter argues that while frequency of occurrence may be useful at a global level for guiding and measuring vocabulary growth, locally approved wordlists can provide a more appropriate and effective foundation for an English vocabulary curriculum and its assessment. It also follows that there is a case to be made for customizing the software programs used to analyse and study vocabulary to enable them to reflect locally approved wordlists.

The chapter describes an attempt to customize the Lexical Frequency Profiler (LFP) software (*Laufer & Nation, 1995*) based on four English wordlists that were developed by the Hong Kong Education Department for each of the four Key Stages of primary and secondary education in Hong Kong. It also reports the results of a study that explores the potential of the customized version as a learning tool for university students and speculates about how the technical vocabulary of academic disciplines might be integrated into local versions of LFP.

2. The Creation of Hong Kong's English Wordlists

These lists consist of 5,000 words that students are expected to know by the end of secondary education. The development of the Hong Kong vocabulary lists was the first part of a longer project to create a new English vocabulary curriculum for the twelve years of compulsory education in Hong Kong (*Curriculum Development Council, 2009, 2012*). While the first part identified the lexical content, the subsequent phases addressed the teaching of vocabulary and produced teaching resources (*McNeill, 2012*). It was assumed that the most appropriate sources of potential words were corpora and existing wordlists, including *West's (1953)* General Service List, the British National Corpus (BNC) (*Leech et al., 2002*) and *Coxhead's (2000)* Academic Wordlist (AWL). The identification of the target words relied heavily on the judgements of local English teachers who were invited to indicate their preferences concerning the potential items. A series of teacher decision-making tasks took place with groups of teachers, each representing one of the four Key Stages. Each Key Stage group consisted of at least 70 teachers and the teacher sample represented about 25% of Hong Kong schools. The teachers were asked to respond on-line to frequency-based selections of words and were asked to indicate whether the items were suitable for inclusion in the wordlist for students of the Key Stage they represented. Each Key Stage group of teachers then took part in a focus group discussion, in which they were asked to give their reasons for rejecting potential items in the decision-making task.

An unexpected outcome of the teacher-decision-making task was the scale of the teachers' rejection of potential items. For example, it was observed that the teachers rejected almost 50% of the BNC words at 4000 level, judging them to be unsuitable for a Hong Kong English vocabulary list. When analyzing the patterns of response from teachers, it soon became apparent that the number of words rejected was far greater than expected (*McNeill, 2011*). The inclusion of the BNC corpus was, at first sight, attractive to the research team because of its spoken component, since the Hong Kong word lists were intended to reflect vocabulary used in spoken as well as written English. However, because BNC is representative of contemporary usage within UK, a large number of the words were judged to be inappropriate in the S.E. Asian context. Many of the items were considered to be restricted to users of colloquial British English or relied on familiarity with contemporary British culture. The high number of rejected items from BNC points to the enormous difference that appears to exist between the high-frequency English vocabulary used by British people for everyday communication among themselves and the kind of English vocabulary which ESL learners might be expected to learn for the purpose of education and employment in their own countries.

3. Lexical Richness and the Lexical Frequency Profile

The original purpose of LFP was to measure the lexical richness of texts. The classic version of the software provides a profile of a text's lexical content by grouping the vocabulary items into four categories: (a) words from the first 1000 frequency level, (b) words from the second 1000 frequency level, (c) words included in the Academic Wordlist (AWL) (*Coxhead, 2000*), and (d) words not included in the previous three categories, i.e. "off-list". The words included in the first and second 1000 frequency levels are basically the items in the General Service List (GSL) (*West, 1953*). A later version of LFP divides a text's lexis into twenty levels based on the British National Corpus (BNC) (*Leech et al., 2002*), plus "off-list". LFP has typically been used by teachers to assess texts written by students. It has also been used to scrutinize texts when considering their suitability for use in examinations and textbooks. The LFP performs a quick analysis of a text's lexical content by showing the frequency level of the words used and providing some basic descriptive statistics about the text based on word frequency. The profile shows the extent to which a text consists of low frequency and academic words. Although LFP has proved to be a popular tool among researchers, other approaches to measuring lexical richness have also been adopted (e.g. *Meara, 2001; Meara & Bell, 2001; Miralpeix & Celaya, 2002; Bell, 2003; Šišková, 2012*).

Lexical richness has been identified as one of the most important features of second language writing and can determine the quality of a text (*Koda, 1993*). Many advanced learners of English, in particular undergraduate and postgraduate students studying through the medium of English, also benefit from LFP and use it to check the vocabulary content of course assignments and academic papers before submitting them. Unfortunately, however, this use of the software for checking drafts is currently less accessible to intermediate level learners because the wordlists used in the original LFP are based on the frequency of occurrence of words within the language in general, rather than a particular L2 vocabulary syllabus where the prescribed lexical content may vary considerably from frequency lists such as GSL and BNC, which comprise the databases of LFP. Developing local versions of LFP based on the approved local wordlists should make the software more useful to learners around the globe.

Many university writing courses adopt a process approach, whereby a student submits a draft of a writing assignment to the instructor, who then provides formative feedback on the written text so that the student can re-draft and improve it. The pedagogical advantages of process writing are undisputed and it has long been established that re-drafting a text in the light of feedback results in improved writing quality (e.g.

Raimes, 1983; *White & Arndt, 1991*). However, giving feedback on drafts can be time-consuming on the part of the instructor. In some respects, LFP allows students to learn to write in a process mode by providing them with an individual lexical profile of a draft. Students can then decide whether they need to enrich the lexical content by substituting items of vocabulary.

4. Customizing the LFP Software

4.1. Technical Considerations

At first sight, the task of replacing one wordlist with another in the LFP software looks straightforward. However, one of the challenges for LFP, particularly when serving as a learning tool, is to assign a text's lexis to the prescribed lists, as accurately as possibly. Basically, the software needs to list all morphological variations of the words in each list, i.e. all members of the word family (*Bauer & Nation, 1993*). If the lists contain 5000 word families, all derived forms of each headword need to be included in the database so that the LFP will recognize them and place them in the correct category when profiling users' texts. If a word form is not recognized, LFP places it in the "Off-List Words" category, which may be inappropriate if the particular word form has simply not been included in the list. The "Familizer" software (available free from Tom Cobb's "Compleat Lexical Tutor" website, www.lextutor.ca) generates the various forms of a headword. However, not all forms of all words are generated by "Familizer", so the proposed LFP wordlists need to be subjected to careful testing before any new customized version goes live.

As in many countries where English is taught for academic purposes within an English-medium education system, it was assumed in the Hong Kong customization that academic vocabulary is present throughout the vocabulary curriculum and is not well served by a separate "academic" vocabulary database. However, other education systems may find it helpful for the LFP to report academic word use separately. The components of the Hong Kong version of LFP are shown in *Table 1*.

Table 1. Categories used to profile lexis based on Hong Kong's local wordlists

	Tokens	***Percentage***
KS1 Words		
KS2 Words		
KS3 Words		
KS4 Words		
KS1+KS2+KS3+KS4		
Total		

4.2. Post-Secondary Customization

The main appeal of producing a customized version of an assessment software program such as LFP is the opportunity to focus learners' attention on the language they are expected to know according to their local curriculum, rather than being judged according to knowledge of words that may not be relevant to their own situation and needs. Indeed, for students who proceed to post-secondary education, it is possible to include additional lists, such as the prescribed words of English courses that focus on academic literacy and lists of discipline-specific lexis, such as the technical vocabulary of STEM subjects.

5. The Study

5.1. Design

Two writing samples were examined in the light of students' experience of using LFP. The first consisted of 20 400-word texts produced by Year

2 undergraduate (UG) students of engineering. The second consisted of 20 200-word texts written by research postgraduate (RPG) students majoring in science. The UG students were asked to write about their experience of learning English vocabulary. The writing task was completed at home and submitted electronically to their English instructor. The students knew that the task was not part of their assessed coursework and was simply intended to provide them with writing practice. The students then attended a workshop in which they learned how to use the LFP software and undertook an analysis of their own writing sample. They were then asked to try to improve the vocabulary content of their texts and re-submit them to their instructor. The 20 RPGs were PhD students from the School of Science. They were given a 200-word structured writing task, which asked them to describe their research topic and explain how their research was expected to contribute to their field.

The design of the study is shown in *Figure 1*.

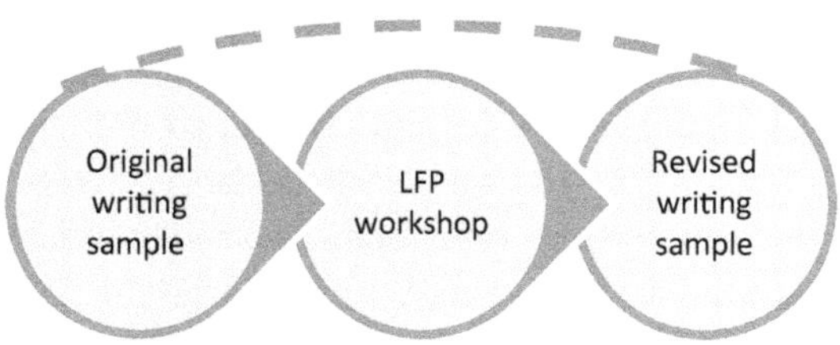

Figure 1. Design of the study

5.2. Results and Discussion

5.2.1. Undergraduate Writing and LFP

The lexical profiles of the first and second drafts of UG writing are summarized in *Table 2*.

Table 2. Comparison of lexical profiles of initial and revised drafts (UG)

	Initial Draft (Mean %)	***Revised Draft (Mean %)***
KS1 Words	73	59
KS2 Words	12	15
KS3 Words	10	14
KS4 Words	2	9
KS1+KS2+KS3+KS4	97	96
Off-List Words	3	4
Total	100	100

As the results indicate, the lexical richness of the texts increased substantially in the revised draft. In particular, there was a marked reduction in the proportion of KS1 words used (from 73 % to 59 %). Since the KS1 list contains most of the grammar words, such as pronouns, auxiliary verbs and conjunctions, it was apparent that students made a serious attempt to increase the lexical content of their writing by substituting words from KS2, KS3 and KS4 for the relatively "easy" words of KS1 when they made their revisions. Two independent judges were asked to compare the revised texts with the original drafts. They confirmed that the overall quality of the revised texts was higher than the first drafts. The results of the undergraduate writing task suggest that students typically produce first drafts with an over-reliance on familiar high-frequency items, then, when prompted to do so, make a serious effort to monitor their lexical choices and improve the sophistication of the vocabulary in the light of their LFP profile.

Figure 2 provides an illustration of the editing process that LFP promotes: (a) a reduction in the number of high-frequency words, and (b) a corresponding increase in the number of low-frequency words added to the text.

Figure 3 presents the LFP results in the form of a bar chart which confirms the pattern of reduction of KS1 words and increase in KS2, KS3 and KS4 words.

Figure 2. Anticipated adjustment to lexical profile during revisions

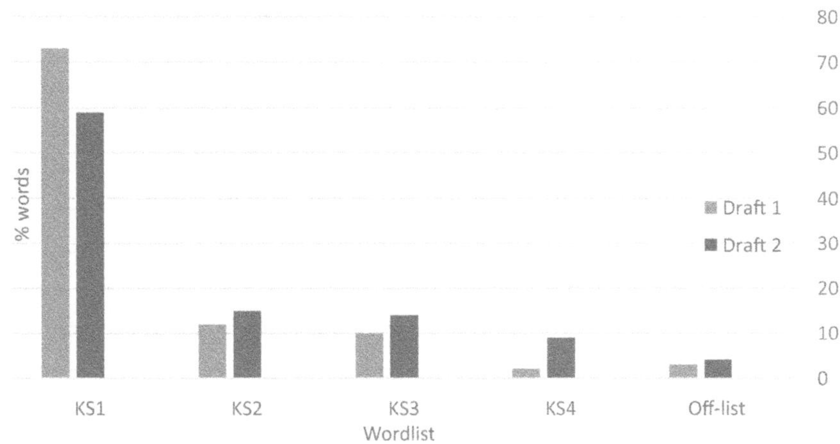

Figure 3. Lexical profiles of initial and final drafts (undergraduates)

Since LFP uses different colours to represent the words from the various lists when displaying the analyzed text on the screen (e.g. KS1 - blue; KS2 - green; KS3 – yellow; KS4 words – brown; off-list words – red), students receive a visual indication of a text's lexical profile, which makes it easy to interpret. When editing the vocabulary of their draft, their task is to reduce the number of words in the lower-level lists (e.g. blue KS1 and green KS2 words) and replace them with more "advanced" vocabulary from KS3, KS4 and any institutional lists that have been included (e.g. prescribed words of a particular course). This lexically-focused editing also gives students the opportunity to review the vocabulary of a topic when substituting words in the original draft. The conscious engagement with lexical choice is a meaningful activity as far as students' L2 vocabulary growth is concerned and can contribute to new word acquisition at university level.

5.2.2. Research Postgraduate Writing and LFP

The lexical profile of the students' first drafts is shown in *Table 3.*

Table 3. Lexical profile of initial drafts (RPG)

	Initial Draft (Mean %)
KS1 Words	47
KS2 Words	12
KS3 Words	16
KS4 Words	10
KS1+KS2+KS3+KS4	85
Off-List Words	15
Total	100

As the results show, the lexical richness of the RPG students' first drafts was already very high. In fact, it is considerably higher than the revised versions of the UG writing task. When the first drafts were examined, it was obvious that it would not have been appropriate to ask the students to try to improve the lexical content of their writing. Because each of the texts was about a focused research topic, much of the lexis was discipline-related and low-frequency in nature. The fact that 15 % of the lexis fell into the "Off-List" category suggests that many of the words were highly technical in nature. The participants in the study were not asked to take a test of vocabulary size, so the actual differences between the size of the RPG and UG lexicons are not available. However, it is apparent from the differences in the lexical richness of the two groups that RPG students have a superior productive vocabulary. For the RPG students, the language issues which required attention related mainly to grammar and syntax rather than lexis.

6. Conclusion

This chapter has argued that carefully developed local English wordlists can serve a valuable purpose in supporting the teaching and learning of English as a second language around the world. Creating coherent and effective English curricula requires an understanding of the needs, opportunities and aspirations that exist in particular communities. In terms of vocabulary software, the pioneering work of *Laufer and Nation (1995)* in creating the Lexical Frequency Profiler has provided both scholars and learners with an instrument which allows us to analyse and manipulate the lexis of the texts we read and write. With the addition of local wordlists in LFP, learners have a valuable resource for building their own productive vocabularies in keeping with their local needs.

The empirical work reported in the chapter suggests that university students can benefit from customized versions of LFP by using the software to enrich the lexis of their written texts. Encouraging students to edit their draft texts based on customized (i.e. local) LFP software is a worthwhile activity which is likely to contribute to vocabulary growth. However, it appears that undergraduates have more to gain from LFP than postgraduates, whose command of discipline-related vocabulary tends to be well developed following years of familiarity with the subject.

References

Bauer, L., & Nation, I. S. P. (1993). Word families. *International Journal of Lexicography, 6*(3), 253–279.

Bell, H. (2003). *Using frequency lists to assess L2 texts* (Unpublished Thesis). University of Wales Swansea.

Coxhead, A. (2000). A new academic word list. *TESOL Quarterly, 34*(2), 213–238.

Curriculum Development Council. (2009). *Enhancing English vocabulary learning and teaching at primary level*. Hong Kong: Government Logistics Department.

Curriculum Development Council. (2012). *Enhancing English vocabulary learning and teaching at secondary level*. Hong Kong: Government Logistics Department.

Koda, K. (1993). Task-induced variability in FL compositions: Language-specific perspectives. *Foreign Language Annals, 26*(3), 332–346.

Koirala, C. (2015). The word frequency effect on second language vocabulary learning. In F. Helm, L. Bradley, M. Guarda, & S. Thouësny (Eds.), *Critical CALL – Proceedings of the 2015 EUROCALL conference, Padova, Italy* (pp. 318–323). Dublin: Research-Publishing.net. http://dx.doi.org/10.14705/rpnet.2015.000352.

Laufer, B., & Nation, I. S. P. (1995). Vocabulary size and use: Lexical Richness in L2 written production. *Applied Linguistics, 16*(3), 307–322.

Leech, G., Rayson, P., & Wilson, A. (2002). Companion website for word frequencies in written and spoken English: Based on the British National Corpus. Retrieved from http://ucrel.lancs.ac.uk/bncfreq.

Masrai, A., & Milton, J. (2018). Measuring the contribution of academic and general vocabulary knowledge to learners' academic achievement. *Journal of English for Academic Purposes, 31*, 44–57.

McNeill, A. (2011). From corpus to language curriculum: A data-based or data-driven exercise? In International Association for Technology, Education and Development, *Proceedings of EDULEARN11 international conference on education and new learning technologies* (pp. 519–525). ISBN: 978-84-615-0441-1.

McNeill, A. (2012). Theoretical underpinnings of vocabulary learning and teaching. In Curriculum Development Institute, *Enhancing English vocabulary learning and teaching at secondary level* (pp. 3–7). Hong Kong: Education Bureau.

Meara, P. (2001). *PLEX v1.1*. University of Wales Swansea.

Meara, P., & Bell, H. (2001). P_Lex: A simple and effective way of describing the lexical characteristics of short L2 texts. *Prospect, 16*(3), 323–337.

Miralpeix, I., & Celaya, M. L. (2002). The use of P_Lex to assess lexical richness in compositions written by learners of English as an

L3. In I. Palacios (Ed.), *Actas del XXVI Congreso de AEDEA* (pp. 399–406). Santiago de Compostela: University of Santiago de Compostela Press.

Raimes, A. (1983). *Techniques in teaching writing*. Oxford: Oxford University Press.

Šišková, Z. (2012). Lexical richness in EFL students' narratives. *University of Reading Language Studies Working Papers, 4*, 26–36.

West, M. (1953). *A general service list of English words*. London: Longman.

White, R., & Arndt, V. (1991). *Process writing*. London: Longman.

DAVID RODRIGUEZ VELASCO / MARÍA CECILIA AINCIBURU

Queen Mary University of London / Universidad Antonio de Nebrija

The Expression of Disagreement of Chinese Students in a Foreign Language: Writing Emails to Their Spanish Lecturer

1. Introduction

The pragmatic competence for a foreign student implies the knowledge of a series of extralinguistic factors, specific to the target language, which are essential both in the codification and decoding of the pragmalinguistics and sociopragmatics phenomena (*Thomas, 1983*, p. 92). In the first case, we consider knowledge of the most conventionalised and ritualised aspects of interpersonal relations, for example, speech acts, idioms or proverbs. In the same sense, examples of pragma-linguistic knowledge are the elements that allow for implicit relationships or chains of discursive argumentation, given that they depend more on the linguistic structure of the statements and the elements that introduce or mark them than on their semantic content or their strict logical structure (*Anscombre & Ducrot, 1983*). In the case of sociopragmatic factors, a series of social perceptions and behavioural expectations are indicated which, as contextual factors, can significantly change the interpretation of a result, as is the case with forms of politeness. In the case that the student does not acquire this competence, or does so partially, we can speak of inadequacy, pragmatic error or pragmatic interference (*Bou-Franch, 2012*, p. 932).

Many studies indicate that pragmatic target language strategies tend not to be explicitly taught in institutional contexts, which would explain the lack of linguistic resources when interacting appropriately in the foreign university context, for example when writing to a foreign language professor or when conducting academic exchanges (*Economidou-Kogetsidis, 2011*; *Betti, 2013*; Nikleva, 2018; *Codina-Espurz & Salazar-Campillo, 2019*). The lack of pragmatic resources to disagree with the assessment of a teacher, an act that implies a vulnus with respect to the professionalism of the assessor and in which a strong attenuation capacity is expected, is generally resolved with direct speech acts that do not seem adequate in the level of communicative formality that the asymmetric situation requires (*Xuehua, 2006*).

The main objective of this research is to describe the resources with which students of Spanish as a foreign language (SFL) at a Chinese university disagree with their foreign lecturers. In contrast to previous studies, not only the sentence containing the act of disagreement will be studied, but also other generally formulaic parts of the emails (*opening* and *closing*) which give a pattern of other elements that are usually functionally acquired at lower levels of competence. Where possible, in addition to the actual act of disagreement, the justification or reaction that completes the pragmatic sequence should be analysed[1].

Despite the fact that the number of Chinese students who carry out university exchanges in Spanish-speaking countries is always greater, studies dedicated to these learners are very scarce and this forces us to build a state of affairs based on empirical data on the learning of English as a foreign language. We assume that this will constitute the first limitation in the reading of the results considering that they come from a textual analysis. On the other hand, most of the studies carried out with which our results can be compared involve Western students who study English (*Economidou-Kogetsidis, 2011*; *Betti, 2013*; Nikleva, 2018) and who can transfer linguistic schemes probably more in line with the target language.

Asian societies have been defined by virtue of their greater component of social cohesion as strongly mitigating, more aware of the need to resolve conflicts by protecting the public image of both partners

1 This study is part of the project: "Emotion, memory, linguistic identity and emotional acculturation: Their influence on the learning of Spanish as a language of migration (EMILIA)" (Ref. FFI2017-83166-C2-2-R, R+D+i Projects, of the State Program for Research, Development and Innovation Oriented to the Challenges of Society, Government of Spain).

(*Zhu & Boxer, 2013*; *Zhu, 2014*; *Yan, 2016*). However, studies by *Zhu (2014)*, which analyze 50 hours of natural interactions between friends, show that Mandarin speakers can present their disagreement in a very direct, probably discourteous way, "without any manifestation of negative signs" and that, in communicative terms, "these face-threatening instances still functioned to maintain the interactants' relationships" (*Zhu, 2014*, p. 97). These results seem difficult to transpose to an asymmetric situation such as that of a student with his teacher, but they could identify a first source of transfer.

The most detailed study of speaking acts of Chinese students of English as a foreign language that we have is that of *Xuehua (2006)*, carried out on the basis of DCT in which two groups of beginners and senior participants gave answers of disagreement in model cases of symmetrical and asymmetrical relations. The analysis of the derived speech acts is based on the classical categorization and therefore, these are classified according to whether they contain (a.) *direct strategy* of disagreement, imply (b.) *negative* or (c.) *positive politeness strategies* and also according to whether they are capable to (d.) *hint* or (e.) *avoid* dissent. The results show that direct acts of speaking English as a foreign language are the most frequent in both public and private contexts and that, although the amount of resources to mitigate is greater in older students, most of the time they would be inadequate in native communication. Unfortunately, in the publication of the research we do not have analyzable samples and the results are strongly aggregated, so we cannot know if any of the situations of the DCT could be assimilated to the one presented in this study.

With regard to other elements of the macro-textual structure of formal e-mail in the academic environment and strongly linked to courtesy (such as the use of subject lines, greetings and farewell formulas), previous research shows that foreign language students tend to ignore basic information about their own and the teacher's identity and qualifications (*Economidou-Kogetsidis, 2011*; *Betti, 2013*; *Codina-Espurz & Salazar-Campillo, 2019*). *Li and Chen (2016)* discuss the perceived level of courtesy of an email request from a Taiwanese student of English as a foreign language. The results are obtained through a semi-directed interview with a group of 13 teachers. The teachers consider that a successful academic email contains a number of decisive pragmatic elements which can be seen in *Figure 1.*

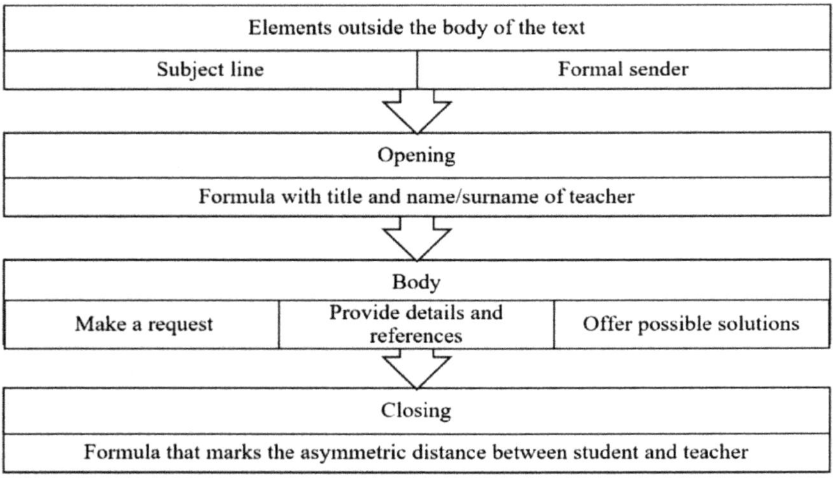

Figure 1. Pragmatic elements that teachers expect in an academic email (own elaboration from *Li & Chen, 2016*)

It is a formulation that in the body of the text assumes the act of ordering and not of disagreement, as in our case, but beyond the function studied it is possible that external elements and opening and closing formulas can be assumed as typical of the expected emails in the academic environment. Similar studies with speakers of other languages show that, although students use these highly formal formulas in their mother tongue, they do not transfer them to the foreign language (*Economidou-Kogetsidis, 2011*; *Betti, 2013*; *Níkleva & Núñez Delgado, 2013*; *Codina-Espurz & Salazar-Campillo, 2019*). This is a strong argument against language interference. The phenomenon could be partly explained by the fact that the student accesses informal communication and its conventions at lower levels of competence.

This research analyses the disagreement emails written by Chinese students in Spanish as a foreign language and, for the reasons already explained, compares its results with those produced by university students in other mother tongues and in other foreign languages. Since this study carried out the construction of a textual corpus with public access, we hope to provide a double contribution to the study of communication in the academic field.

2. Method

The present study analyses the uses and preferences of subject lines, opening and closing moves in messages and aims at investigating the strategies used by Chinese university students of Spanish in order to perform the speech act of disagreement in their L2 in an unequal situation (student/lecturer). This research aims to answer the following questions:

1. What macro and microstructure pattern do senior Chinese students choose when writing an email to their lecturer in Spanish?
2. Which strategies do they use and prefer when dissenting with their lecturer?

To answer these questions, a corpus of 135 emails was collected during the academic year 2017/2018. This corpus, published and still in progress in TalkBank[2], includes emails written by senior students who were studying Spanish as a foreign language at Heilongjiang International University and whose language proficiency was a B1 (Common European Framework of Reference for Languages). The group analysed consisted in 116 females and 12 males aging from 18 to 20. Both groups were native Chinese speaking coming from different regions of China.

In order to identify their macrostructure, a cualitative analysis of the pre-opening moves, opening moves, main text and closing moves was done. The study of the microstructure was focus on the uses of subject lines, greetings, self-identification, disagreement strategies, farewells and signature. The examination of the subject lines was determined inductively based on the use or lack of it. For the analysis of the opening and closing moves, *Economidou-Kogetsidis' (2011)* and *Codina-Espurz and Salazar-Campillo's (2019)* typology was adapted to identify the distribution of greetings and farewells and the uses of self-identification and the signature. To analyse the adequacy and the status-congruent language in their greetings and farewells, a questionnaire

2 For more information, please visit https://slabank.talkbank.org/access/Spanish/Nebrija-WOCAE.html

was completed by 10 Spanish-native university teacher (8 female and 2 male) from Universidad Antonio de Nebrija (4), Heilongjian International University (4), Universidad Complutense de Madrid (1) and Universidad Estatal Paulista (1). Their age ranged from late 20s to 40s (2 were in their 20s, 7 in their 30s and 1 in her 40s). Their teaching experience in higher education varied from 1 to 17 years. The questionnair was administrated via online where they were asked to provide their perception on the politeness and appropiateness of the greeting formulas (*Table 2*) and farewell formulas (*Table 3*). Participants were asked to imagine that they were Dr Pedro Rodríguez Torres, who had received a number of email from his student. More specific, they are asked to evaluate the formulas registered on the corpus based on a 5 scale Likert (being 1 very umpolite/inadecuate and 5 very polite/adecuate). A cuantitative anylisis was also held to examine on one hand, the distribution of dissenting strategies in the corpus and, on the other hand, the conditions of joint variability of opening and closing movements and the correlation between the the forms of farewell with the presence of the signature. The analysis of the distribution of dissenting strategies was done using SPSS while the conditions of joint variability and the correlation were done using the Spearman range correlation coefficient (non-parametric).

The uses of disagreement strategies and the pragmalinguistic competence of the senior Chinese students was analysed by a pedagogical framework based task in which they were asked to put themselves in the following situation:

> Imagine your lecturer has sent you the following email. You obtained a mark of 4 out of 10 (FAIL) in the final examination for the module of 'Oral Spanish' and you do not agree with the mark given. Write an email to your lecturer, Dr Pedro Rodríguez Torres, showing your opinion along with any request you feel is necessary.

As emails are a type of asynchronous communication, students were allowed to take time to reflect on their lecturer utterance and to plan and write their own response. Therefore, in pursuit of more realistic outcomes, students were able to use their dictionaries and online resources to search for vocabulary, politeness formulas and overcome any grammatical deficiency. Finally, to examine the disagreement strategies, *Xuehua's (2006)* taxonomy was used, which identifies five categories: Direct Strategy, where the disagreement is expressed boldly without mitigation devices; Negative Politeness Strategy, which is orientated to the hearer's negative face; Positive Politeness Strategy, orientated to the hearer's positive face; Hinting Strategy, where the dissenting act is implicitly expressed by hints or indirect language and Avoidance Strategy, where no disagreement act is made. However, as the task asked students to directly disagree to their lecturer, *Xuehua's (2006)* fifth strategy was removed. Instead, Strategy 5 was selected to identify the expression of feelings used by students in their emails.

3. Results

3.1. Macro and Microstructure Pattern Found in the Corpus

The complete corpus is integrated with 21785 words (M= 143.2; DS= 10.7) that have been processed in mixed form (by categories and with quantification), using the annotation tools of NVivo7. A first lexical analysis shows that the type/token ratio is low, at 0.53, which indicates that the formulaic composition of emails is prevalent. In order to answer the first question, *Table 1* shows the macro and microstructure pattern senior Chinese students chose when writing an email to their lecturer in Spanish. Examples that help the reader to understand our results will be provided from the Nebrija-WOCAE corpus, however, since the loading of the corpus has not been yet fully completed, some example may be missing, but will be visible soon[3].

3 The labels in the examples coincide with those of the WOCAE corpus and after the two dots the line of the transcript in which the example is included.

Table 1. Macro and microstructure pattern

Macrostructure	**Microstructure**		**Overall results**	
Sections	*Movement*	*Submovement*	*N= 135*	*(%)*
Pre-opening	Subject line	Use of Subject Line	25	18.5 %
		Omission of Subject Line	110	81.5 %
Opening	Greetings	Use of Greetings	134	99.3 %
		Omission of Greetings	1	0.7 %
	Self-identification	Use of identification	37	27.4 %
		Omission of Identification	98	72.6 %
Main text	Disagreement Strategies	Direct Strategy	113	39 %
		Negative politeness Strategy	25	9 %
		Positive politeness Strategy	22	8 %
		Hinting Strategy	66	23 %
		Emotional Strategy	61	21 %
Closing	Farewell	Use of Farewell	119	88 %
		Omission of Farewell	16	12 %
	Signature	Use of Signature	85	63 %
		Omission of Signature	50	37 %

Regarding the pre-opening section, our results show that only 18.5 % of the students used subject lines in their emails while 81.5 % of them preferred to leave it blank. These results lead us to think that either they lack the knowledge of its uses or they are unaware of its importance in academic communication. Although *Sappleton & Lourenço (2016)* suggested that a blank subject may be a good method to attract the attention of the recipient, it may not be the most effective way since, although it seems to provoke a greater curiosity in the participants, the reaction it elicits is not necessarily positive. Other studies, such as *Phelps et al. (2004)* or *Burgess et al. (2005)* based on the impact of the subject line on the recipients, have revealed the need to send emails with sufficiently detailed and personalized issues to know the content of the message and assess its importance.

In term of the opening section, our results showed a great variation of greetings formulas similar to what it was found in *Bou-Franch (2011)* and *Economidou-Kogetsidis' (2011)* findings. The formulas in *Table 2* are taken from the latter author (*Economidou-Kogetsidis, 2011*, p. 12) in order to increase the comparability of results. A total number of 40 different greetings were used in our corpus, as *Table 2* shows.

Table 2. Forms of address (in gray the appropriate ones according to the native judgment)

Submovement	***Formula***	***Example***	***N=135***	***Overall %***
Use of "dear" (*Estimado/Querido*)	Dear + Academic Title + Full Name	*Estimado Dr. Pedro Rodríguez Torres*	4	73.3 %
	Dear + Academic Title + Last Name	*Estimado profesor Rodríguez*	2	
	Dear + Academic Title + Fist Name	*Estimado Dr. Pedro*	3	
	Dear + Academic Title	*Estimado profesor*	64	
	Dear + Wrong Academic Title	*Estimado señor*	4	
	Dear + Wrong Academic Title + Full Name	*Estimado señor Pedro Rodríguez Torres*	1	
	Dear + Wrong Academic Title + First Name	*Estimado señor Pedro*	3	
	Dear + Wrong Academic Title + Last Name	*Estimado señor Rodríguez*	1	
	Dear + Full Name	*Estimado Pedro Rodríguez Torres*	10	
	Dear + Last Name	*Estimado Rodríguez*	1	
	Dear + First Name	*Estimado Pedro*	4	
	Other	*Estimatos profesor*	2	

Continued

Table 2. *Continued*

Submovement	*Formula*	*Example*	*N=135*	*Overall %*
Ommission of "dear"	Academic Title	*Profesor*	2	5.9 %
	Academic Title + Full Name	*Profesor Pedro Rodríguez Torres*	1	
	Academic Title + Last Name	*Profesor Rodríguez*	2	
	Academic Title + First Name	*Profesor Pedro*	1	
	Wrong Academic Title + Full Name	*Señor Pedro Rodríguez Torres*	1	
	Wrong Academic Title + First Name	*Señor Pedro*	1	
Usage of greetings (*Hola*)	Hi/Hello + Academic Title + Full Name	*Hola profesor Pedro Rodríguez Torres*	1	20 %
	Hi/Hello + Academic Title	*Hola profesor*	7	
	Hi/Hello + Academic Title + First Name	*Hola profesor Pedro*	2	
	Hi/Hello + First Name	*Hola Pedro*	10	
	Hi/Hello + Last Name	*Hola Rodríguez*	2	
	Hi/Hello	*Hola*	3	
	Other	*Pedro Rodríguez Torres*	2	
Zero greetings	Ø		1	0.8 %

As data shows, the most chosen formula was *Estimado profesor* [Dear + Academic Title], used 64 times, although considered neutral by the majority of the academics (6/10). As in *Economidou-Kogetsidis' (2011*, p. 12) findings, our data also showed formulas which were grammatically unacceptable in Spanish (e.g. *Estimito profesor* [CH-ES_4_30:8];

Estimado profesora [CH-ES_4_132]). However, in spite of their grammatical deficiencies, they were not seen as a possible cause of pragmatic infelicities. Formulas which could cause them were also found in the corpus such *Hola Rodriguez* [Hi/Hello + Last Name]; *Profesor* [Ademic Title]; *Profesor Pedro* [Academic Title + Frist Name] or *Pedro Rodriguez Torres* [Full name]. Some of them were seen as too informal (e.g. *Hola Rodriguez* [CH-ES_4_58]; *Profesor Pedro* [CH-ES_4_7:8]) while others were seen as too abrup due to the lack of deference (e.g. Profesor [CH-ES_4_17:8]; Pedro Rodríguez Torres [CH-ES_4_5:8]). In constrast to *Economidou-Kogetsidis' (2011)* findings, where the overall preference was the omission of term of address, our results seem to be closer to *Félix-Brasdefer's (2012)* and Salazar-Campillo's (2018), where the vast majority preferred to address their lecture with a greeting formula.

Within the opening moves and with respect to the usage of self-identification, data has shown that most of the students (72.6 %) did not identify themselves when writing to their lecturer. When self-identification was used, the most used formula was "I am + First Name" (e.g. *Soy Blanca* [CH-ES_4_12:9]; *Soy Luna* [CH-ES_4_15:9]) follower by "My name is + First Name" (e.g. *Me llamo Sergio* [CH-ES_4_120]; *Me llamo Nati* [CH-ES_4_135]). Some of the students made a more alaborated reference by naming what they studied, however, a closer look to the self-identification formulas revealed that the majority of them were too vague (e.g. *Me llamo Elsa, soy una estudiante de español* [My name is Elsa, I am a Spanish student] [CH-ES_4_54]). Self-identification is also necessary in any email to faculty. As *Li and Chen (2016*, p. 105) pointed out "professors may consider the student sender to be irresponsible if he/she does not provide any information about him/herself". Due to the large number of students in grammar classes, where is likely than several pupils has the same forename, the mere use of the first name to identify oneself seems almost impractical to its purpose. As *Codina-Espurz and Salazar-Campillo (2019)* explained, this behaviour may be due to the fact that students tend to rely on their username to be recognised by the faculty member when replying to an existing message.

Respecting the closing section, our results also revealed a great variation of farewells, with a total number of 20 formulas. As *Table 3* shows, the majority of the students chose a polite formula to end their messages (e.g. *Un cordial saludo* [warm regards] [CH-ES_4_13:19]; *atentamente* [sincerely] [CH-ES_4_20:18]; *un saludo* [greetings] [CH-ES_4_29:24]). In line to *Codina-Espurz and Salazar-Campillo (2019,* p. 87) findings, "the results for closing formulae seem to suggest, on the one hand, students' concern about formality attempting to mitigate the imposition of the [disagreement], and on the other, the tendency to adhere to traditional epistolary format". Our results also showed that, similar to what was registered previously in the greetings' submovements, some of the constructions employed were grammatically unacceptable but could not be neither seen as causing pragmatic infelicities (e.g. *Un braza* [CH-ES_4_22:19]*; un brazo* [CH-ES_4_111]*; un salud* [CH-ES_4_89]). However, according to the answers in the questionnair, some of the popular formulas chosen by the students were considered as too informal (e.g. *Un abrazo* [Hugs] [CH-ES_4_1:19]) or inadequate to the situation (e.g. *Un beso* [a kiss] [CH-ES_4_2:27]), which could suggest that Chinese SFL learners still struggle to be fully pragmatically competent in an academic context.

Table 3. Farewells and signature formulas used in the closing section

Movement	***Formula***	***N=135***	***Overall %***
Farewell	*Un cordial saludo* [Warm regards]	38	28 %
	Atentamente [Sincerely]	23	17 %
	Un saludo [Greetings]	12	9 %
	Tu estudiante [Your student]	3	2 %
	Tu alumno [Your student]	2	1 %
	Un abrazo [A hug]	17	13 %
	Un beso [A kiss]	16	12 %
	Other (e.g. *Un braza; Un brazo; Un salud*)	8	6 %
	Zero farewell	16	12 %
Signature	First Name	77	57 %
	Other (e.g. *J.X; X*)	8	6 %
	Zero signature	50	37 %

As for the signature, 57 % of the students chose their First Name to close their emails, while 37 % left it blank. Other type of signatures, but much less common, were also found in the corpus (e.g. J.X [CH-ES_4_3:25]; X [CH-ES_4_30:21]), however, surprisigly none them used the student's full name to end the messages. As we comented before, the use of their forename seems insufficient to their recognition.

In order to observe conditions of joint variability of opening and closing movements, which constitute the external framework to the use of disagreement strategies, the Spearman range correlation coefficient (non-parametric) has been used. The rho derived from the test indicates that there is a strong correlation between the omission of the identification at the opening and the inclusion of the signature (rho value 0.86, p=0.012). This indicates that students sometimes fail to show up, probably relying on institutional email and signature identification to be sufficient. Also correlated are the forms of farewell that are considered more formal (e.g. *Un cordial saludo* [warm regards]; *atentamente* [sincerely]) with the presence of the signature (rho value 0.91, p=0.008). While this might indicate that those who write in a more formal register are more respectful of the epistolary form of an e-mail, the data should be interpreted with caution, since the fact that it is a simulated task could bias its reading.

Unfortunately the studies reviewed do not contain statistical processing of the data and the quantitative description contains only percentages. Nevertheless, the frequency seen in our results follow the same line of *Economidou-Kogetsidis' (2011), Níkleva and Núñez Delgado's (2013)* and *Rodríguez-Velasco's (2019)* studies, which pointed out the difficulties that the vast majority of students manifest in the use of language when it comes to adequate and achieve their communicative purpose to the context. It would be important to have a study on the perception of native teachers with a consistent number of informants that overcomes the possible biases of idiosyncratic sensitivity. Currently the results about which traits are irritating to natives is almost nil, and although everyone agrees that explicit instruction is necessary to prevent pragmatic unhappiness, the truth is that it is difficult to know when the student will obtain his or her communicative objective.

3.2. Dissenting Strategies Used by the Students

Table 1 showed how many e-mails contain one type of strategy, but since the same text can contain more than one strategy, a more detailed analysis of the strategies is needed. The category "strategy" has 459 occurrences in this corpus, with the distribution shown in Figure 2.

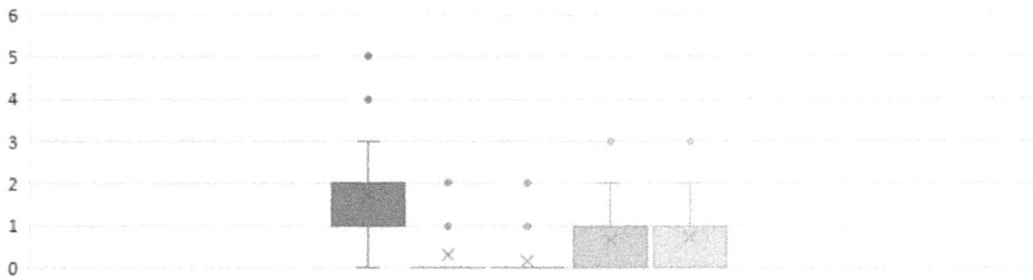

	Direct Strategy	Negative Politeness Strategy	Positive Politeness Strategy	Hinting Strategy	Emotional Strategy
Media	1,77	0,22	0,00	0,61	0,61
SD	1,20	0,48	0,44	0,71	0,78

Figure 2. Boxplot for distribution of disagreement strategies' p in the corpus (n=459)

The average distribution of strategies by email is 2.3 and there is an outlier among the 135 participants whose production does not contain strategies. Since in some cases the presence of one type of strategy is very low, the distribution is heterogeneous and shows very high standard deviations.

The direct strategy is the most widely used and has the most homogeneous distribution (high SD but below average). According to our data and in line to *Xuehua's (2006)* findings, students did not have the skill to dissent in an indirect and subtle way. The analysis shows that senior Chinese students prefered to disagree directly using bald-on record statements. Among the 459 strategies found in the 135 emails, 239 were realeted to Direct Strategy. This strategy was divided into four substrategies: direct disagreement, contradiction, counterattacks and other types of disagreement. Among these substrategies, the direct disagreement was the most used 116 occurrences (e.g. *No estoy de acuerdo de las notas del Español Oral* [I do not agree with the Oral Spanish's grades] [CH-ES_4_23:10]). "Other types of disagreement" was the second substretegy most frequent with 59 instances. This substrategy grouped those cases in which students attack their lecturer's prefessionalism by asking them, for instance, to change his minds on their marks or to double-check their grades (e.g. *Creo que la nota posiblemente equivocada* [I think my grade is probably wrong] [CH-ES_4_87]). The use of contradictions, found 58 times (e.g. *Creo que mi puntuación debe más mayor y no es 4.* [I think my score should be higher and it's not 4] [CH-ES_4_14:11]), and counterattacks, used 6 times (e.g. *En caso contrario, yo podré denunciarte. Necesito justicia.* [Otherwise, I can report you. I need justice] [CH-ES_4_39:25]), were also some of the substrategies used to express directly their contrasting ideas.

The second most used strategy was Emotional Strategy, which was found in 83 instances in 61 emails. This strategy was implemented when *Xuehua's (2006)* taxonomy could not be applied. It was used to cluster those examples in which students exhibited their feelings (e.g. sadness, shame or forgiveness) as a strategy to persuade their lecturer. It may overlap with other categories, such as Xuehua's Hinting Strategy. Unfortunately we cannot be certain if this author, or any other of the litarature mentioned before, has considered it under another label because these were purely quanlitative studies with no published corpus. Moreover, it may not be considered as a dissenting act by itself. However, the quantity and quality of these sentences make them a separate phenomenon that deserves further inquiry. Therefore, as foregoing mentioned, it seems that students appealed to the expression of sadness, (e.g. *Estoy muy triste porque la nota es muy baja* [I am very sad because the grade is so low] [CH-ES_4_29:11]), shame (e.g. *Creo que suspenso en cualquier examen es muy vergonzoso* [I think failure on any test is very embarrassing] [CH-ES_4_87]) or forgivenes (e.g. *Espero que puedas perdonarme por este error* [I hope you can forgive me for this mistake] [CH-ES_4_72]) to seek their lecturer's sympathy or support hooping for a change of mind. The expression of anger was also widely displayed (e.g. *De verdad, estoy muy enfadada a causa de este asunto* [I am really very angry about this matter] [CH-ES_4_64]), which contyradict the believe that Chinese people avoid confrontational communication in order to maintain harmonious interpersonal relationships (*Freshley, 2005*; *Gao, 2008*; *Cheng & Tsui, 2009*; *Liu, 2014*).

Following very close to the previous strategy was Hinting Strategy, linked to the expression of disagreement indirectly and found 82 times in 66 out of 135 emails. As data showed, students used this strategy to perform the dissenting act implicitly by using hints or indirect language. A closer look to the corpus revealed that, when students wanted to contradict their lecturer but did not want to do it directly, they appealed to question (e.g. *Tengo una pregunta sobre el examen* [I have a question about the exam [CH-ES_4_24:10]) or express doubts (e.g. *Tengo algunas dudas* [I have some doubts] [CH-ES_4_13:9]) about the results of their final exam. These two substrategies aligns with *Yeung's (2000)* hypothesis which points out that contrasting each other's opinion was a common practice amongs the Chinese society when the speeach act of disagreement takes place.

Finally, the two least chosen strategies were Negative Politeness and Positive Politeness Strategy (see Figure 2). By looking at the students' emails, it seems that they preferred to use negative politeness to express their opinions objectively without taking into account their lecturer's higher social status. Although supportive moves such as preparators (e.g. *Me permito molestarle en una hora tan inoportuna* [I allow myself to disturb you at such an inappropriate time] [CH-ES_4_59]) and apologies (e.g. *Perdone que le moleste* [Sorry to bother you] [CH-ES_4_130]), as well as syntactic downgraders (ex. *Me gustaría saber por qué he suspendido* [I would like to know why I fail the exam] [CH-ES_4_59]) and lexical modifiers (ex. please, some, any, maybe or possible) were seen in their emails, its scarcity gives an overall sense of rudeness due to the predominance of direct strategies. It was also notice that when "please" was used, it tended to be followed by an imperative clause which, as *Hartford and Bardovi-Harlig (1996)*, *Economidou-Kogetsidis (2011)* and *Rodriguez-Velasco (2019)* pointed out, it could sound harsh as this lexical modifier is not enough to mitigate the force of the imperative.

Regarding the Positive Politeness Strategies, data reaffirmed *Xue-hua's (2006)* observations, which claimed that students were hardly aware of the possibility of using it to prevent potential distressful consequences in their lecture's public face. As data showed, students agreed totally (e.g. *Acabo de recibir tu carta, y sabía que no pasaba el examen oral de español* [I just received your letter, and I knew I was not passing the oral Spanish exam] [CH-ES_4_65]), partially (e.g. *Es probable que mi vocabulario es muy insuficiente. Pero en todo, creo que todo el examen fue bien acabado* [Probably my vocabulary is poor. However, I think that I finished it correctly] [CH-ES_4_77]) or explained themselves as a way to disagree with their teacher's judgement (e.g. *Creo que las notas no son altas porque no puedo expresar correctamente mis pensamientos* [I think my grades are not high because I can't correctly express my thoughts] [CH-ES_4_51]). This "weak disagreement" (*Pomerantz, 1984*) resembles *Yang's (2009)* results in which Chinese students also agreed before introducing their dissenting clause.

The results show that Chinese students have a wide repertoire of dissenting strategies and that, among them, they prefer direct ones. Given that the second nucleus of strategies, that of exposing an emotional situation, is a finding with respect to the classic categorization reused by *Xuehua (2006)* we believe that a wider discussion of these results is necessary since the problem is not found in the linguistic competence, but in the pragmatic one.

4. Discussion

As we have seen in our results, in terms of the microstructure in the pre-opening section, students preffered not to use subject lines when writing to their lecturer, which made us believe that they are unaware of their uses nor their importance in netiquette. The absence of subjects lines could cause pragmatic infelicities as there are part of the minimum essential elements which guarantee courtesy in email comunication (*Li & Chen, 2016*). In addition, due to the large number of emails that lecturers receive daily, the need to prioritize what is relevant becomes harder, "so the effect of poorly worded emails and inadequate subject lines compounds the situation through additional time spent dealing with emails with defects" (*Burgess et al., 2005*, p. 82).

With regards to the greetings and self-identification moves, data showed that students, in general, may feel lost when they start to write an emails. In terms of greeting formulas, it seems that thay have difficulties to differentiate what is appropriate for this context. Although most of the students (64/135) chose one of the formulas described as "neutral" by the Spanish-native teachers, the wide selection displayed in *Table 2* reflect the lack of standardization and understanding of what is preferred. Greeting formulas are regarded as important as they serve to catch the recipient's attention and to indicate the relationship between interlocutors (*Li & Chen, 2016*). The empirical data that we have analyzed reveal that, as far as verbal courtesy is concerned, the linguistic features used to reflect the social distance between the interlocutors can lead to misunderstandings due to the lack of pragmalinguistic competence. The scarcity of the formulas considered by the survey respondents as polite and adequate, combine with the use of those seen as too informal or abrup and the tendency towards lack of self-identification, reinforce the need to include in the classroom the sociocultural norms of virtual courtesy used in the target language.

Respecting the main text section, data has show that students did not have the skill to adequate their disagreements to an academic context. In contrast to *Cheng and Tsui (2009)* or Shum y *Lee (2013)*, *Yan (2016)* findings, which pointed out how Asian society emphasized conflict resolution through strategies that avoid damaging the public image of both parties, our results showed that Chinese students were prone to use a direct language without enough mitigating devices to soften their dissention. These findings resemble those of *Xuehua (2006)*, *Zhu and Boxer (2013)* or *Zhu (2014)* which highlighted that, despite the high value Chinese society has for harmony, depending on the context and what is at stake, the Chinese community does not hesitate to adopt direct strategies to openly express disagreement. These results refute the generalization that discourages the use of dissenting acts in this culture in favour of a more harmonious, ambiguous or non-confrontational strategy. Therefore, the preference seen in our corpus for direct strategies combined with the tendency to express their feeling to make their lecturer to change his mind and the scarcity of mitigating devices made their emails unsuitable for an academic context.

As for the closing section, although the majority of the students include a form of farewell which was considered by the Spanish-native lectures as polite and adequate, the informality of some of the formulas chosen by a number of students made their farewell movements inadequate to the context. These results combined to the wide construction of fomulas seen in *Table 3* reflects once more the lack of standarization and understanding of what is preferred in virtual communication in academia. Finally, as it was seen in their self-identification movements, in terms of signature movements, the scarcity of identification or the simple use of their first name manifest the lack of understanding on how important these elements are. The use of signature is the essential to ensure email effectiveness. Adding a full signature at the end of an email would increase its efficiency because it helps the recipient to address that person without wondering who the sender is or adding an extra hassle. Therefore, the tendency towards the use of only their forename seems insufficient to its purpose.

5. Conclusion

All these results have reflected the obstacles that the vast majority of students manifest in the use of language when it comes to adequate and achieve their communicative purpose to the context. They have confirm the strong link between the different pragmatic strategies used by students and the sociocultural context in which they are developed. All these issue highlighted the necessity of explicit instruction in virtual communication and culture norms among university students as the context we have exposed in this paper plays a vital role in academia and the form students interact to their teachers might change from one culture to another (*Economidou-Kogetsidis, 2011*; *Betti, 2013*; *Rodriguez-Velasco, 2019*; *Codina-Espurz & Salazar-Campillo, 2019*). Therefore, the present study concludes by pointing out the following observations:

1. When subject lines were used, senior Chinese student preferred to leave it in black, which gives us the impression that they are unaware of its importance in computer mediate communication. Opening moves were widely used, being *Dear + Academic Title* the most chosen form of address (47.40%). Self-identification was also seen but limited and when used it was rather vague. In terms of Closing moves, students included a form of farewell which was considered as polite and adequate, nonetheless a number of cases were also seen

as too informal and out of context. When the signature was used, their first name was the most chosen formulas (57%) followed by zero signature (37%).

2. Results showed that, when senior Chinese student had to disagree with their lecture they use direct strategies with scare use of mitigation. Out of the 459 strategies found in the corpus, Direct Disagreement Strategies were employed 239 times in 113 emails, followed by Emotional Strategies (used 83 and found in 61 emails), Hint Strategies (adopted 82 times and found in 66 emails), Negative Politeness Strategies (employed 30 times and found in 25 emails) and Positive Politeness Strategies (used 25 times and found in 22 emails). The analysis of their emails proved that the group studied did not take in consideration factors that may influence their pragmalinguistic moves, such as degree of imposition or relative power and social distance when they write to their lecturer. Their wide use of allegations against their lecture's professionalism, their tendency towards imperative closes, summed to the use of emotions to seek their lecturer's support and the scarcity of deference made their emails inadequate to this particular context.

This research has contributed to Spanish language teaching research and has evidenced the lack of student competence in the sociopragmatic aspect. Nonetheless, it has not the intention to cite evidence in representation of Chinese interactional behaviour, as the corpus is too small to represent the typical methods of handling disagreement within the country. Therefore, it is hoped that in the future larger scale studies will be conducted where both native and non-natives students were analysed to support our claims and highlight the strategy patterns used by groups.

References

Anscombre, J. C., & Ducrot, O. (1983). *L'argumentation dans la langue*. Bruxelles: Editions Mardaga.

Betti, S. (2013). "Hola profe!" ¿Son corteses los jóvenes en el correo electrónico? Estudio de mensajes virtuales españoles e italianos (enseñanza y aprendizaje de la pragmática de una lengua extranjera). *RESLA, 26*, 67–89.

Bou-Franch, P. (2011). Openings and closings in Spanish email conversations. *Fuel and Energy Abstracts, 43*, 1772–1785.

Bou-Franch, P. (2012). Pragmatic transfer. In C. A. Chapelle (Ed.), *The encyclopedia of applied linguistics* (pp. 931–934). Oxford: Blackwell/Wiley.

Burgess, A. K., Jackson, T., & Edwards, J. (2005). Email training significantly reduces email defects. *International Journal of Information Management, 25*, 71–83.

Cheng, W., & Tsui, A. B. M. (2009). "ahh ((laugh)) well there is no comparison between the two I think": How do Hong Kong Chinese and native speakers of English disagree with each other? *Journal of Pragmatics, 41*(11), 2365–2380.

Codina-Espurz, V., & Salazar-Campillo, P. (2019). Openings and closings in emails by CLIL students: A pedagogical proposal. *English Language Teaching, 12*(2), 57–67.

Economidou-Kogetsidis, M. (2011). "Please answer me as soon as possible": Pragmatic failure in non-native speakers' e-mail requests to faculty. *Journal of Pragmatics, 43*(13), 3193–3215.

Félix-Brasdefer, C. (2012). Email openings and closings: Pragmalinguistic and gender variation in learner-instructor cyber consultations. In E. Alcón & M. P. Safont (Eds.), *Discourse and language learning across L2 instructional settings* (pp. 223–248). Amsterdam: Rodopi.

Freshley, D. (2005). A crosscultural study of identification of emotions: China and the United States. *Intercultural Communication Studies, 14*(1), 171–175.

Gao, X. (2008). Teachers' professional vulnerability and cultural tradition: A Chinese paradox. *Teaching and Teacher Education, 24*(1), 154–165.

Hartford, B. S., & Bardovi-Harlig, K. (1996). "At your earliest convenience:" A study of written student requests to faculty. *Pragmatics and Language Learning, 7*, 55–69.

Li, W., & Chen, Y. S. (2016). Politeness and effectiveness of English email requests: Taiwanese professors' perspectives. In Y. Chen, D. H. Rau, & G. Rau (Eds.), *Email discourse among Chinese using English as a Lingua Franca* (pp. 91–113). Springer, Singapore.

Liu, C. (2014). Chinese, why don't you show your anger? A comparative study between Chinese and Americans in expressing anger. *International Journal of Social Science and Humanity, 4*(3), 206–209.

Nikleva, D. (2018). Pragmatic strategies and institutional contexts: A study of target language use in academic exchanges. Journal of Pragmatics, 134, 1–14. https://doi.org/10.1016/j.pragma.2018.07.003

Níkleva, D. G., & Núñez Delgado, P. (2013). El correo electrónico como género discursivo: percepciones y habilidades para su composición en estudiantes universitarios. *RESLA, 26*, 385–407.

Phelps, J., Lewis, R., Mobilio, L., Perry, D., & Raman, N. (2004). Viral marketing or electronic word-of-mouth advertising: Examining consumer responses and motivations to pass along email. *Journal of Advertising Research, 44*, 333–348.

Pomerantz, A. (1984). Agreeing and disagreeing with assessments: Some features of preferred/dispreferred turn shapes. In M. Atkinson (Ed.), *Structures of social action: studies in conversation analysis* (pp. 57–101). Cambridge: Cambridge University Press.

Rodríguez-Velasco, D. (2019). Análisis de los elementos pragmáticos en la interacción escrita académica: el caso de los correos electrónicos de universitarios norteamericanos. *Revista Nebrija De Lingüística Aplicada a La Enseñanza De Lenguas, 13*(26), 198–225.

Salazar-Campillo, P. (2018). Pragmatic variation in email communication: A focus on student requests. *Journal of Pragmatics, 124*, 83–95. https://doi.org/10.1016/j.pragma.2017.11.013

Sappleton, N., & Lourenço, F. (2016). Email subject lines and response rates to invitations to participate in a web survey and a face-to-face interview: The sound of silence. *International Journal of Social Research Methodology, 19*(5), 611–622.

Shum, W., & Lee, C. (2013). (Im)politeness and disagreement in two Hong Kong Internet discussion forums. *Journal of Pragmatics, 50*, 52–83.

Thomas, J. (1983). Cross-cultural pragmatic failure. *Applied Linguistics, 4*(2), 91–112.

Xuehua, W. (2006). A study of strategy use in showing agreement and disagreement to others opinions. *CELEA Journal, 29*(5), 55–65.

Yan, C. (2016). A contrastive pragmatic study of politeness strategies in disagreement between native speakers of English and Chinese EFL Learners. *Chinese Journal of Applied Linguistics, 39*(2), 231–249.

Yang, R. R. (2009). Other-repair in Chinese conversation: A case of web-based academic discussion. *Intercultural Pragmatics, 6*(3), 315–343.

Yeung, L. N. (2000). The question of Chinese indirectness: A comparison of Chinese and English participative decision-making discourse. *Multilingua, 19*(3), 221–264.

Zhu, W. (2014). Managing relationships in everyday practice: The case of strong disagreement in Mandarin. *Journal of Pragmatics, 64*, 85–101.

Zhu, W., & Boxer, D. (2013). Strong disagreement in Mandarin and ELFP: Aggressive or politic? *Journal of Language Aggression and Conflict, 1*(2), 194–224.

CONCHI HERNÁNDEZ GUERRA

Universidad de Las Palmas de Gran Canaria

Intensification and Euphemisms in American Opinion Articles about Weinstein's Accusations

1. Introduction

Harvey Weinstein's trial has been one of the most overwhelming mass media event in the last decades, not only for the relevance of the character himself who was prosecuted but also, and consequently, because of the worldwide repercussion in the national and international media. Every single country has provided different viewpoints and perspectives towards the event and the culture of every single country also reflects the bias towards the event. This happened in Hollywood. One of the most remarkable moguls, thanks to whom lots of Oscars and money have been earned by different actors, actresses and other professionals, was accused of perpetrating sexual abuse to different actresses during decades. Many questions have arisen from different agents, but one of the most repeated has been: why now? If this had been happening during so many years. Interpretations are varied and quite personal. In this paper I am not dealing with the reasons or opinions expressed on the subject. The primary goal of this study is to analyse the degree of intensification provided.

My interest in this phenomenon lies in the fact that intensification is a personal choice of the writer so, apart from the use of the more or less formal grammar or other syntactic structures, intensification also reveals aspects concerning cultural layers in the country of origin. In this context, the study of intensification will benefit from a discursive analysis approach. I would like to unveil the extent of authorial objectivity.

The degree of personal opinion and impromptu in the publications will be matter of consideration. The use of intensification, as we shall see, may fulfil such functions as to present events in an exaggerated matter or to manipulate them to gain a particular perspective. A related concept to intensification is euphemism. In the corpus analysed, rather than emphasis, euphemisms are used to present the information in an ironical way. The main reason seems to be avoidance of offensive descriptions. This element, not being an intensifier, also plays a part, and will be considered in the analysis of the corpus.

2. Literature

Intensification is produced when there is a reinforcement in the expression (*Renkema, 2001*). *Zhiber* (*2019*, p. 71) also quotes Beltrama & *Bochnak (2015)* when he says that "intensification helps highlight what is being said and is related to the basic human need to make an impact to the interlocutor." *Zhiber* bases his study on the different layers of intensification in spoken and written British and American English. The written expression is analysed in the news. In his study, he concludes that the decline in intensification is higher as the formality of the register increases and that an overuse of intensifying adverbs negatively affects the credibility of a legal argument. The definition and study of intensification has undergone an evolution since their origins with *Quirk et al. (1987)*. In the origins intensifiers were classified into two subdivisions: amplifiers and downtoners. Amplifiers were divided into maximizers (i.e., *utterly*) and boosters (i.e., *violently*) but the borderline appeared to be fuzzy, as this is often a matter of semantic choice following from the speaker's intention (*Mahmood, 2015*).

Speaking about intensification is closely related to speaking about evidential and epistemic markers, as claimed in González et al.: "Whereas epistemicity involves the speaker's or writer's evaluation, judgment and degree of commitment attached to the truth-value of a piece of information, evidentiality involves the speaker's or writer's assertion of the source and kind of evidence at their disposal" (*González et al., 2017*, p. 68). Evidential markers signal the source of the information. For some people, evidentials also report on value judgments. In a way, the speaker detaches himself from the information given; and the epistemic value is the degree of certainty of the speaker with regard to the message (*Sanromán, 2020*). These features are not only found in the lexis and semantics but the context and other expressions have to be considered. Furthermore, they are better distinguished in the oral expression due to the spontaneity it owns (*González et al., 2017*, p. 70). Taken both as elements of intensification, there have been long discussions about the pertinence of including epistemicity and evidentiality as one set or, on the contrary, contrasting them due to the fact that one expresses opinion and the other, facts. Indeed, Palmer stated:

> Epistemic modality and evidential modality are concerned with the speaker's attitude to the truth-value or factual status of the proposition and may thus be described as 'propositional modality'. The basic difference between epistemic modality and evidential modality is that with epistemic modality speakers make judgments about the factual status of the proposition, whereas with evidential modality they indicate what the evidence is that they have for it (*Palmer, 2001*, 24).

This distinction is useful whether we want to show the intentionality of the author; that is, the distinction between what is an opinion or a fact, and has been used widely in the analysis of corpora (i.e., *Alonso-Almeida, 2015*; *Álvarez-Gil, 2018*, among many others). In the work we present here the aim is not to distinguish between both manifestations of intensification but to consider them as a whole. For that reason, a strict classification will not be established between epistemic devices and evidentials. The analysis will, however, cover the different grammatical structures involving intensification, including nouns, as these seem to play an important role in enhancing a particular authorial stance, albeit semantically. Indeed, the study of intensification in different corpora is always interesting in the light of what it reveals about the culture in a country. Another attractiveness is that intensification can also be analysed from different perspectives and all of them complement each other. As a demonstration, Zhiber (2019), for instance, states that "intensifying adverbs [...] possess grammatical properties, although are insufficiently defined unless we describe their functional significance" (70). To sum up, every perspective considered requires its classification (*Albelda Marco, 2014*).

This study has been performed from the analysis of mood in the media. Related to this, it is an interesting fact that the literature has dedicated more pages to attenuation than to intensification (e.g., *Samper-Hernández, 2013*). It seems much more popular in this genre trying not to overreact the opinion but to mitigate the information provided. The large number of examples of linguistic attenuation in the written texts found state this assertion. Just to cite a few examples, *Samper-Hernández (2013)* distinguishes the attenuation between *modus,* how it is said; and *dictum,* what it is said. Her study was done on an academic corpus and makes a deep study on the difference between attenuation and politeness. *Cabedo Nebot (2018)* distinguishes three types of mitigators: *bushes* (soften the propositional content), *hedges* (deny the speech act), and *shields* (establish a distance between the sender and the message). Different papers have dealt with the study of mitigators. One case in point is *Helfrich (2017)*. His study of mitigation as element of politeness is remarkable.

Added to this, we cannot miss the information provided by *Hyland* on metadiscourse (*2005*) as this is closely related to the information provided on next section. He talks about the concept of community as a "metaphor" that joins writers, texts and readers (139). He distinguishes key aspects of context that are crucial to the interpretation of texts. They are

> The *situational context* in terms of what people 'know about what they can see around them'; the *background knowledge context,* including cultural knowledge and interpersonal knowledge of what people know about the world, what they know about aspects of life, and what they know about each other; and the co-textual context in terms of what people 'know about what they have been saying' (*2005*, p. 139).

In the paper methodological procedure relies on *Albelda Marco*'s classification on lexical, semantic and expressions (*2014*), as her research recollects earlier works by *Briz (1998)* and *Mancera Rueda (2009)*. The result of the application of Albeda Marco's taxonomy to our corpus is given in a table containing examples of, say, exaggeration, repetition, and metaphors.

On the other hand, we shall also make an overlook on the euphemisms used in these papers. The use of euphemisms is a recurrent tool in order to veil the truth and "camouflaging the reality", replacing rude words by neutral ones (*Shenshurenko & Shafigullina, 2015*). Indeed, the study of this resource has been widely used to analyse socio-political articles and its relation with political correctness. These same authors define euphemism as the "language phenomenon that is permitted by norms of verbal behaviour, socially acceptable and used for replacing forbidden, improper and incorrect words, or a taboo." (2) Related to this, *Crespo Fernández (2008)* also offer a stimulating paper on the use of euphemisms and dysphemisms in sex-related terms and taboos along the recent centuries, whose conclusions concerning metaphors related to food and animals may illustrate our understanding of this linguistic phenomenon.

Euphemisms have traditionally been familiar to politics and politicians. This is a very common resource to avoid conflicts, confrontations, to soften the bad news or to mask unpleasant concepts. As *Ryabova* (*2011*, p. 36) aptly states

> The language of politicians [. . .] must consist to a large extent of euphemisms, rhetorical repression of the actual problems, empty words, nebulous half- statements, stereotyped expressions and common places. Euphemisms are periphrastic manipulation on the lexical level, and is motivated by an assumption that a change of name can also impact new and different qualities to a thing or to a person; hence euphemism is a sort of semantic camouflage [. . .] or/and an instrument of ideological framing.

Researchers have highlighted the proliferation in the use of euphemisms as a dominating process in modern communication for attenuating claims in conversations, for instance. *Ryabova* (*2011*, 39) distinguishes six functions of euphemisms that can be summarized as follows: (1) Change words with terrifying connotations (*departure* instead of *death*); (2) Replace words with unpleasant repulsive meaning (*insect* instead of *louse*); (3) Things considered impolite (*sleep together* instead of *sexual intercourse*); (4) Avoid using the direct name (*not very clever* instead of *silly*); (5) To camouflage the truth (*collateral* damage instead of *killed people*); (6) To elevate unskilled jobs (model for someone who shows clothes). As we can see, at a basic level, euphemisms apparently serve positive ends.

But euphemism is not simply a polite approach for stating and highlighting unpleasant things to say. It is also a way of covering the meaning it signifies and, consequently, of avoiding the knowledge of the moral implications (*Lukas & Fyke, 2014*, p. 554). In this paper, I focus on euphemisms used in reference to sexual scandals, and there is much research literature in the topic. One example is *Lucas and Fyke (2014)*, where the authors made a comprehensive study on the euphemisms used on Penn State's sexual abuse scandal and the limits with ethics. In this case, the authors perform an analysis of two clusters: those reported by the eye-witnesses, and the other by the key leaders during the (in) action in the course of the subsequent events. They state that "When unethical action already has occurred, euphemism provides a shield to protect individuals from the psychological consequences of those actions." (*Lucas & Fyke, 2014*, p. 555)

Secondly, *Crespo Fernández (2008)* presents a research based on the euphemistic and dysphemistic use of sexual metaphorization within the frame of the well-known "Conceptual Metaphor Theory" (CMT) initiated by *Lakoff and Johnson (1980)*. She concludes that "CMT is of paramount importance in euphemistic and dysphemistic use and interpretation, given that cognitive representation affects evasive and abusive referent manipulation in a remarkable way" (*Crespo Fernández, 2008*, p. 108). The examples she provides, as said above, are sex-related and demonstrates, for instance, how sex reference can be related to hostility and dominance and so, the metaphors will be concepts about war (*sex is war*, *sex is horse-riding*) but when violence is not highlighted but the idea of "a work", business-related concepts are used (*did the business*, *work on*). She concludes that in the examples she provides women are considered as inferiors as sex is reduced to an exchange.

3. American Legislation, Sexual Harassment and Communication Media: An Overview

In this section I explain American legislation relevant to this topic and how previous examples have been seen by the American society.

The American *Model Penal Code* does not distinguish between sexual aggression and sexual abuse, and this leads to endless discussion about where is the limit between consensual or non-consensual. Secondly, the question of whether there is more suffering when violence is used than other circumstance as power abuse against the victim's will. *Philadelphia Sexual Assault*,[1] for instance, denies there is more suffering in the second scenario. So, here we find two starting points for the analysis of the texts: the legal differences between the States themselves and the lack of detailed legislation in the different situations like lack of violence but intimidation. As a consequence of all this, it has been demonstrated that there are more cases of depression in victims that consider that in a way they could have avoided it (*Ros Cordón, 2016*).

In the political domain, *Van der Linden and Panagopoulos (2019)* conclude that conservatives are generally less concerned with sexual harassment in society and, more importantly, conservatives are more likely to condemn out-group (that is, liberals prosecuted) than in-group, while liberals condemn both equally. They also conclude that conservatives support their representatives even whether they have been accused of this crime and, also, there is a lack of consensus on what is sexual harassment and their boundaries. American communication media have had an important role in disseminating cases of sexual abuse as reported in *McDonald and Charlesworth (2012)*. These authors examine particularly mainstream news media texts reporting sexual harassment in four industrialized countries. This article evaluates the content of, and discourses evident in, mainstream news media texts reporting sexual harassment in 311 articles published in the United States, the United Kingdom, Canada, and Australia during a six-month period in 2010. They analyse how media characterizes these newsworthy examples. One of the conclusions is that they are seen as individualized examples, not as a systemic issue.

For all stated in this section, summarized in the lack of consensus in the legislation, there may be differences in the way of interpreting the law and, consequently, this leads to a varied criticism to the decisions

1 This is a private, not-for-profit centre whose mission is to provide expertise in the assessment and evaluation of sexual assault victims in Philadelphia.

taken by judges. When truism overcomes legislation euphemisms arise as a powerful tool to condemn injustice.

4. Data and Method

4.1. Data

We have chosen ten articles published online from October 2017 to December 2018 amounting to 13.109 words. They have been chosen from different sources in order to avoid the same political bias. In the primary sources found at the end of the paper, references are given. The following table offers information concerning source, authorship and summary of contents:

Table 1. Description of the corpus

#	**Source**	**Author**	**Description of contents**
1	*The New York Times*	Editorial Board of *The New York Times*	This is an extensive account of the issue during last decades. It shows the evolution from the first popular complaints not taken seriously and the steps taken in the most remarkable companies. They also give some clues about how to change the culture.
2	*The New York Times*	Nicholas Kristof	This focuses on how men can be part of a solution. He asked different women what they thought was the solution and the answers are quoted literally. They can be summarized in having more empathy with women and not patronize the problem.

Table 1. *Continued*

#	Source	Author	Description of contents
3	*The New York Times*	Jodi Kantor and Megan Twohey	Intensification is reflected in the direct quotations. That is, victims' opinions on Weinstein, not themselves. This is a resource to state the general vision of this character but not in first person. They even name the big number of employees that speak positively about him. What these journalists do is to.
			name several examples in which women complaint about Weinstein's misconduct. Not taken in isolation but a fact that grew constantly.
4	*The Hollywood Reporter*	Matthew Belloni	It focuses on Weinstein´s lawyer and all the expositions to the public opinion he has reported. Shortly, he takes the pain out of the complaints by questioning the veracity of the complaint.
5	*The Hollywood Reporter*	Eriq Gardner	He entitles his paper with a euphemism stated by Weinstein about the claims. He declares that it was a "commercial sex act" and the paper is a reflection about what can be considered sex trafficking as long as lawyers consider that different opinions may lead to misinterpretation of the intention.
6	*The Hollywood Reporter*	Tatiana Siegel	This, entitled "Harvey Weinstein Criminal Case may be Crumbling, Experts Say", reflects all the weak points of the accusations. How, for instance, one of the accusers sent him caring messages after the facts she alleges.
7	*Hasting Women's Law Journal*	Rochelle Dornatt	This is surprisingly entitled "Thank you, Harvey Weinstein". Despite the title, she mentions all the unfair situations women have overcome in relevant jobs until quite recently. She considers this case a turning point in the women's employment rights.

Table 1. *Continued*

#	Source	Author	Description of contents
8	*CNN*	Michelle Threadgould	"Harvey Weinstein Allegations: it's all about Power, not Sex" summarizes the mistreatment that she and other women have suffered at work. She doesn't question the allegations. On the contrary, she agrees and recognises that this has happened during last decades.
9	*The Loyalist*	Liam Miller	He wonders why this was not demanded earlier but offers a detailed summary of the allegations. He condemns hypocrisy and that famous women don't speak up these cases.
10	*USA Today*	Christian Schneider	"Men are complicit in the Harvey Weinstein Scandal as Enablers and Abusers." The title is as straight as the content of the paper. He accuses Weinstein as much as the men who kept silent and describes in a raw way this behaviour.

4.2. Method

This research has focused on the contents of these articles published in popular online American newspapers. Examples of intensifiers have been excerpted after manual analysis of these documents. Results have been then divided into three main groups: semantic items, lexical items and idiomatic expressions. The last group includes examples of repetition and hypeboles. Basic statistics has been calculated to reveal the degree of intensification the authors use in their articles.

5. Results

The following table contains the results of the number of examples seen in every category after several readings of the articles.

Table 2. Intensifiers in every paper

Paper	N. words	Lexical	Semantic	Expressions	Total	%
1	1641	39	7	1	47	2.86 %
2	839	12	5	1	18	2.14 %
3	3390	24	6	–	30	0.88 %
4	1364	26	3	1	30	2.19 %
5	762	13	4	–	17	2.23 %
6	1247	13	4	–	17	1.36 %
7	1731	14	9	1	24	1.38 %
8	747	5	3	1	9	1.20 %
9	633	11	4	–	15	2.36 %
10	755	6	11	–	17	2.25 %
	13.109	**163**	**56**	**5**	**224**	**1.70 %**

This table offers data about the examples of intensification in the sample and the percentage of intensification in each text. So this has been calculated according to the number of words used in every paper. Doing simple statistical calculations, we have seen that the use of lexical resources is much bigger than the use of semantics and expressions but the analysis of variance suggests that there is not a common pattern in all the authors. Furthermore, the longer texts do not mean the larger use of intensifiers as we can see, for instance, in text three. Being the longest in extension (3390 words) is the shortest in the use of intensifiers (0.88 % of the words in the text). On the contrary, shorter texts reflect an extensive use of intensifiers and words related to harassment. For instance, text five, that is quite short (762 words) and with a lot of examples of intensification (2.23 %).

6. Discussion

6.1. Intensification

The topic of sexual harassment may trigger the use of certain unpopular expressions that are impossible to avoid, even though one does not want to speak straightforwardly about it. In the examples analysed, formality and plain description of the facts seem to be the constant characteristics. Intensification is seen in the repetition of the facts themselves and the use of euphemisms that mitigate the importance of the criminal offence. For instance, in text one the expression "sexual harassment" appears twelve times and the different combinations with these two terms, in several occasions: "sexual misconduct", "constant harassment", "sex-based harassment". That is why the analysis of the expressions used may not represent intensification in themselves but description of the facts. The topic is intense in what is deviated from normality.

The lexical limits are key in this paper. Intensifiers alone work well in the texts analyzed, and their function is enhanced by the presence of certain value-laden words that contribute to reinforce the idea of crime. The term "rape" is a value-laden word. Considering the act referred to has been consensual; and, on the other hand, this can be descriptive if we are talking about a sexual crime. On this, we have in text five next quotation: "Yes, rape is illegal as is sexual assault. But there are reasons (jurisdiction, statute of limitations, specific facts, damages, etc.) that a plaintiff like Noble would assert a seemingly exotic claim like sex trafficking in court."

At the same time, presumption of innocence is difficult to defend in the case we are analysing due to the extended number of victims that accuse him of the same acts during several decades, so reporters do not question the facts so much as they avoid the spread of evidence-based analysis of the issue. As the papers are normally focused on the limits in the law that judges discuss on issues like the difference between consensual sex and offences, reporters play with the appropriate words to describe facts and opinions. Even in text six the term "unethically" in the sentence "it was the prosecutor who unethically withheld this information from the Grand Jury and it is they who are lying in the Court" is used to avoid the illegal content of the action. Another example could be the expression "decades of sexual harassment" in the sentence "On Oct. 5, 2017, the New York times published a scathing report detailing decades of sexual harassment by Oscar-winning producer Harvey Weinstein" (text nine). This expression in isolation indicates a neutral stand as facts happened like this, but it also conveys the idea of the continuity in time of a crime that may have affected countless women.

The line that divides the term from being neutral to strengthened is very thin. The first problem faced was to decide whether a term like "sexual abuse" could be considered in one or the other category. When we face texts that deal with Weinstein's prosecution it is unavoidable to name these terms, as this is the reason for the trial. Said once in isolation could not be considered strengthening but repeated several times in the same text creates a tense atmosphere. Anyhow, authors hardly want to name the facts as a criminal offense.

Another example related to this is the word "harassment". Again, it does not reflect an intensifier in itself but the big amount of examples and the adjectives pivoting around this noun, e.g. "sexual harassment", "constant harassment", "sex-based harassment", "harassment complaints", "workplace harassment" permeate the action raising the seriousness of the misconduct, and there is therefore the sense of semantic intensification of an idea. Notwithstanding, the common attitude in the authors is said to be the use of much mitigating descriptors like "inappropriate behaviour", "grave misconduct", "unwanted sexual conduct", "sexual office games", among others.

Within the group of semantic examples, the number is even shorter. When talking about actions the authors show themselves more reluctant to use strong verbs. So, we have examples like "forcibly performed oral sex" (text four), "perpetrating non-consensual sexual acts" (text five), "to scorer sexual favours" (text five), "sexually exploited" (text five), "forced her to perform oral sex" (text six), "groped, grabbed and fondled" (text seven), with others as surprising as "to overcome sexual obstacles" (text seven).

The examples of intensifying expressions are scarce. The repetition of a structure is used twice, in "let's not forget; let's even not forget" (text one) and "personal account after personal account of abuses" (text eight); in other example, the repetition of the same grammatical structure is used: "passionately, eloquently and something tearfully" (text two). In this group there are others like "quintessential non-victims" (text four) and "dressing `nicely´" (text seven).

6.2. Euphemisms

Contrary to what could be expected, euphemisms are a resource often used due to the nature of the data. Indeed, almost every single paper makes use of euphemisms at least once. In most of the cases, they are even named between inverted commas to make reference to the original words. So, we have examples like "unwanted sexual attention", "unwanted physical contact", "unwelcome advances", "serve at the pleasure of the member", "harmless flirtation" to refer to the criminal offence. They appear in sentences like "If she accepted his sexual advances, he would boost her career" (text three); "As a key hearing approach, the disgraced mogul's defence hinges on discrediting accusers with emails and preventing "prior bad act" [inverted commas in the original] witnesses –which helped convict Cosby- from speaking."(-text six); "Dinners where women were expected to provide a diversion from the day's heavy policy business through light conversation and "harmelss" [inverted commas in the original, and next] flirtations." These euphemisms make reference to the acts themselves. The contrast between the seriousness of the facts and the description by some of the commentators is relevant.

Other group could include expressions related to how we perceive them. For instance, "attempt at humour" in "Former President George Bush, now 93 and using a wheelchair, apologized last week after multiple women said he groped them and whispered a crude joke during photo ops. He described it as an `attempt of humour´" (text one); "excusing mentality" in the sentence "Bloom went on [. . .] doubling-down on the idea that Weinstein didn't know any better [. . .]. This 'excusing mentality' can, too often, be found in our friends, family, or other people who are known for their integrity." (text eight) and "unethically", as seen above, try to make a criticism on the people who cover these acts are irrelevant.

7. Conclusions

The use of intensifiers in American papers dealing with the relevant trial of Weinstein is scarce. Journalists prefer to establish a barrier between the facts themselves and the opinion they deserve. The only action of speaking about it contains the degree of intensification due to the characteristics of the offences. Added to this, there is no relationship between the words devoted and the use of intensification. On the contrary, the shorter texts focus on the inappropriateness of the actions more straightforwardly than the longer ones, that show themselves being more informative. That is, that relate the facts plainly. But consciously or not, the insistence on the facts produce an intensifying effect. We have also seen that euphemisms themselves can have positive purposes but also unethical ends. For their very nature, they can be ambiguous, and the writers know and play with it. In the papers analysed this is the resource used to intensify how absurd some allegations are.

Primary Sources (Corpus references)

Belloni, M. (2018, October 19). Harvey Weinstein criminal lawyer previews defense strategy: Police misconduct and 'non-victim' actresses. *The Hollywood Reporter*. https://www.hollywoodreporter.com (Artículo 4)

Dornatt, R. (2018). Thank you Harvey Weinstein. *Hastings Women's Law Journal, 29*(1), 3–6. (Artículo 7)

Gardner, E. (2018, August 28). Harvey Weinstein wants appeals court to define a 'commercial sex act'. *The Hollywood Reporter*. https://www.hollywoodreporter.com (Artículo 5)

Kantor, J., & Twohey, M. (2017, October 5). Harvey Weinstein paid off sexual harassment accusers for decades. *The New York Times*. https://www.nytimes.com (Artículo 3)

Kristof, N. (2017, October 25). Steinem, Sandberg and Judd on how to end sex harassment. *The New York Times*. https://www.nytimes.com (Artículo 2)

Miller, L. (2017, November 10). On the Harvey Weinstein scandal. *The Loyalist*. https://www.loyalist.com (Artículo 9)

Schneider, C. (2017, October 14). Men are complicit in the Harvey Weinstein scandal as enablers and abusers. *USA Today*. https://www.usatoday.com (Artículo 10)

Siegel, T. (2018, December 18). Harvey Weinstein criminal case may be crumbling, experts say. *The Hollywood Reporter*. https://www.hollywoodreporter.com (Artículo 6)

The Editorial Board. (2017, October 28). Will Harvey Weinstein's fall finally reform men? *The New York Times*. https://www.nytimes.com (Artículo 1)

Threadgould, M. (2017, October 6). Harvey Weinstein allegations: It's all about power, not sex. *CNN*. https://www.cnn.com (Artículo 8)

References

Albelda Marco, M. (2014). Ficha Metodológica para el Análisis Pragmático de la Atenuación en Corpus Discursivos del Español. *Oralia, 17*, 7–62.

Alonso-Almeida, F. (2015). On the mitigating function of modality and evidentiality. Evidence from English and Spanish medical research papers. *Intercultural Pragmatics, 12*(1), 33–57.

Álvarez-Gil, F. J. (2018). Epistemic modals in Early Modern English history texts. Analysis of gender variation. *Revista de Lingüística y Lenguas Aplicadas, 13*(1), 13–20.

Briz Gómez, A. (1998). *El Español Coloquial en la Conversación. Esbozo de Pragmapragmática*. Madrid: Ariel.

Cabedo Nebot, A. (2018). Creación de un modelo estadístico predictivo para la determinación de las funciones de atenuación en español hablado. (Spanish). *RILCE. Revista de Filología Hispánica, 34*(3), 1009.

Crespo Fernández, E. (2008). Sex-related euphemism and dysphemism: An analysis in terms of conceptual metaphor theory. *Atlantis: Revista de La Asociación Española de Estudios Anglo-Norteamericanos, 30*(2), 95–110.

González, M., Roseano, P., Borràs-Comes, J., & Prieto, P. (2017). Epistemic and evidential marking in discourse: Effects of register and debatability. *Lingua, 186*, 68–87. https://doi.org/10.1016/j.lingua.2014.11.008

Helfrich, S. (2017). Mitigation as an element of politeness in discourse. *Journal of Pragmatics, 117*, 48–62. https://doi.org/10.1016/j.pragma.2017.07.005

Hyland, K. (2005). *Metadiscourse. Exploring interaction in writing*. London: Continuum.

Lakoff, G., & Johnson, M. (1980). *Metaphors we live by*. Chicago: Chicago University Press.

Lucas, K., & Fyke, J. P. (2014). Euphemisms and ethics: A language-centered analysis of penn state's sexual abuse scandal. *Journal of Business Ethics, 122*(4), 551. https://doi.org/10.1007/s10551-013-1777-0.

Mahmood, A. A. (2015). Linguistic intensification and its role in interlingual translation of speech acts between English and Arabic. *Advances in Language and Literary Studies, 6*(3), 23–32.

Mancera Rueda, A. (2009). Una Aproximación al Estudio de los Procedimientos de Intensificación Presentes en el Discurso Periodístico. *Revista Electrónica de Estudios Filológicos, 17*, 1–26.

McDonald, P., & Charlesworth, S. (2012). Workplace sexual harassment at the margins. Work, *Employment & Society, 26*(1), 74–93. https://doi.org/10.1177/0950017011426313

Nikleva, D. (2018). Pragmatic strategies and institutional contexts: A study of target language use in academic exchanges. *Journal of Pragmatics, 134*, 1–14. https://doi.org/10.1016/j.pragma.2018.07.003

Palmer, F. R. (2001). *Mood and modality*. Cambridge: Cambridge University Press.

Quirk, R., Greenbaum, S., Leech, G., & Svartvik, J. (1987). *A comprehensive grammar of the English language*. London: Longman.

Renkema, J. (2001). Intensificadores: un marco de análisis. *Revista electrónica discurso, 1*(1), 17.

Ros Cordón, E. (2016). Agresión vs. abuso sexual: ¿Qué diferencia hay? *Crime and Law*. https://crimeandlawblog.com/2016/06/21/agresion-vs-abuso-sexual-que-diferencia-hay/

Ryabova, M. (2011). Politeness strategy in political discourse. *Rhetorical Studies, 5*(3), 34–45.

Samper-Hernández, M. (2013). La atenuación lingüística en el Español de Las Palmas de Gran Canaria. *Lingüística Española Actual, 2*, 325–48.

Sanromán Vilas, B. (2020). Do evidential markers always convey epistemic values? A look into three Ibero-Romance reportatives. *Lingua, 238*. https://doi.org/10.1016/j.lingua.2020.102832.

Shemshurenko, O. V., & Shafigullina, L. S. (2015). Politically correct euphemisms in mass media (based on American and Turkish online periodicals of the beginning of the 21st century). *Journal of Sustainable Development, 8*(5), 128–135. https://doi.org/10.5539/jsd.v8n5p128.

Van der Linden, S., & Panagopoulos, C. (2019). The O'Reilly factor: An ideological bias in judgments about sexual harassment. *Personality and Individual Differences, 139*, 198–201.

Zhiber, A. (2019). The decline of intensification in formal British and American English: A comparative study. *English Studies, 100*(1), 70–87.

Zhiber, E. V., & Korotina, L. V. (2019). Intensifying adverbs in the English language. *TLC Journal, 3*(3), 70–88.

FRANCISCO J. ÁLVAREZ-GIL / MARTA ISABEL GONZÁLEZ-BLANCO

Universidad de Las Palmas de Gran Canaria / Universidad de Las Palmas de Gran Canaria

The Translation of Deontic Modals into English of Nicolas de Blegny's *Le Remede Anglois pour la Guerison des Fievres*

1. Introduction

In this chapter, we study the translation of deontic modal verbs from seventeenth-century French into Modern English. Instances of modal devices have specifically been excerpted from the Nicolas de Blegny's *Le Remede Anglois pour la Guerison des Fievres* (1682a), and from a contemporary English translation, i.e. *The English Remedy or Talbor's Wonderful Secret for Cureing of Agues and Feavers* (Blegny, 1682b). The main goal of this paper is to compare the uses and functions of deontic modal verbs in these texts in order to identify possible deviations between the source text and the target text. For this, we follow previous research in the field of modality to indicate our understanding of the notion (Palmer, 2001; Collins, 2009; Alonso-Almeida, 2015; Álvarez-Gil, 2018; Alonso-Almeida & Álvarez-Gil, 2019). Our methodology of enquiry will also involve corpus linguistics methodology in order to offer a quantitative and a qualitative interpretation of deontic modals in French and their equivalents in English in the texts analysed. The identification of deontic modals in the original text requires the analysis and characterisation of all the modals in this text. The figures obtained in this analysis will be offered in the relevant section, even though we shall concentrate on the translation of deontic modals alone in our discussion of data.

The chapter is structured as follows: section 2 presents a revision of previous literature dedicated to the definition and categories of modality. The following section presents some information about Nicolas de Blegny, author of *Le Remede Anglois pour la Guerison des Fievres* (1682a), and about this work in particular. After that, the analysis of the data obtained from the corpus and the discussion of those findings concerning deontic modals are given. Finally, the conclusions drawn from this study is presented.

2. Modality: definition and categories.

The concept of modality is a rather complex term that may refer to both semantic and pragmatic phenomena. Precisely, this complexity explains the lack of unanimous agreement among scholars as to its scope. Many linguists have attempted to provide their own definition for the notion of modality, as this is the case of Palmer (2001); Depraetere and Reed (2006) and Collins (2009). Some of these definitions share some points in common, as seen in what follows:

> The term 'modality' is a cover term for a range of semantic notions such as ability, possibility, hypotheticality, obligation, and imperative meaning. [...] If, however, we wish to provide a more theoretically useful definition, we need to find what it is that all modal utterances have in common (Depraetere and Reed, 2006, p. 1).

> Modality embraces a range of semantic notions, including possibility, necessity, ability, obligation, permission, and hypotheticality. What they have in common is that they all involve some kind of non-factuality: a situation is represented not as a straightforward fact, as not being known (Collins, 2009, p. 11).

These two definitions refer to modality within a semantic approach. The authors agree on such certain semantic notions as possibility, ability, obligation and hypothesis. However, they differ on imperative meaning, as given in the first definition, and permission, in the second one. Wilmet (1998) presents a more formalized view of modality:

> Mode et son doublet modalité décrivent la valeur de vérité d'une proposition p – de la nécessité de p à la possibilité de p, et de l'impossibilité de p (ou necessité de non-p) à la contingence de p (possibilité de non-p ou non- necessité de p). (Wilmet, 1998, p. 288)

Wilmet's study shows that modality may present different forces. The concept involves such notions as necessity and possibility, which also insist on the non-factual quality of modality as modality describes the value of truth of a proposition p – from the necessity of p to the possibility of p, and from the impossibility of p (or necessity of non-p) to the contingence of p (possibility of non-p or non-necessity of p). This coincides with Collins' definition and with the fact that both scholars claim that the speaker's knowledge and intentions are fundamental in the use of modality. As stated in Turnbull and Saxton (1997, p. 147), 'the use of modal expressions allows speakers to qualify their commitment to what they say'. In this context, the term of modality would make reference to a semantic as well as to a pragmatic dimension. In this context, an important function of modality, especially that indicating attenuation of the propositional contents, is the indication of politeness (Brown & Levinson, 1987). The authors of scientific reports try to mitigate the strength of the illocutionary force of propositions in order to avoid face-threatening acts leading to further critical stance against their own writing in reply (Nuyts, 2001; Cornillie & Delbecque, 2008; Alonso-Almeida, 2015; Carrió-Pastor, 2019).

There exist different taxonomies of modality, but one of the most extended tends to divide it into three categories, namely deontic, epistemic, and dynamic. This threefold distinction is followed in the present chapter.

2.1. Deontic modality

Modality is classified as deontic when the speaker tries to convey some kind of force of obligation to the proposition expressed. According to Palmer (2001, p. 10), deontic modality might also be instantiated by an external source as well as by an internal motivation of the speaker. However, Depraetere and Reed (2006, p. 274) argue that 'deontic modality also implies an authority, or "deontic source" – which may be a person, a set of rules, or something as vague as a social norm – responsible for imposing the necessity (obligation) or granting the possibility (permission)'. The following example illustrates this definition:

(1) I must, however, as to climate, bear testimony to its salubrity generally (from Alonso-Almeida and Vázquez, 2015, p. 143).

In (1), we can observe that the author, by using the modal verb *must*, indicates some kind of obligation or duty that comes from an unclear source. This might be based on the speaker's previous experience.

2.2. Epistemic modality

Epistemic modality is related to the expression of possibilities and what is thought to be true. Turnbull and Saxton (1997, p. 149) state that 'epistemic modality relativizes the truth of the proposition' and its use 'conveys speakers' judgments about their state of knowledge, belief, or opinion'. Additionally, Alonso-Almeida (2015, p. 34) explains that epistemic modality may have a mitigating function of the proposition, as shown in the following instance:

(2) There may be some truth in this view of the case (from Alonso-Almeida and Vázquez, 2015, p. 147).

In this utterance, we can see that the modal verb *may* indicates the possibility of the fact being described to be true and, at the same time, attenuates the illocutionary force of the proposition hedged. A pragmatic function of *may* in this context is to suggest politeness.

2.3. Dynamic modality

The last subgroup in this taxonomy is dynamic modality. Dynamic modality refers to the ability of the speaker to carry out an action. This type of modality also relies on the conditions enabling the realization of an action. According to Palmer (2001, p. 179), "the dynamic ability is less central to modality than deontic permission in that it does not involve the speaker's attitude to the factuality or actualization of the situation". In fact, some linguists do not consider the dynamic modality as a type of modal meaning, because of its closeness to factuality. In this paper, dynamic modality is considered as one type of modal meaning. One example is given in (3):

(3) We operate what might be described as a gigantic tutorial system (from Palmer, 1990, p. 110).

In this statement, we can see that the modal verb *might* is deployed to indicate dynamic possibility. In this case, *might* is not really implying that the system described is likely to be described or not. It rather refers to the potentiality of this label, i.e. a gigantic tutorial system, to suit what these people manage.

In what follows, we analyse the modal verbs used in a French medical text from the seventeenth century and its translation into English. We examine how these forms are rendered in the target language and culture.

3. Data: Nicolas de Blegny's *Le remede Anglois pour la guerison des fievres*

As stated by Kronick (2004, p. 1), there is a considerable amount of information regarding Nicolas de Blegny's works and biography. However, there are some specific areas of his life and accomplishments of which there are hardly any records. In this section, we will explain some of his most important landmarks and success in the medical field.

Nicolas de Blegny, brother of the famous French writer Étienne de Blegny, was born in the mid-seventeenth century in Lyon. However, this fact is controversial and depending on the source consulted, it may vary. He died in Avignon in 1722. There is not a great amount of information available about his early years, but he attended the surgical College of Saint-Côme as a clerk or apprentice during his early manhood (Nicholls, 1934, p. 198). He started there as a designer of trusses in the treatment of hernia and also gave discourses and demonstrations in surgery, pharmacy and wigs; but later was named surgeon of Queen Maria Theresa (1678) and doctor of the Duke d'Orleans (1683) and of King

Louis XIV (1687). Throughout his life, he was an essayist, historian and surgeon.

Blegny was the founder of the first medical bulletin written in French entitled *Les Nouvelles découvertes sur toutes les parties de la médicine* published in Paris from 1679 to 1685. Indeed, as stated by Nicholls (1934, p. 198), 'it seems highly probable that it was the first of its kind to be published in any language'. Scientific articles and reports were published monthly, and due to the journal's popularity, it was even translated into German under the title of *Monatliche neueröffnete Anmerckungen* and into Latin with the title *Zodiacus Medico- Gallicus*. Moreover, he published *Le livre commode des addresses de Paris pour 1692* under the pseudonym of Abraham du Pradel. In this work, he talks about places designated for the maniacs and people who should be deprived of their freedom. He opened his own establishment in 1690, which was one of the first health centres accepting insane people in France.

The work that is due to study, *Le Remède Anglois pour la guerison des fièvres*, was published in 1682. It was written by command of the King of France, Louis XIV, who had bought that remedy and his formula from Sir Robert Talbor, court physician of King Charles II, for 2000 louis d'or and 2000 French livres annually, but could not be published until his death. As stated by Nicholls (1934, p. 200), Talbor 'had successfully treated the Dauphin in 1680 for fever with chinchona [always referred in the work as "Quinquina"]'. Talbor died in 1681 and the book was immediately published.

The relevance of this specific text lies in an innovative observation by de Blegny of Talbor's remedy on how to use *Quinquina* to cure high fevers. According to Bricheteau (1859, p. 300), after the publication of this work, *'le quinquina devint dès lors à la mode, on ne parla plus que de Talbot et de son vin'*. In other words, this means that the quinquina became very relevant and people kept talking about Talbot and his wine, therefore demonstrating the importance of the discovery Talbor's remedy for the medical world. This is why a translation into the English language was chiefly needed and, subsequently, it was published in 1682, the same year as the original paper. In the following section, an analysis of data from *Le Remède Anglois pour la guerison des fièvres* will be performed, paying special attention to the modal verbs used through both the original and the translated text.

4. Analysis of data

This section of the chapter presents the study of the modal verbs used by Nicolas de Blegny's in *Le Remede Anglois pour la Guerison des Fievres* and the ones deployed in its English translation. This will allow the analysis of the frequency of use of those modal verbs in the original text (OT) and the strategies used by the translator to interpret them in the target text (TT). In the following graphic, the distribution of modal verbs according to the categories they belong to are shown:

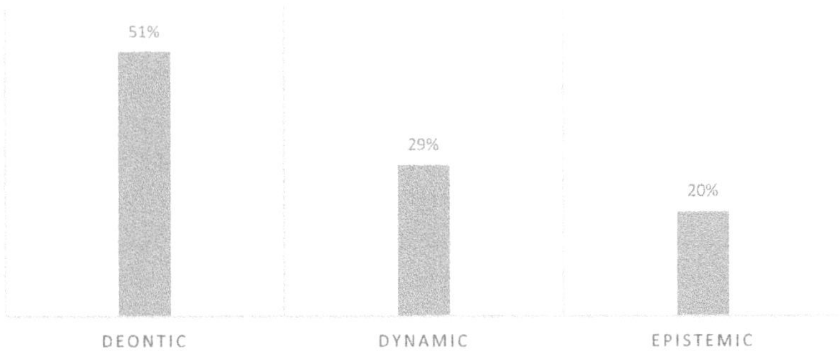

Figure 1. Modal meanings, as realized by modal verbs in the original text.

As can be observed from the graph above, deontic modality is by far the most common type, filling more than half of the graphic (used fifty-seven times in the text, in other words, 51 per cent). The next kind of modality, which entails almost one-third of the total (thirty-eight times used in the text – 29 per cent), is dynamic modality. Epistemic modality appears less often throughout the text, only reaching 20 per cent of the total (twenty-seven times used in the text). Through our analysis, we will show how these meanings have been differently transferred to the TT, as shown in Figure 2:

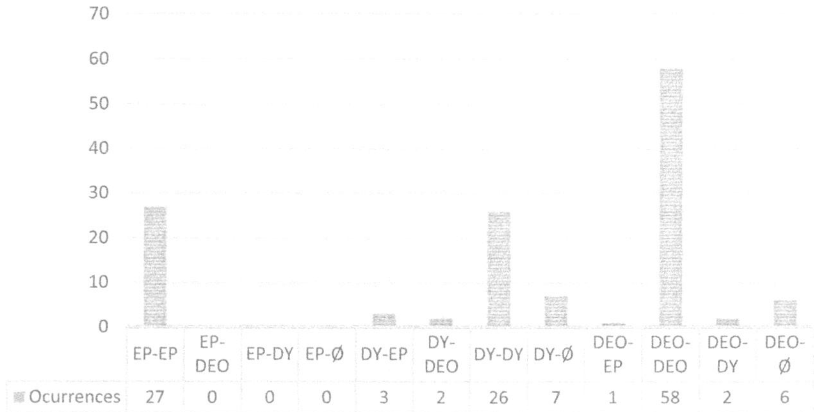

Figure 2. Translation of modal meanings as realized by modal verbs in the OT in the TT (key: EP: epistemic, DEO: deontic, DY: dynamic, Ø: omission of OT modal form in the TT).

The deontic type is the most frequent kind of modality employed in the original text. Likewise, the most common strategy is from deontic in the original text to deontic in the translated text, with fifty-eight cases in the text. However, there are other strategies as well which are used to translate deontic modals, like from deontic to nothing, in other words, the omission of the modality in the translated text of which there are six cases, from deontic to dynamic modality there are two cases or from deontic to epistemic modality which is used only once. Regarding dynamic possibility, the main strategy present in the text is also translating from dynamic to dynamic modality, applied twenty-six times. In the fashion of the results obtained, dynamic modality to non-translation is the next most common type; it is used seven times; followed by dynamic to epistemic modality, used three times and dynamic to deontic modality, used twice. In the case of epistemic modality, this modal meaning is preserved in the translation of modal verbs in the TT.

Quantitatively, in the OT, written in French, we find a variety of verbs used with deontic meaning. The largest number of cases corresponds to the verb *devoir* with twenty-seven occurrences. Besides, we find other verbs such as *falloir* with twenty instances, *pouvoir* with nineteen and finally *vouloir* with only one case. Concerning dynamic modality, we find the verb pouvoir predominantly with thirty-two cases in this work, followed by *vouloir* with four cases and both *falloir* and *devoir* appearing in only one occasion. Finally, within the domain of epistemic modality, the verb *pouvoir* is used twenty-five times, being almost the exclusive representative of this type except for the verbs *vouloir* and *devoir* which appear one time each.

As for the translated text in English, as we have seen above, the deontic type is the most common, and this is reflected in the variety of verbs used and its frequency through the text. The modalising expression *to be to* is the most frequently used with nineteen occurrences, followed by both modal verbs *must* and *cannot* with thirteen instances each. *Ought to* is next with ten appearances and *should* and *could* are present on two occasions, each. Finally, the modal *can* is used once within this modality. As for dynamic modality, the largest number of cases corresponds to the verb *may* appearing a total of fourteen. Again, the modalising expression *to be to* is very representative of this type of modality, with five occurrences while *would* and *cannot* is present with three cases, each. Finally, *can* and *should* are the least commonly used with two and one uses, respectively. In epistemic modality, as in dynamic modality, *may* is the most representative modal verb, appearing in twenty-one occasions. *Would* and *migh*t are next with three occurrences each, *can* with two and both *to be to* and *should* only appear once.

The following section is devoted to comment on the translation strategies deployed in the target texts to render cases of deontic modality. Examples will be provided to exemplify variation in the translated versions.

5. Discussion of findings

As commented on the analysis of data, there are samples, in which the translator decided to change the modality type to another one, keep the same sense of modality or simply omit it. Through a selection of examples from both the OT and the TT, we will analyse the diverse types of modality and the strategies used by the translator when dealing with them.

5.1. Deontic Modality

From our study we have been able to verify that deontic modality is the most frequent one. At this point, we are going to check the cases in which the modality is translated to another modal type, remain in a similar way or is plainly omitted.

5.1.1. Deontic to Deontic Translation

Within the deontic domain, the translation from deontic to deontic is the most used, with a total amount of fifty-eight samples. The first instance shows the rendering of *faut* into *must*:

(4) OT: Au reste, lors qu'on a commence à donner de cette infusion, il faut continuer à la faire prendre en mesme dose de trois en trois heures (p. 55).
TT: After one hath began to give of this infusion, he must continue to make the Patient take it once every three hours (p. 34).

In (4), we find that both the modal verb *falloir* in French and *must* in English imply a sense of obligation to the reader. The deontic force is external to the participant, as recovery is only possible following the directions of taking the infusion every three hours. The semantic space in this particular example relates deontic possibility since a positive outcome relies on procedure. The rendering strategy followed by the translator is compensation within a focalisation procedure. As stated in Alonso and Sánchez (2015, p. 13), the purpose of this is to rephrase the sentence in the TT to produce the same cognitive effects in the sentence in the OT.

The example below shows the literal translation of the modal verb *pouvoir* into *cannot* in the TT.

(5) OT: La sang ne peut estre arresté long-temps en un lieu (p. 116).
TT: The Blood cannot be long stopt in a place (p. 83).

In (5), we can find an example of deontic force with the modal verbs *pouvoir* in French and *cannot* in English. Unlike the previous example, the subject does not refer to a person, yet we can see that the sense of obligation is still external to it. In this case, the heart is the subject and forces the blood to move when it pumps. The semantic space in this particular example relates deontic impossibility since the blood is always moving through the body and it is unable to stop circulating. Regarding the rendering strategy, the translator opts for a literal, word-for-word translation.

5.1.2. Deontic to omission in the translation

This strategy presents six occurrences in the TT. The following examples can serve to illustrate this kind of translation strategy. The first instance shows the rendering of *ne pouvoir plus* that is subsequently omitted in the TT.

(6) OT: [. . .] il ne cause aucun trouble dans l'oeconomie naturelle, ne pouvant non plus que les autres drogues ameres temperées (p. 87).
TT: [. . .] it causes no trouble in the oeconomy of Nature, being like other bitter temperate medicaments (p. 59).

In (6), we can observe how, even though there is a deontic force in the OT conveyed by the structure *ne pouvoir plus*, it is entirely omitted in the TT. In this sample, the verb conveys a sense of obligation by denying that the effect of this drug cannot be different than the rest. However, in the TT, as the modal verb is omitted, we cannot find any force of obligation. The semantic space relies on deontic factuality, since the author is stating that this drug is like the other drugs. The rendering strategy followed by the translator is equivalence, a substitution procedure. The aim of this strategy, as explained in Alonso-Almeida and Sánchez-Hernández (2015, p. 8), is to 'indicate the use of an expression in the TT, which is pragmatically similar but differs in form and meaning'. As stated in this definition, both examples refer to the same concept but, while the English version is more vague about the meaning, the OT uses a modal verb that makes the meaning clearer.

In (7), whilst in the OT the author employs the French modal verb *pouvoir*, in the TT we are unable to find any translation of the modal verb. The force of obligation is represented here by declaring that this poison cannot be extracted by any means unless the liquor is perverted. Again, the translator decided to use the equivalence strategy to point out a similar expression to the one in the OT. One difference caused by the use of this strategy is that, in the OT, the author rejects any possibility of the poison being extracted without changing the composition of the liquor, in this case the Quinquina. However, in the TT, the translator marks an alternative by using *would*.

(7) OT: [. . .] & de resoudre ce venin; mais cet Autheur n'a pas pris garde, que si effectivement le Quinquina estoit capable de détruire ou mesme de pousser dehors les acides qui sont dans le sang, il ne pourroit estre pris sans pervertir entierement cette liqueur (p. 43).
TT: [. . .] and resolving that Poison, but that Author hath not minded, that if in effect *Quinquina* were able to destroy or even to expel the Acides that are in the blood, it would not be taken without entirely perverting that Liquor (p. 24).

5.1.3. Deontic to dynamic translation

The third most common type of translation strategy used is from a deontic sense to dynamic modality. In example 8, we can observe how the translator transforms the obligation implied with the modal verb *devoir* in the OT to a modal verb (*would have*) with less strong force.

(8) OT: Pour mieux faire comprendre l'importance de toutes les regles & de toutes les observations precedentes, je dois faire remarquer [. . .] (p. 81).
TT: For the better understanding of the above mentioned directions and observations, I would have it remarked [. . .] (p. 54).

In this example, by carefully observing both the OT and TT extracts, we can determine a difference between the modal verb *devoir* in French and the expression *would have* in English. In the OT, the force of the modal verb is deontic, through the use of the modal verb *devoir,* which could be translated as *must*, because the obligation is rendered as an internal motivation of the author to explain the conclusions of his work to the reader. However, in the TT, the translator opts for a more subtle expression that takes into account the previous work of the author and gives him the knowledge to write the subsequent conclusion. In this excerpt, we find two translation strategies: condensation and equivalence. The aim of the condensation strategy within the reduction procedure is to 'use a shorter number of morphemes in the TT' (Alonso-Almeida and Sánchez-Hernández 2015, p. 8). We can observe this procedure in the extract when the translator decides to shorten '*l'importance de toutes les regles & de toutes les observations precedentes*' by writing 'of the above mentioned directions and observations' instead. Moreover, the equivalence strategy is seen in the part related to the modal verb or expression, where the translator uses a similar sentence but, as it was explained above, with a difference in meaning.

In the following instance, we can also observe a difference between the original text and its translation, specifically in what concerns the meaning of the French modal verb *pouvoir* and the English modal verb *might*:

(9) OT: [...] les mauvaises dispositions du corps, qui pourroient estre opposes au benefice qu'on en doit attendre (p. 74).
TT: [...] correct the bad dispositions of the body, that might hinder the benefit which is to be expected from it (p. 48).

In (9), the use of the verb *pouvoir* in the OT, implies a strong force of obligation by compelling the person to do as said. Meanwhile, in the TT we can observe that by using the modal verb *might,* the sense of the sentence has changed from an obligation point into an expected necessity for the reader, which involves dynamic modality. The rendering strategy for this is amplification within the extension procedure. This technique consists in using more morphemes in the TT than in the OT (Alonso-Almeida and Sánchez-Hernández 2015, p. 8). In the final part of the extract, in the OT the author writes '*qu'on en doit attendre*'. In the TT, the translator decides to change the emphasis of the expression while extending this sentence by adding more words resulting in 'which is to be expected from it'. By doing so, the translator transforms the deontic modality in the OT into dynamic modality in the TT.

5.1.4. Deontic to epistemic translation

Finally, the least used translation within the deontic modality is the deontic to epistemic type, only appearing once in the whole work. The instance below shows a change in meaning with the rendering of the modal verb *falloir* into the modal expression *to be to.*

(10) OT: Mais il <u>faut</u> remarquer que cette odeur est beaucoup moins forte & moins aromatique que celle du Cassia Cariophilata (p. 22).

> TT: But it is to be observed that smell is much weaker and less aromatick than the scent of Cassia Cariophilata (p. 6).

As seen in (10), the probability of the event to happen is different in the OT than in the TT. This idea is reinforced by the French modal verb *falloir* that entails a force of obligation, which holds a difference with the English modal expression *to be to* that involves probability. There is an obligation in the OT because the author wants to sustain the idea of the smell being weaker and not as aromatized as the Cassia Cariophilata. Regarding the rendering strategies, there are two examples of modulation (included in the focalisation procedure) in this extract. According to Alonso-Almeida and Sánchez-Hernández (2015, p. 8), this strategy aims to modify the perspective or the emphasis concerning the OT. The first case is the part including the modal verb or expression, where the translator decides to change the emphasis, allowing more space to the possibility of it being true or not. The second case refers to the following excerpt '*beaucoup moins forte*' in the OT and 'much weaker' in the TT. In them, we can clearly see a difference in perspective. While they are expressing the same, in the OT the author takes the adjective 'strong' as a referent and degrades it, but in the TT the translator uses the adjective 'weak' and upgrades it.

6. Conclusion

This chapter has focused on an analysis of the modal devices in Nicolas de Blegny's *Le Remede Anglois pour la Guerison des Fievres* written in French and its English translation, *The English Remedy or Talbor's Wonderful Secret for Cureing of Agues and Feavers* (Blegny, 1682b), with an emphasis on deontic modals in French and their renderings in English. Deontic modality appears in 51% of the modals cases analysed. Deontic modals seem to be used to indicate authority and necessity in contexts showing an objective perspectivisation of the propositions modulated. This objective stance towards information is crucial to add rigour to the arguments presented. The usage of both the dynamic and epistemic modalities in the translated text as the equivalents of the deontic modals in the original text was levelled through the work demonstrating the necessity of attenuating and giving a more subjective perspective of some ideas. In the specific case of epistemic modality, this allows the tentative presentation of ideas in the translated material, and this obviously mitigates the effect of authorial imposition that the use of deontic modality may imply.

Even if there is an intention to attenuate the deontic force of some modals in the original text, deontic modals have been retained in the translated version. A reason for this is the use of deontic modality to give a sense of authority by expressing certainty and confidence in what he writes. This appeal to authority as realised by deontic modality has been claimed by different linguists to be a feature of scientific texts, as put forward in Alonso-Almeida and Mulligan (2015, p. 46). In the specific case of the translation of deontic modals into dynamic modals, the sense of authority is conveyed in the use of modals designating dynamic possibility. This meaning indicates that the contents of the proposition occur, and this may be understood in terms of factuality. At the same time, dynamic possibility refers to certain enabling conditions that allow the fulfilment of the action, and this has a clear attenuating function, which may also report on the translator's intentions to avoid potential face-threatening acts. All in all, this study has shown that perspectivisation concerning deontic modal meanings in the original texts may be altered in order to gain certain communicative needs so that the book and its contents are likely to find wide acceptance in the target culture.

References

Alonso-Almeida, F. (2015) On the mitigating function of modality and evidentiality. Evidence from English and Spanish medical research papers. *Intercultural Pragmatics*, *12* (1), 33–57.

Alonso-Almeida, F., & Sánchez-Hernández, A. (2015) "If they have not the French": translation choices in The Happy Deliverie of Women (1612). *The Translator*, 22(1), 1–19.

Alonso-Almeida, F., & Álvarez Gil, F. (2019) Modal verb categories in CHET. In I. Moskowich, B. Crespo, L. Puente-Castelo, L. Monaco (Eds.), Writing History in Late Modern English: Explorations of the Coruña Corpus (pp. 149–166). Amsterdam, Philadelphia: John Benjamins Publishing Company.

Alonso-Almeida, F., & Mele-Marrero, M. (2014) Stancetaking in seventeenth-century prefaces on obstetrics. *Journal of Historical Pragmatics*, 15(1), 1–35.

Alonso-Almeida, F., & Mulligan, M. (2015) Meeting Readers. Promoting the Use of English in Early Modern Utilitarian and Scientific Books (1500-1699). Revista canaria de estudios ingleses, 71, 41–56.

Alonso-Almeida, F., & Vázquez, N. (2015). Legitimising linguistic devices in *A Cheering Voice from Upper Canada (1834)*. In M. Dossena (Ed.), *Transatlantic Perspectives on Late Modern English* (Advances in Historical Sociolinguistics 4), (pp. 135–151). Amsterdam, Philadelphia: John Benjamins Publishing Company.

Álvarez Gil, F. (2018). Epistemic modals in early modern English history texts. Analysis of gender variation. *Revista de Lingüística y Lenguas Aplicadas*, 13, 13–20.

Blegny, N. (1682a). *Le remède anglais pour la guérison des fièvres : avec les observations de Monsieur le premier médecin de sa majesté, sur la composition, les vertus, l'usage, de ce remède.* Cambridge: Omnysis.

Blegny, N. (1682b). *The English Remedy or Talbor's Wonderful Secret for Cureing of Agues and Feavers*. Cornhill: Black Bull.

Bricheteau, F. (1859). *Bulletin général de thérapeutique médicale et chirurgical. Vol. 56*. Paris: Baillière.

Carrió-Pastor, M. L. (2019). Different ways to express personal attitudes in Spanish and English engineering papers: An analysis of metadiscourse devices, affective evaluation and sentiment analysis. *Lodz Papers in Pragmatics, 15*(1), 45–67.

Brown, P., & Levinson, S. (1987). *Politeness: Some universals in language usage*. Cambridge: Cambridge University Press.

Coates, J. (1983). *The Semantics of Modal Auxiliaries*. London: Croom Helm.

Collins, P. (2009). *Modals and Quasi-modals in English*. Amsterdam, New York: Rodopi.

Cornille, B., & Delbecque, N. (2008) Speaker Commitment: Back to the Speaker Evidence from Spanish Alternations. *Belgian Journal of Linguistics*, 22, 37–62. doi: 10.1075/bjl.22.03cor.

Depraetere, I., & Reed, N. (2006). Mood and Modality in English. In B. Aarts & A. McMahon (Eds.), *The Handbook of English Linguistics*, (pp. 269–290). Oxford: Blackwell Publishing.

Kronick, D. (2004). *'Devant le Deluge' and Other Essays on Early Modern Scientific Communication*. Maryland: Scarecrow Press.

Leech, G. (1971). *Meaning and the English Verb*. London: Longman.

Nicholls, N. (1934) Nicolas de Blegny and the First Medical Periodical. *The Canadian Medical Association Journal*, Aug, 198–202.

Nuyts, J. (2001). *Epistemic Modality, Language and Conceptualization: A Cogni-tive-Pragmatic Perspective*. Amsterdam, Philadelphia: John Benjamins Publishing Company.

Palmer, F. R. (1990). *Modality and the English Modals*. New York: Routledge.

Palmer, F. R. (2001). *Mood and Modality*. Cambridge: Cambridge University Press.

Turnbull, W., & Saxton, K. L. (1997) Modal expressions as facework in refusals to comply with requests: I think I should say "no" right now. *Journal of Pragmatics*, 27, 145–181.

Wilmet, M. (1998). *Grammaire critique du français*. Paris: Hachette – Duculot.

Linguistic Insights

Studies in Language and Communication

This series aims to promote specialist language studies in the fields of linguistic theory and applied linguistics, by publishing volumes that focus on specific aspects of language use in one or several languages and provide valuable insights into language and communication research. A cross-disciplinary approach is favoured and most European languages are accepted.

The series includes two types of books:

- Monographs – featuring in-depth studies on special aspects of language theory, language analysis or language teaching.
- Collected papers – assembling papers from workshops, conferences or symposia.

Each volume of the series is subjected to a double peer-reviewing process.

Vol. 1 Maurizio Gotti & Marina Dossena (eds)
Modality in Specialized Texts. Selected Papers of the 1st CERLIS Conference.
421 pages. 2001. ISBN 3-906767-10-8 · US-ISBN 0-8204-5340-4

Vol. 2 Giuseppina Cortese & Philip Riley (eds)
Domain-specific English. Textual Practices across Communities and Classrooms.
420 pages. 2002. ISBN 3-906768-98-8 · US-ISBN 0-8204-5884-8

Vol. 3 Maurizio Gotti, Dorothee Heller & Marina Dossena (eds) Conflict and Negotiation in Specialized Texts. Selected Papers of the 2nd CERLIS Conference.
470 pages. 2002. ISBN 3-906769-12-7 · US-ISBN 0-8204-5887-2

Vol. 4 Maurizio Gotti, Marina Dossena, Richard Dury, Roberta Facchinetti & Maria Lima
Variation in Central Modals. A Repertoire of Forms and Types of Usage in Middle English and Early Modern English.
364 pages. 2002. ISBN 3-906769-84-4 · US-ISBN 0-8204-5898-8

Editorial address:
Prof. Maurizio Gotti Università di Bergamo, Dipartimento di Lingue, Letterature e Culture Straniere Piazza Rosate 2, 24129 Bergamo, ItalyFax: +39 035 2052789, E-Mail: m.gotti@unibg.it

Vol. 5 Stefania Nuccorini (ed.)
Phrases and Phraseology. Data and Descriptions.
187 pages. 2002. ISBN 3-906770-08-7 · US-ISBN 0-8204-5933-X

Vol. 6 Vijay Bhatia, Christopher N. Candlin & Maurizio Gotti (eds) Legal Discourse in Multilingual and Multicultural Contexts. Arbitration Texts in Europe.
385 pages. 2003. ISBN 3-906770-85-0 · US-ISBN 0-8204-6254-3

Vol. 7 Marina Dossena & Charles Jones (eds)
Insights into Late Modern English. 2nd edition.
378 pages. 2003, 2007. ISBN 978-3-03911-257-9 · US-ISBN 978-0-8204-8927-8

Vol. 8 Maurizio Gotti
Specialized Discourse. Linguistic Features and Changing Conventions.
351 pages. 2003, 2005.ISBN 3-03910-606-6 · US-ISBN 0-8204-7000-7

Vol. 9 Alan Partington, John Morley & Louann Haarman (eds)
Corpora and Discourse.
420 pages. 2004. ISBN 3-03910-026-2 · US-ISBN 0-8204-6262-4

Vol. 10 Martina Möllering
The Acquisition of German Modal Particles. A Corpus-Based Approach.
290 pages. 2004. ISBN 3-03910-043-2 · US-ISBN 0-8204-6273-X

Vol. 11 David Hart (ed.)
English Modality in Context. Diachronic Perspectives.
261 pages. 2003. ISBN 3-03910-046-7 · US-ISBN 0-8204-6852-5

Vol. 12 Wendy Swanson
Modes of Co-reference as an Indicator of Genre.
430 pages. 2003. ISBN 3-03910-052-1 · US-ISBN 0-8204-6855-X

Vol. 13 Gina Poncini
Discursive Strategies in Multicultural Business Meetings.
2nd edition. 338 pages. 2004, 2007.
ISBN 978-3-03911-296-8 · US-ISBN 978-0-8204-8937-7

Vol. 14 Christopher N. Candlin & Maurizio Gotti (eds)
Intercultural Aspects of Specialized Communication.
2nd edition. 369 pages. 2004, 2007.
ISBN 978-3-03911-258-6 · US-ISBN 978-0-8204-8926-1

Vol. 15 Gabriella Del Lungo Camiciotti & Elena Tognini Bonelli (eds)
Academic Discourse. New Insights into Evaluation.
234 pages. 2004. ISBN 3-03910-353-9 · US-ISBN 0-8204-7016-3

Vol. 16 Marina Dossena & Roger Lass (eds)
Methods and Data in English Historical Dialectology.
405 pages. 2004. ISBN 3-03910-362-8 · US-ISBN 0-8204-7018-X

Vol. 17 Judy Noguchi
The Science Review Article. An Opportune Genre in the Construction of Science.
274 pages. 2006. ISBN 3-03910-426-8 · US-ISBN 0-8204-7034-1

Vol. 18 Giuseppina Cortese & Anna Duszak (eds)
Identity, Community, Discourse. English in Intercultural Settings.
495 pages. 2005. ISBN 3-03910-632-5 · US-ISBN 0-8204-7163-1

Vol. 19 Anna Trosborg & Poul Erik Flyvholm Jørgensen (eds)
Business Discourse. Texts and Contexts.
250 pages. 2005. ISBN 3-03910-606-6 · US-ISBN 0-8204-7000-7

Vol. 20 Christopher Williams
Tradition and Change in Legal English. Verbal Constructions in Prescriptive Texts.
2nd revised edition. 216 pages. 2005, 2007. ISBN 978-3-03911-444-3.

Vol. 21 Katarzyna Dziubalska-Kolaczyk & Joanna Przedlacka (eds)
English Pronunciation Models: A Changing Scene.
2nd edition. 476 pages. 2005, 2008. ISBN 978-3-03911-682-9.

Vol. 22 Christián Abello-Contesse, Rubén Chacón-Beltrán,
M. Dolores López-Jiménez & M. Mar Torreblanca-López (eds)
Age in L2 Acquisition and Teaching.
214 pages. 2006. ISBN 3-03910-668-6 · US-ISBN 0-8204-7174-7

Vol. 23 Vijay K. Bhatia, Maurizio Gotti, Jan Engberg & Dorothee Heller (eds)
Vagueness in Normative Texts.
474 pages. 2005. ISBN 3-03910-653-8 · US-ISBN 0-8204-7169-0

Vol. 24 Paul Gillaerts & Maurizio Gotti (eds)
Genre Variation in Business Letters. 2nd printing.
407 pages. 2008. ISBN 978-3-03911-681-2.

Vol. 25 Ana María Hornero, María José Luzón & Silvia Murillo (eds)
Corpus Linguistics. Applications for the Study of English.
2nd printing. 526 pages. 2006, 2008. ISBN 978-3-03911-726-0

Vol. 26 J. Lachlan Mackenzie & María de los Ángeles Gómez-González (eds)
Studies in Functional Discourse Grammar.
259 pages. 2005. ISBN 3-03910-696-1 · US-ISBN 0-8204-7558-0

Vol. 27 Debbie G. E. Ho
Classroom Talk. Exploring the Sociocultural Structure of Formal ESL Learning.
2nd edition. 254 pages. 2006, 2007. ISBN 978-3-03911-434-4

Vol. 28 Javier Pérez-Guerra, Dolores González-Álvarez, Jorge L. Bueno-Alonso &
Esperanza Rama-Martínez (eds)
'Of Varying Language and Opposing Creed'. New Insights into Late Modern English.
455 pages. 2007. ISBN 978-3-03910-788-9

Vol. 29 Francesca Bargiela-Chiappini & Maurizio Gotti (eds)
Asian Business Discourse(s).
350 pages. 2005. ISBN 3-03910-804-2 · US-ISBN 0-8204-7574-2

Vol. 30 Nicholas Brownlees (ed.)
News Discourse in Early Modern Britain. Selected Papers of CHINED 2004.
300 pages. 2006. ISBN 3-03910-805-0 · US-ISBN 0-8204-8025-8

Vol. 31 Roberta Facchinetti & Matti Rissanen (eds)
Corpus-based Studies of Diachronic English.
300 pages. 2006. ISBN 3-03910-851-4 · US-ISBN 0-8204-8040-1

Vol. 32 Marina Dossena & Susan M. Fitzmaurice (eds)
Business and Official Correspondence. Historical Investigations.
209 pages. 2006. ISBN 3-03910-880-8 · US-ISBN 0-8204-8352-4

Vol. 33 Giuliana Garzone & Srikant Sarangi (eds)
Discourse, Ideology and Specialized Communication.
494 pages. 2007. ISBN 978-3-03910-888-6

Vol. 34 Giuliana Garzone & Cornelia Ilie (eds)
The Use of English in Institutional and Business Settings. An Intercultural Perspective.
372 pages. 2007. ISBN 978-3-03910-889-3

Vol. 35 Vijay K. Bhatia & Maurizio Gotti (eds)
Explorations in Specialized Genres.
316 pages. 2006. ISBN 3-03910-995-2 · US-ISBN 0-8204-8372-9

Vol. 36 Heribert Picht (ed.)
Modern Approaches to Terminological Theories and Applications.
432 pages. 2006. ISBN 3-03911-156-6 · US-ISBN 0-8204-8380-X

Vol. 37 Anne Wagner & Sophie Cacciaguidi-Fahy (eds)
Legal Language and the Search for Clarity / Le langage juridique et la quête de clarté.
Practice and Tools / Pratiques et instruments.
487 pages. 2006. ISBN 3-03911-169-8 · US-ISBN 0-8204-8388-5

Vol. 38 Juan Carlos Palmer-Silveira, Miguel F. Ruiz-Garrido & Inmaculada Fortanet-Gómez (eds)
Intercultural and International Business Communication. Theory, Research and Teaching.
2nd edition. 343 pages. 2006, 2008. ISBN 978-3-03911-680-5

Vol. 39 Christiane Dalton-Puffer, Dieter Kastovsky, Nikolaus Ritt & Herbert Schendl (eds)
Syntax, Style and Grammatical Norms. English from 1500–2000.
250 pages. 2006. ISBN 3-03911-181-7 · US-ISBN 0-8204-8394-X

Vol. 40 Marina Dossena & Irma Taavitsainen (eds)
Diachronic Perspectives on Domain-Specific English.
280 pages. 2006. ISBN 3-03910-176-0 · US-ISBN 0-8204-8391-5

Vol. 41 John Flowerdew & Maurizio Gotti (eds)
Studies in Specialized Discourse.
293 pages. 2006. ISBN 3-03911-178-7

Vol. 42 Ken Hyland & Marina Bondi (eds)
Academic Discourse Across Disciplines.
320 pages. 2006. ISBN 3-03911-183-3 · US-ISBN 0-8204-8396-6

Vol. 43 Paul Gillaerts & Philip Shaw (eds)
The Map and the Landscape. Norms and Practices in Genre.
256 pages. 2006. ISBN 3-03911-182-5 · US-ISBN 0-8204-8395-4

Vol. 44 Maurizio Gotti & Davide Giannoni (eds)
New Trends in Specialized Discourse Analysis.
301 pages. 2006. ISBN 3-03911-184-1 · US-ISBN 0-8204-8381-8

Vol. 45 Maurizio Gotti & Françoise Salager-Meyer (eds)
Advances in Medical Discourse Analysis. Oral and Written Contexts.
492 pages. 2006. ISBN 3-03911-185-X · US-ISBN 0-8204-8382-6

Vol. 46 Maurizio Gotti & Susan Šarcević (eds)
Insights into Specialized Translation.
396 pages. 2006. ISBN 3-03911-186-8 · US-ISBN 0-8204-8383-4

Vol. 47 Khurshid Ahmad & Margaret Rogers (eds)
Evidence-based LSP. Translation, Text and Terminology.
584 pages. 2007. ISBN 978-3-03911-187-9

Vol. 48 Hao Sun & Dániel Z. Kádár (eds)
It's the Dragon's Turn. Chinese Institutional Discourses.
262 pages. 2008. ISBN 978-3-03911-175-6

Vol. 49 Cristina Suárez-Gómez
Relativization in Early English (950-1250). the Position of Relative Clauses.
149 pages. 2006. ISBN 3-03911-203-1 · US-ISBN 0-8204-8904-2

Vol. 50 Maria Vittoria Calvi & Luisa Chierichetti (eds)
Nuevas tendencias en el discurso de especialidad.
319 pages. 2006. ISBN 978-3-03911-261-6

Vol. 51 Mari Carmen Campoy & María José Luzón (eds)
Spoken Corpora in Applied Linguistics.
274 pages. 2008. ISBN 978-3-03911-275-3

Vol. 52 Konrad Ehlich & Dorothee Heller (Hrsg.)
Die Wissenschaft und ihre Sprachen.
323 pages. 2006. ISBN 978-3-03911-272-2

Vol. 53 Jingyu Zhang
The Semantic Salience Hierarchy Model. The L2 Acquisition of Psych Predicates
273 pages. 2007. ISBN 978-3-03911-300-2

Vol. 54 Norman Fairclough, Giuseppina Cortese & Patrizia Ardizzone (eds)
Discourse and Contemporary Social Change.
555 pages. 2007. ISBN 978-3-03911-276-0

Vol. 55 Jan Engberg, Marianne Grove Ditlevsen, Peter Kastberg & Martin Stegu (eds)
New Directions in LSP Teaching.
331 pages. 2007. ISBN 978-3-03911-433-7

Vol. 56 Dorothee Heller & Konrad Ehlich (Hrsg.)
Studien zur Rechtskommunikation.
322 pages. 2007. ISBN 978-3-03911-436-8

Vol. 57 Teruhiro Ishiguro & Kang-kwong Luke (eds)
Grammar in Cross-Linguistic Perspective.
The Syntax, Semantics, and Pragmatics of Japanese and Chinese.
304 pages. 2012. ISBN 978-3-03911-445-0

Vol. 58 Carmen Frehner Email – SMS – MMS
294 pages. 2008. ISBN 978-3-03911-451-1

Vol. 59 Isabel Balteiro
The Directionality of Conversion in English. A Dia-Synchronic Study.
276 pages. 2007. ISBN 978-3-03911-241-8

Vol. 60 Maria Milagros Del Saz Rubio
English Discourse Markers of Reformulation.
237 pages. 2007. ISBN 978-3-03911-196-1

Vol. 61 Sally Burgess & Pedro Martín-Martín (eds)
English as an Additional Language in Research Publication and Communication.
259 pages. 2008. ISBN 978-3-03911-462-7

Vol. 62 Sandrine Onillon
Pratiques et représentations de l'écrit.
458 pages. 2008. ISBN 978-3-03911-464-1

Vol. 63 Hugo Bowles & Paul Seedhouse (eds)
Conversation Analysis and Language for Specific Purposes.
2nd edition. 337 pages. 2007, 2009. ISBN 978-3-0343-0045-2

Vol. 64 Vijay K. Bhatia, Christopher N. Candlin & Paola Evangelisti Allori (eds)
Language, Culture and the Law.
The Formulation of Legal Concepts across Systems and Cultures.
342 pages. 2008. ISBN 978-3-03911-470-2

Vol. 65 Jonathan Culpeper & Dániel Z. Kádár (eds)
Historical (Im)politeness.
300 pages. 2010. ISBN 978-3-03911-496-2

Vol. 66 Linda Lombardo (ed.)
Using Corpora to Learn about Language and Discourse.
237 pages. 2009. ISBN 978-3-03911-522-8

Vol. 67 Natsumi Wakamoto
Extroversion/Introversion in Foreign Language Learning. Interactions with Learner Strategy Use.
159 pages. 2009. ISBN 978-3-03911-596-9

Vol. 68 Eva Alcón-Soler (ed.)
Learning How to Request in an Instructed Language Learning Context.
260 pages. 2008. ISBN 978-3-03911-601-0

Vol. 69 Domenico Pezzini
The Translation of Religious Texts in the Middle Ages.
428 pages. 2008. ISBN 978-3-03911-600-3

Vol. 70 Tomoko Tode
Effects of Frequency in Classroom Second Language Learning. Quasi-experiment and stimulated-recall analysis.
195 pages. 2008. ISBN 978-3-03911-602-7

Vol. 71 Egor Tsedryk
Fusion symétrique et alternances ditransitives.
211 pages. 2009. ISBN 978-3-03911-609-6

Vol. 72 Cynthia J. Kellett Bidoli & Elana Ochse (eds)
English in International Deaf Communication.
444 pages. 2008. ISBN 978-3-03911-610-2

Vol. 73 Joan C. Beal, Carmela Nocera & Massimo Sturiale (eds)
Perspectives on Prescriptivism.
269 pages. 2008. ISBN 978-3-03911-632-4

Vol. 74 Carol Taylor Torsello, Katherine Ackerley & Erik Castello (eds)
Corpora for University Language Teachers.
308 pages. 2008. ISBN 978-3-03911-639-3

Vol. 75 María Luisa Pérez Cañado (ed.)
English Language Teaching in the European Credit Transfer System. Facing the Challenge.
251 pages. 2009. ISBN 978-3-03911-654-6

Vol. 76 Marina Dossena & Ingrid Tieken-Boon van Ostade (eds)
Studies in Late Modern English Correspondence. Methodology and Data.
291 pages. 2008. ISBN 978-3-03911-658-4

Vol. 77 Ingrid Tieken-Boon van Ostade & Wim van der Wurff (eds)
Current Issues in Late Modern English.
436 pages. 2009. ISBN 978-3-03911-660-7

Vol. 78 Marta Navarro Coy (ed.)
Practical Approaches to Foreign Language Teaching and Learning.
297 pages. 2009. ISBN 978-3-03911-661-4

Vol. 79 Qing Ma
Second Language Vocabulary Acquisition.
333 pages. 2009. ISBN 978-3-03911-666-9

Vol. 80 Martin Solly, Michelangelo Conoscenti & Sandra Campagna (eds)
Verbal/Visual Narrative Texts in Higher Education.
384 pages. 2008. ISBN 978-3-03911-672-0

Vol. 81 Meiko Matsumoto
From Simple Verbs to Periphrastic Expressions:
The Historical Development of Composite Predicates, Phrasal Verbs, and Related Constructions in English.
235 pages. 2008. ISBN 978-3-03911-675-1

Vol. 82 Melinda Dooly
Doing Diversity. Teachers' Construction of Their Classroom Reality.
180 pages. 2009. ISBN 978-3-03911-687-4

Vol. 83 Victoria Guillén-Nieto, Carmen Marimón-Llorca & Chelo Vargas-Sierra (eds)
Intercultural Business Communication and Simulation and Gaming Methodology.
392 pages. 2009. ISBN 978-3-03911-688-1

Vol. 84 Maria Grazia Guido
English as a Lingua Franca in Cross-cultural Immigration Domains.
285 pages. 2008. ISBN 978-3-03911-689-8

Vol. 85 Erik Castello
Text Complexity and Reading Comprehension Tests.
352 pages. 2008. ISBN 978-3-03911-717-8

Vol. 86 Maria-Lluisa Gea-Valor, Isabel García-Izquierdo & Maria-José Esteve (eds)
Linguistic and Translation Studies in Scientific Communication.
317 pages. 2010. ISBN 978-3-0343-0069-8

Vol. 87 Carmen Navarro, Rosa Ma Rodríguez Abella, Francesca Dalle Pezze & Renzo Miotti (eds)
La comunicación especializada.
355 pages. 2008. ISBN 978-3-03911-733-8

Vol. 88 Kiriko Sato
The Development from Case-Forms to Prepositional Constructions in Old English Prose.
231 pages. 2009. ISBN 978-3-03911-763-5

Vol. 89 Dorothee Heller (Hrsg.)
Formulierungsmuster in deutscher und italienischer Fachkommunikation. Intra- und interlinguale Perspektiven.
315 pages. 2008. ISBN 978-3-03911-778-9

Vol. 90 Henning Bergenholtz, Sandro Nielsen & Sven Tarp (eds)
Lexicography at a Crossroads. Dictionaries and Encyclopedias Today, Lexicographical Tools Tomorrow.
372 pages. 2009. ISBN 978-3-03911-799-4

Vol. 91 Manouchehr Moshtagh Khorasani
The Development of Controversies. From the Early Modern Period to Online Discussion Forums.
317 pages. 2009. ISBN 978-3-3911-711-6

Vol. 92 María Luisa Carrió-Pastor (ed.)
Content and Language Integrated Learning. Cultural Diversity.
178 pages. 2009. ISBN 978-3-3911-818-2

Vol. 93 Roger Berry
Terminology in English Language Teaching. Nature and Use.
262 pages. 2010. ISBN 978-3-0343-0013-1

Vol. 94 Roberto Cagliero & Jennifer Jenkins (eds)
Discourses, Communities, and Global Englishes
240 pages. 2010. ISBN 978-3-0343-0012-4

Vol. 95 Facchinetti Roberta, Crystal David, Seidlhofer Barbara (eds)
From International to Local English – And Back Again.
268 pages. 2010. ISBN 978-3-0343-0011-7

Vol. 96 Cesare Gagliardi & Alan Maley (eds)
EIL, ELF, Global English. Teaching and Learning Issues
376 pages. 2010. ISBN 978-3-0343-0010-0

Vol. 97 Sylvie Hancil (ed.)
The Role of Prosody in Affective Speech.
403 pages. 2009. ISBN 978-3-03911-696-6

Vol. 98 Marina Dossena & Roger Lass (eds)
Studies in English and European Historical Dialectology.
257 pages. 2009. ISBN 978-3-0343-0024-7

Vol. 99 Christine Béal
Les interactions quotidiennes en français et en anglais.
De l'approche comparative à l'analyse des situations interculturelles.
424 pages. 2010. ISBN 978-3-0343-0027-8

Vol. 100 Maurizio Gotti (ed.)
Commonality and Individuality in Academic Discourse.
398 pages. 2009. ISBN 978-3-0343-0023-0

Vol. 101 Javier E. Díaz Vera & Rosario Caballero (eds)
Textual Healing. Studies in Medieval English Medical, Scientific and Technical Texts.
213 pages. 2009. ISBN 978-3-03911-822-9

Vol. 102 Nuria Edo Marzá
The Specialised Lexicographical Approach. A Step further in Dictionary-making.
316 pages. 2009. ISBN 978-3-0343-0043-8

Vol. 103 Carlos Prado-Alonso, Lidia Gómez-García, Iria Pastor-Gómez & David Tizón-Couto (eds)
New Trends and Methodologies in Applied English Language Research. Diachronic, Diatopic and Contrastive Studies.
348 pages. 2009. ISBN 978-3-0343-0046-9

Vol. 104 Françoise Salager-Meyer & Beverly A. Lewin
Crossed Words. Criticism in Scholarly Writing?
371 pages. 2011. ISBN 978-3-0343-0049-0.

Vol. 105 Javier Ruano-García
Early Modern Northern English Lexis. A Literary Corpus-Based Study.
611 pages. 2010. ISBN 978-3-0343-0058-2

Vol. 106 Rafael Monroy-Casas
Systems for the Phonetic Transcription of English. Theory and Texts.
280 pages. 2011. ISBN 978-3-0343-0059-9

Vol. 107 Nicola T. Owtram
The Pragmatics of Academic Writing.
A Relevance Approach to the Analysis of Research Article Introductions.
311 pages. 2009. ISBN 978-3-0343-0060-5

Vol. 108 Yolanda Ruiz de Zarobe, Juan Manuel Sierra & Francisco Gallardo del Puerto (eds)
Content and Foreign Language Integrated Learning. Contributions to Multilingualism in European Contexts
343 pages. 2011. ISBN 978-3-0343-0074-2

Vol. 109 Ángeles Linde López & Rosalía Crespo Jiménez (eds)
Professional English in the European context. The EHEA challenge.
374 pages. 2010. ISBN 978-3-0343-0088-9

Vol. 110 Rosalía Rodríguez-Vázquez
The Rhythm of Speech, Verse and Vocal Music. A New Theory.
394 pages. 2010. ISBN 978-3-0343-0309-5

Vol. 111 Anastasios Tsangalidis & Roberta Facchinetti (eds)
Studies on English Modality. In Honour of Frank Palmer.
392 pages. 2009. ISBN 978-3-0343-0310-1

Vol. 112 Jing Huang
Autonomy, Agency and Identity in Foreign Language Learning and Teaching.
400 pages. 2013. ISBN 978-3-0343-0370-5

Vol. 113 Mihhail Lotman & Maria-Kristiina Lotman (eds)
Frontiers in Comparative Prosody. In memoriam: Mikhail Gasparov.
426 pages. 2011. ISBN 978-3-0343-0373-6

Vol. 114 Merja Kytö, John Scahill & Harumi Tanabe (eds)
Language Change and Variation from Old English to Late Modern English. A Festschrift for Minoji Akimoto
422 pages. 2010. ISBN 978-3-0343-0372-9

Vol. 115 Giuliana Garzone & Paola Catenaccio (eds)
Identities across Media and Modes. Discursive Perspectives.
379 pages. 2009. ISBN 978-3-0343-0386-6

Vol. 116 Elena Landone
Los marcadores del discurso y cortesía verbal en español.
390 pages. 2010. ISBN 978-3-0343-0413-9

Vol. 117 Maurizio Gotti & Christopher Williams (eds)
Legal Discourse across Languages and Cultures.
339 pages. 2010. ISBN 978-3-0343-0425-2

Vol. 118 David Hirsh
Academic Vocabulary in Context.
217 pages. 2010. ISBN 978-3-0343-0426-9

Vol. 119 Yvonne Dröschel
Lingua Franca English. The Role of Simplification and Transfer.
358 pages. 2011. ISBN 978-3-0343-0432-0

Vol. 120 Tengku Sepora Tengku Mahadi, Helia Vaezian & Mahmoud Akbari
Corpora in Translation. A Practical Guide.
135 pages. 2010. ISBN 978-3-0343-0434-4

Vol. 121 Davide Simone Giannoni & Celina Frade (eds)
Researching Language and the Law. Textual Features and Translation Issues.
278 pages. 2010. ISBN 978-3-0343-0443-6

Vol. 122 Daniel Madrid & Stephen Hughes (eds)
Studies in Bilingual Education.
472 pages. 2011. ISBN 978-3-0343-0474-0

Vol. 123 Vijay K. Bhatia, Christopher N. Candlin & Maurizio Gotti (eds)
The Discourses of Dispute Resolution.
290 pages. 2010. ISBN 978-3-0343-0476-4

Vol. 124 Davide Simone Giannoni
Mapping Academic Values in the Disciplines. A Corpus-Based Approach.
288 pages. 2010. ISBN 978-3-0343-0488-7

Vol. 125 Giuliana Garzone & James Archibald (eds)
Discourse, Identities and Roles in Specialized Communication.
419 pages. 2010. ISBN 978-3-0343-0494-8

Vol. 126 Iria Pastor-Gómez
The Status and Development of N+N Sequences in Contemporary English Noun Phrases.
216 pages. 2011. ISBN 978-3-0343-0534-1

Vol. 127 Carlos Prado-Alonso
Full-verb Inversion in Written and Spoken English.
261 pages. 2011. ISBN 978-3-0343-0535-8

Vol. 128 Tony Harris & María Moreno Jaén (eds)
Corpus Linguistics in Language Teaching.
214 pages. 2010. ISBN 978-3-0343-0524-2

Vol. 129 Tetsuji Oda & Hiroyuki Eto (eds)
Multiple Perspectives on English Philology and History of Linguistics. A Festschrift for Shoichi Watanabe on his 80th Birthday.
378 pages. 2010. ISBN 978-3-0343-0480-1

Vol. 130 Luisa Chierichetti & Giovanni Garofalo (eds)
Lengua y Derecho. líneas de investigación interdisciplinaria.
283 pages. 2010. 978-3-0343-0463-4

Vol. 131 Paola Evangelisti Allori & Giuliana Garzone (eds)
Discourse, Identities and Genres in Corporate Communication. Sponsorship, Advertising and Organizational Communication.
324 pages. 2011. 978-3-0343-0591-4

Vol. 132 Leyre Ruiz de Zarobe & Yolanda Ruiz de Zarobe (eds)
Speech Acts and Politeness across Languages and Cultures.
402 pages. 2012. 978-3-0343-0611-9

Vol. 133 Thomas Christiansen
Cohesion. A Discourse Perspective.
387 pages. 2011. 978-3-0343-0619-5

Vol. 134 Giuliana Garzone & Maurizio Gotti
Discourse, Communication and the Enterprise. Genres and Trends.
451 pages. 2011. ISBN 978-3-0343-0620-1

Vol. 135 Zsuzsa Hoffmann
Ways of the World's Words.
Language Contact in the Age of Globalization.
334 pages 2011. ISBN 978-3-0343-0673-7

Vol. 136 Cecilia Varcasia (ed.) Becoming Multilingual.
Language Learning and Language Policy between Attitudes and Identities.
213 pages. 2011. ISBN 978-3-0343-0687-5

Vol. 137 Susy Macqueen
The Emergence of Patterns in Second Language Writing. A Sociocognitive Exploration of Lexical Trails.
325 pages. 2012. ISBN 978-3-0343-1010-9

Vol. 138 Maria Vittoria Calvi & Giovanna Mapelli (eds)
La lengua del turismo. Géneros discursivos y terminología.
365 pages. 2011. ISBN 978-3-0343-1011-6

Vol. 139 Ken Lau
Learning to Become a Professional in a Textually-Mediated World. A Text-Oriented Study of Placement Practices.
261 pages. 2012. ISBN 978-3-0343-1016-1

Vol. 140 Sandra Campagna, Giuliana Garzone, Cornelia Ilie & Elizabeth Rowley-Jolivet (eds)
Evolving Genres in Web-mediated Communication.
337 pages. 2012. ISBN 978-3-0343-1013-0

Vol. 141 Edith Esch & Martin Solly (eds)
The Sociolinguistics of Language Education in International Contexts.
263 pages. 2012. ISBN 978-3-0343-1009-3

Vol. 142 Forthcoming.

Vol. 143 David Tizón-Couto
Left Dislocation in English. A Functional-Discoursal Approach.
416 pages. 2012. ISBN 978-3-0343-1037-6

Vol. 144 Margrethe Petersen & Jan Engberg (eds)
Current Trends in LSP Research. Aims and Methods.
323 pages. 2011. ISBN 978-3-0343-1054-3

Vol. 145 David Tizón-Couto, Beatriz Tizón-Couto, Iria Pastor-Gómez & Paula Rodríguez-Puente (eds)
New Trends and Methodologies in Applied English Language Research II.
Studies in Language Variation, Meaning and Learning.
283 pages. 2012. ISBN 978-3-0343-1061-1

Vol. 146 Rita Salvi & Hiromasa Tanaka (eds)
Intercultural Interactions in Business and Management.
306 pages. 2011. ISBN 978-3-0343-1039-0

Vol. 147 Francesco Straniero Sergio & Caterina Falbo (eds)
Breaking Ground in Corpus-based Interpreting Studies.
254 pages. 2012. ISBN 978-3-0343-1071-0

Vol. 148 Forthcoming.

Vol. 149 Vijay K. Bhatia & Paola Evangelisti Allori (eds)
Discourse and Identity in the Professions. Legal, Corporate and Institutional Citizenship.
352 pages. 2011. ISBN 978-3-0343-1079-6

Vol. 150 Maurizio Gotti (ed.)
Academic Identity Traits. A Corpus-Based Investigation.
363 pages. 2012. ISBN 978-3-0343-1141-0

Vol. 151 Priscilla Heynderickx, Sylvain Dieltjens, Geert Jacobs, Paul Gillaerts & Elizabeth de Groot (eds)
The Language Factor in International Business.
New Perspectives on Research, Teaching and Practice.
320 pages. 2012. ISBN 978-3-0343-1090-1

Vol. 152 Paul Gillaerts, Elizabeth de Groot, Sylvain Dieltjens, Priscilla Heynderickx & Geert Jacobs (eds)
Researching Discourse in Business Genres. Cases and Corpora.
215 pages. 2012. ISBN 978-3-0343-1092-5

Vol. 153 Yongyan Zheng
Dynamic Vocabulary Development in a Foreign Language.
262 pages. 2012. ISBN 978-3-0343-1106-9

Vol. 154 Carmen Argondizzo (ed.)
Creativity and Innovation in Language Education.
357 pages. 2012. ISBN 978-3-0343-1080-2

Vol. 155 David Hirsh (ed.)
Current Perspectives in Second Language Vocabulary Research.
180 pages. 2012. ISBN 978-3-0343-1108-3

Vol. 156 Seiji Shinkawa
Unhistorical Gender Assignment in Lahamon's Brut. A Case Study of a Late Stage in the Development of Grammatical Gender toward its Ultimate Loss.
186 pages. 2012. ISBN 978-3-0343-1124-3

Vol. 157 Yeonkwon Jung
Basics of Organizational Writing: A Critical Reading Approach.
151 pages. 2014. ISBN 978-3-0343-1137-3.

Vol. 158 Bárbara Eizaga Rebollar (ed.)
Studies in Linguistics and Cognition.
301 pages. 2012. ISBN 978-3-0343-1138-0

Vol. 159 Giuliana Garzone, Paola Catenaccio, Chiara Degano (eds)
Genre Change in the Contemporary World. Short-term Diachronic Perspectives.
329 pages. 2012. ISBN 978-3-0343-1214-1

Vol. 160 Carol Berkenkotter, Vijay K. Bhatia & Maurizio Gotti (eds)
Insights into Academic Genres.
468 pages. 2012. ISBN 978-3-0343-1211-0

Vol. 161 Beatriz Tizón-Couto
Clausal Complements in Native and Learner Spoken English. A corpus-based study with Lindsei and Vicolse.
357 pages. 2013. ISBN 978-3-0343-1184-7

Vol. 162 Patrizia Anesa
Jury Trials and the Popularization of Legal Language. A Discourse Analytical Approach.
tt. 2012. ISBN 978-3-0343-1231-8

Vol. 163 David Hirsh
Endangered Languages, Knowledge Systems and Belief Systems.
153 pages. 2013. ISBN 978-3-0343-1232-5

Vol. 164 Eugenia Sainz (ed.)
De la estructura de la frase al tejido del discurso. Estudios contrastivos español/italiano.
305 pages. 2014. ISBN 978-3-0343-1253-0

Vol. 165 Julia Bamford, Franca Poppi & Davide Mazzi (eds)
Space, Place and the Discursive Construction of Identity.
367 pages. 2014. ISBN 978-3-0343-1249-3

Vol. 166 Rita Salvi & Janet Bowker (eds)
Space, Time and the Construction of Identity.
Discursive Indexicality in Cultural, Institutional and Professional Fields.
324 pages. 2013. ISBN 978-3-0343-1254-7

Vol. 167 Shunji Yamazaki & Robert Sigley (eds)
Approaching Language Variation through Corpora. A Festschrift in Honour of Toshio Saito.
421 pages. 2013. ISBN 978-3-0343-1264-6

Vol. 168 Franca Poppi
Global Interactions in English as a Lingua Franca. How written communication is changing under the influence of electronic media and new contexts of use.
249 pages. 2012. ISBN 978-3-0343-1276-9

Vol. 169 Miguel A. Aijón Oliva & María José Serrano
Style in syntax. Investigating variation in Spanish pronoun subjects.
239 pages. 2013. ISBN 978-3-0343-1244-8

Vol. 170 Inés Olza, Óscar Loureda & Manuel Casado-Velarde (eds)
Language Use in the Public Sphere. Methodological Perspectives and Empirical Applications
564 pages. 2014. ISBN 978-3-0343-1286-8

Vol. 171 Aleksandra Matulewska
Legilinguistic Translatology. A Parametric Approach to Legal Translation.
279 pages. 2013. ISBN 978-3-0343-1287-5

Vol. 172 Maurizio Gotti & Carmen Sancho Guinda (eds)
Narratives in Academic and Professional Genres.
513 pages. 2013. ISBN 978-3-0343-1371-1

Vol. 173 Madalina Chitez
Learner corpus profiles. The case of Romanian Learner English.
244 pages. 2014. ISBN 978-3-0343-1410-7

Vol. 174 Chihiro Inoue
Task Equivalence in Speaking Tests.
251 pages. 2013. ISBN 978-3-0343-1417-6

Vol. 175 Gabriel Quiroz & Pedro Patiño (eds.)
LSP in Colombia: advances and challenges.
339 pages. 2014. ISBN 978-3-0343-1434-3

Vol. 176 Catherine Resche
Economic Terms and Beyond: Capitalising on the Wealth of Notions.
How Researchers in Specialised Varieties of English Can Benefit from Focusing on Terms.
332 pages. 2013. ISBN 978-3-0343-1435-0

Vol. 177 Wei Wang
Media representation of migrant workers in China. Identities and stances
198 pages. 2018. 978-3-0343-1436-7

Vol. 178 Cécile Desoutter & Caroline Mellet (dir.)
Le discours rapporté: approches linguistiques et perspectives didactiques.
270 pages. 2013. ISBN 978-3-0343-1292-9

Vol. 179 Ana Díaz-Negrillo & Francisco Javier Díaz-Pérez (eds)
Specialisation and Variation in Language Corpora.
341 pages. 2014. ISBN 978-3-0343-1316-2

Vol. 180 Pilar Alonso
A Multi-dimensional Approach to Discourse Coherence. From Standardness to Creativity.
247 pages. 2014. ISBN 978-3-0343-1325-4

Vol. 181 Alejandro Alcaraz-Sintes & Salvador Valera-Hernández (eds)
Diachrony and Synchrony in English Corpus Linguistics.
393 pages. 2014. ISBN 978-3-0343-1326-1

Vol. 182 Runhan Zhang
Investigating Linguistic Knowledge of a Second Language.
207 pages. 2015. ISBN 978-3-0343-1330-8

Vol. 183 Hajar Abdul Rahim & Shakila Abdul Manan (eds.)
English in Malaysia. Postcolonial and Beyond.
267 pages. 2014. ISBN 978-3-0343-1341-4

Vol. 184 Virginie Fasel Lauzon
Comprendre et apprendre dans l'interaction. Les séquences d'explication en classe de français langue seconde.
292 pages. 2014. ISBN 978-3-0343-1451-0

Vol. 185 Forthcoming.

Vol. 186 Wei Ren
L2 Pragmatic Development in Study Abroad Contexts
256 pages. 2015. ISBN 978-3-0343-1358-2

Vol. 187 Marina Bondi & Rosa Lorés Sanz (eds)
Abstracts in Academic Discourse. Variation and Change.
361 pages. 2014. ISBN 978-3-0343-1483-1

Vol. 188 Giuditta Caliendo
Rethinking Community. Discourse, Identity and Citizenship in the European Union.
240 pages. 2017. ISBN 978-3-0343-1561-6

Vol. 189 Paola Evangelisti Allori (ed.)
Identities in and across Cultures.
315 pages. 2014. ISBN 978-3-0343-1458-9

Vol. 190 Erik Castello, Katherine Ackerley & Francesca Coccetta (eds).
Studies in Learner Corpus Linguistics. Research and Applications for Foreign Language Teaching and Assessment.
358 pages. 2015. ISBN 978-3-0343-1506-7

Vol. 191 Ruth Breeze, Maurizio Gotti & Carmen Sancho Guinda (eds)
Interpersonality in Legal Genres.
389 pages. 2014. ISBN 978-3-0343-1524-1

Vol. 192 Paola Evangelisti Allori, John Bateman & Vijay K. Bhatia (eds)
Evolution in Genre. Emergence, Variation, Multimodality.
364 pages. 2014. ISBN 978-3-0343-1533-3

Vol. 193 Jiyeon Kook
Agency in Arzt-Patient-Gesprächen. Zur interaktionistischen Konzeptualisierung von Agency
271 pages. 2015. ISBN 978-3-0343-1666-8

Vol. 194 Susana Nicolás Román & Juan José Torres Núñez (eds)
Drama and CLIL. A new challenge for the teaching approaches in bilingual education.
170 pages. 2015. ISBN 978-3-0343-1629-3

Vol. 195 Alessandra Molino & Serenella Zanotti (eds)
Observing Norm, Observing Usage. Lexis in Dictionaries and in the Media.
430 pages. 2015. ISBN 978-3-0343-1584-5

Vol. 196 Begoña Soneira
A Lexical Description of English for Architecture. A Corpus-based Approach.
267 pages. 2015. ISBN 978-3-0343-1602-6

Vol. 197 M Luisa Roca-Varela
False Friends in Learner Corpora. A corpus-based study of English false friends in the written and spoken production of Spanish learners.
348 pages. 2015. ISBN 978-3-0343-1620-0

Vol. 198 Rahma Al-Mahrooqi & Christopher Denman
Bridging the Gap between Education and Employment. English Language Instruction in EFL Contexts.
416 pages. 2015. ISBN 978-3-0343-1681-1

Vol. 199 Rita Salvi & Janet Bowker (eds)
The Dissemination of Contemporary Knowledge in English. Genres, discourse strategies and professional practices.
171 pages. 2015. ISBN 978-3-0343-1679-8

Vol. 200 Maurizio Gotti & Davide S. Giannoni (eds)
Corpus Analysis for Descriptive and Pedagogical Purposes. ESP Perspectives.
432 pages. 2014. ISBN 978-3-0343-1516-6

Vol. 201 Ida Ruffolo
The Perception of Nature in Travel Promotion Texts. A Corpus-based Discourse Analysis.
148 pages. 2015. ISBN 978-3-0343-1521-0

Vol. 202 Ives Trevian
English suffixes. Stress-assignment properties, productivity, selection and combinatorial processes.
471 pages. 2015. ISBN 978-3-0343-1576-0

Vol. 203 Maurizio Gotti, Stefania Maci & Michele Sala (eds)
Insights into Medical Communication.
422 pages. 2015. ISBN 978-3-0343-1694-1

Vol. 204 Carmen Argondizzo (ed.)
European Projects in University Language Centres. Creativity, Dynamics, Best Practice.
371 pages. 2015. ISBN 978-3-0343-1696-5

Vol. 205 Aura Luz Duffé Montalván (ed.)
Estudios sobre el léxico. Puntos y contrapuntos.
502 pages. 2016. ISBN 978-3-0343-2011-5

Vol. 206 Maria Pavesi, Maicol Formentelli & Elisa Ghia (eds)
The Languages of Dubbing. Mainstream Audiovisual Translation in Italy.
275 pages. 2014. ISBN 978-3-0343-1646-0

Vol. 207 Ruth Breeze & Inés Olza (eds)
Evaluation in media discourse. European perspectives.
268 pages. 2017. ISBN 978-3-0343-2014-6

Vol. 208 Vijay K. Bhatia & Maurizio Gotti (eds)
Arbitration Discourse in Asia.
331 pages. 2015. ISBN 978-3-0343-2032-0

Vol. 209 Sofía Bemposta-Rivas, Carla Bouzada-Jabois, Yolanda Fernández-Pena, Tamara Bouso, Yolanda J. Calvo-Benzies, Iván Tamaredo (eds)
New trends and methodologies in applied English language research III. Synchronic and diachronic studies on discourse, lexis and grammar processing.
280 pages. 2017. ISBN 978-3-0343-2039-9

Vol. 210 Francisco Alonso Almeida, Laura Cruz García & Víctor González Ruiz (eds)
Corpus-based studies on language varieties.
285 pages. 2016. ISBN 978-3-0343-2044-3

Vol. 211 Juan Pedro Rica Peromingo
Aspectos lingüísticos y técnicos de la traducción audiovisual (TAV).
177 pages. 2016. ISBN 978-3-0343-2055-9

Vol. 212 Maria Vender
Disentangling Dyslexia. VenderPhonological and Processing Deficit in Developmental Dyslexia.
338 pages. 2017. ISBN 978-3-0343-2064-1

Vol. 213 Zhilong Xie
Bilingual Advantages. Contributions of Different Bilingual Experiences to Cognitive Control Differences Among Young-adult Bilinguals.
221 pages. 2016. ISBN 978-3-0343-2081-8

Vol. 214 Larissa D'Angelo
Academic posters. A textual and visual metadiscourse analysis.
367 pages. 2016. ISBN 978-3-0343-2083-2

Vol. 215 Evelyne Berger
Prendre la parole en L2. Regard sur la compétence d'interaction en classe de langue.
246 pages. 2016. ISBN 978-3-0343-2084-9

Vol. 216 David Lasagabaster and Aintzane Doiz (eds)
CLIL experiences in secondary and tertiary education: In search of good practices.
262 pages. 2016. ISBN 978-3-0343-2104-4

Vol. 217 Elena Kkese
Identifying Plosives in L2 English: The Case of L1 Cypriot Greek Speakers.
317 pages. 2016. ISBN 978-3-0343-2060-3

Vol. 218 Sandra Campagna, Elana Ochse, Virginia Pulcini & Martin Solly (eds)
Languaging in and across Communities: New Voices, New Identities. Studies in Honour of Giuseppina Cortese.
507 pages. 2016. ISBN 978-3-0343-2073-3

Vol. 219 Adriana Orlandi & Laura Giacomini (ed.)
Defining collocation for lexicographic purposes. From linguistic theory to lexicographic practice.
328 pages. 2016. ISBN 978-3-0343-2054-2

Vol. 220 Pietro Luigi Iaia
Analysing English as a Lingua Franca in Video Games. Linguistic Features, Experiential and Functional Dimensions of Online and Scripted Interactions.
139 pages. 2016. ISBN 978-3-0343-2138-9

Vol. 221 Dimitrinka G. Níkleva (ed.)
La formación de los docentes de español para inmigrantes en distintos contextos educativos.
390 pages. 2017. ISBN 978-3-0343-2135-8

Vol. 222 Katherine Ackerley, Marta Guarda & Francesca Helm (eds)
Sharing Perspectives on English-Medium Instruction.
308 pages. 2017. ISBN 978-3-0343-2537-0

Vol. 223 Juana I. Marín-Arrese, Julia Lavid-López, Marta Carretero, Elena Domínguez Romero, Ma Victoria Martín de la Rosa & María Pérez Blanco (eds)
Evidentiality and Modality in European Languages. Discourse-pragmatic perspectives.
427 pages. 2017. ISBN 978-3-0343-2437-3

Vol. 224 Gilles Col
Construction du sens : un modèle instructionnel pour la sémantique.
292 pages. 2017. ISBN 978-3-0343-2572-1

Vol. 225 Ana Chiquito & Gabriel Quiroz (eds)
Pobreza, Lenguaje y Medios en América Latina.
362 pages. 2017. ISBN 978-3-0343-2142-6

Vol. 226 Xu Zhang
English Quasi-Numeral Classifiers. A Corpus-Based Cognitive-Typological Study.
360 pages. 2017. ISBN 978-3-0343-2818-0

Vol. 227 María Ángeles Orts, Ruth Breeze & Maurizio Gotti (eds)
Power, Persuasion and Manipulation in Specialised Genres. Providing Keys to the Rhetoric of Professional Communities.
368 pages. 2017. ISBN 978-3-0343-3010-7

Vol. 228 Maurizio Gotti, Stefania Maci & Michele Sala (eds)
Ways of Seeing, Ways of Being: Representing the Voices of Tourism.
453 pages. 2017. ISBN 978-3-0343-3031-2

Vol. 229 Dino Selvaggi
Plurilingual Code-Switching between Standard and Local Varieties.
A Socio-Psycholinguistic Approach
371 pages. 2018. ISBN 978-3-0343-2663-6

Vol. 230 Anca-Cristina Sterie
Interprofessional interactions at the hospital. Nurses' requests and reports of problems in calls with physicians.
371 pages. 2017. ISBN 978-3-0343-2734-3

Vol. 231 Xiaodong Zhang
Understanding Chinese EFL Teachers' Beliefs and Practices in the Textbook-Based Classroom.
189 pages. 2017. ISBN 978-3-0343-3053-4

Vol. 232 Manuela Caterina Moroni & Federica Ricci Garotti (Hrsg.)
Brücken schlagen zwischen Sprachwissenschaft und DaF-Didaktik.
345 pages. 2017. ISBN 978-3-0343-2667-4

Vol. 233 Dimitrinka Georgieva Níkleva
Necesidades y tendencias en la formación del profesorado de español como lengua extranjera
401 pages. 2017. ISBN 978-3-0343-2946-0

Vol. 234 Juan Santana-Lario & Salvador Valera (Hrsg.)
Competing patterns in English affixation.
272 pages. 2017. ISBN 978-3-0343-2701-5

Vol. 235 Francisco Salgado-Robles
Desarrollo de la competencia sociolingüística por aprendices de español en un contexto de inmersión en el extranjero
241 pages. 2018. ISBN 978-3-0343-2323-9

Vol. 236 Maria Chiara Janner
Sguardi linguistici sulla marca. Analisi morfosintattica dei nomi commerciali in italiano
345 pages. 2017. ISBN 978-3-0343-2667-4

Vol. 237 Bárbara Herrero Muñoz-Cobo & Otman El Azami Zalachi
La primavera del árabe marroquí.
192 pages. 2017. ISBN 978-3-0343-3104-3

Vol. 238 Consuelo Pascual Escagedo
El papel del oyente en la construcción de la conversación espontánea de estudiantes italianos en su interlengua y en su lengua materna
295 pages. 2017. ISBN 978-3-0343-3186-9

Vol. 239 Stefania M. Maci
The MS Digby 133 Mary Magdalene. Beyond scribal practices: language, discourse, values and attitudes.
336 pages. 2017. ISBN 978-3-0343-3256-9

Vol. 240 Eliecer Crespo-Fernández
Taboo in Discourse. Studies on Attenuation and Offence in Communication.
326 pages. 2018. ISBN 978-3-0343-3018-3

Vol. 241 Jana Altmanova, Maria Centrella, Katherine E. Russo (eds)
Terminology & Discourse / Terminologie et discours.
424 pages. 2018. ISBN 978-3-0343-2417-5

Vol. 242 Xavier Blanco et Inès Sfar (dir.)
Lexicologie(s) : approches croisées en sémantique lexicale.
442 pages. 2018. ISBN 978-3-0343-3056-5

Vol. 243 Yunfeng Ge
Resolution of Conflict of Interest in Chinese Civil Court Hearings. A Perspective of Discourse Information Theory.
302 pages. 2018. ISBN 978-3-0343-3313-9

Vol. 244 Carla Vergaro
Illocutionary Shell Nouns in English
322 pages. 2018. ISBN 978-3-0343-3069-5

Vol. 245 Paolo Frassi
L'adjectif en français et sa définition lexicographique.
270 pages. 2018. ISBN 978-3-0343-3394-8

Vol. 246 Suwilai Premsrirat and David Hirsh (eds)
Language Revitalization. Insights from Thailand
328 pages. 2018. ISBN 978-3-0343-3497-6

Vol. 247 Wei Wang
Researching Learning and Learners in Genre-based Academic Writing Instruction
282 pages. 2018. ISBN 978-3-0343-3297-2

Vol. 248 Isusi Alabarte, Alberto & Lahuerta Martínez, Ana Cristina (eds)
La comprensión lectora de lengua extranjera Estudio de los factores de familiaridad, interés, género y métodos de evaluación
336 pages. 2018. ISBN 978-3-0343-3493-8

Vol. 249 Mercedes Eurrutia Cavero
Approche didactique du langage techno-scientifique Terminologie et discours
374 pages. 2018. ISBN 978-3-0343-3512-6

Vol. 250 Aurora Ruiz Mezcua (ed.)
Approaches to Telephone Interpretation Research, Innovation, Teaching and Transference
268 pages. 2018. ISBN 978-3-0343-3330-6

Vol. 251 Morini Massimiliano A Day in the News
A Stylistic Analysis of Newsspeak
188 pages. 2018. ISBN 978-3-0343-3507-2

Vol. 252 Ignacio Guillén-Galve & Ignacio Vázquez-Orta (eds.)
English as a Lingua Franca and Intercultural Communication Implications and Applications in the Field of English Language Teaching
414 pages. 2018. ISBN 978-3-0343-2763-3

Vol. 253 Bianca Del Villano
Using the Devil with Courtesy
Shakespeare and the Language of (Im)Politeness
216 pages. 2018. ISBN 978-3-0343-2315-4

Vol. 254 David Hirsh (ed.)
Explorations in Second Language Vocabulary Research
252 pages. 2018. ISBN 978-3-0343-2940-8

Vol. 255 Tania Baumann (ed.)
Reiseführer - Sprach- und Kulturmittlung im Tourismus / Le guide turistiche - mediazione linguistica e culturale in ambito turistico
270 pages. 2018. ISBN 978-3-0343-3402-0

Vol. 256 Ariadna Sánchez-Hernández & Ana Herraiz-Martínez (eds)
Learning second language pragmatics beyond traditional contexts
376 pages. 2018. ISBN 978-3-0343-3437-2

Vol. 257 Albert Bastardas-Boada, Emili Boix-Fuster, Rosa Maria Torrens (eds)
Family Multilingualism in Medium-Sized Linguistic Communities
336 pages. 2019. ISBN 978-3-0343-2536-3

Vol. 258 Yuyang Cai
Examining the Interaction among Components of English for Specific Purposes Ability in Reading. The Triple-Decker Model
296 pages. 2020. 978-3-0343-2913-2

Vol. 259 Catia Nannoni
Participe présent et gérondif dans la presse française contemporaine
176 pages. 2019. ISBN 978-3-0343-3631-4

Vol. 260 Nieves Rodríguez Pérez & Bárbara Heinsch (eds.)
Contextos multilingües. Mediadores interculturales, formación del profesorado de lenguas extranjeras
289 pages. 2019. ISBN 978-3-0343-3768-7

Vol. 261 Giuliana Elena Garzone, Mara Logaldo, Francesca Santulli (eds.)
Investigating Conflict Discourses in the Periodical Press
244 pages. 2020. ISBN 978-3-0343-3668-0

Vol. 262 Laura Nadal
Lingüística experimental y contraargumentación
233 pages. 2019. ISBN 978-3-0343-3791-5

Vol. 263 Claudia Claridge & Merja Kytö (eds.)
Punctuation in Context – Past and Present Perspectives
288 pages. 2019. ISBN 978-3-0343-3790-8

Vol. 264 Maurizio Gotti, Stefania Maci, Michele Sala (eds.)
Scholarly Pathways
530 pages. 2020. ISBN 978-3-0343-3860-8

Vol. 265 Ruth Breeze, Ana M. Fernández Vallejo (eds.)
Politics and populism across modes and media
350 pages. 2020. ISBN 978-3-0343-3707-6

Vol. 266 Jean Marguerite Jimenez
Understanding the Effects of Immediate Electronic Corrective Feedback on Second Language Development
252 pages. 2020. ISBN 978-3-0343-3815-8

Vol. 267 Sergio Rodríguez-Tapia, Adela González-Fernández (eds)
Lenguas y turismo: estudios en torno al discurso, la didáctica y la divulgación
380 pages. 2020. ISBN 978-3-0343-3881-3

Vol. 268 Ana Bocanegra-Valle (ed.)
Applied Linguistics and Knowledge Transfer. Employability, Internationalisation and Social Challenges
344 pages. 2020. ISBN 978-3-0343-3714-4

Vol. 269 Beatrice Garzelli
La traducción audiovisual español-italiano.Películas y cortos entre humor y habla soez
202 pages. 2020. ISBN 978-3-0343-4013-7

Vol. 270 Iván Tamaredo
Complexity, Efficiency, and Language Contact. Pronoun Omission in World Englishes
292 pages. 2020. ISBN 978-3-0343-3902-5

Vol. 271 Silvia Domenica Zollo,
Origine et histoire du vocabulaire des arts de la table. Analyse lexicale et exploitation de corpus textuels
239 pages. 2020. ISBN 978-3-0343-3890-5

Vol. 272 Paola Paissa, Michelangelo Conoscenti, Ruggero Druetta, Martin Solly (eds.)
Metaphor and Conflict / Métaphore et conflit
385 pages. 2021. 978-3-0343-4068-7

Vol. 273 María Martínez-Atienza de Dios,
Entre el léxico y la sintaxis: las fases de los eventos
178 pages. 2021. 978-3-0343-4173-8

Vol. 274 Noelia Castro-Chao,
Argument Structure in Flux. The Development of Impersonal Constructions in Middle and Early Modern English, with Special Reference to Verbs of Desire.
300 pages. 2021. 978-3-0343-4189-9

Vol. 275 Gabriella Carobbio, Cécile Desoutter, Aurora Fragonara (eds.)
Macht, Ratio und Emotion: Diskurse im digitalen Zeitalter / Pouvoir, raison et émotion: les discours à l'ère du numérique
246 pages. 2020. 978-3-0343-4184-4

Vol. 276 Miguel Fuster-Márquez, José Santaemilia, Carmen Gregori-Signes, Paula Rodríguez-Abru-ñeiras (eds.)
Exploring discourse and ideology through corpora
293 pages. 2021. 978-3-0343-3969-8

Vol. 277 Tamara Bouso
Changes in Argument Structure The Transitivizing Reaction Object Construction
392 pages. 2021. 978-3-0343-4095-3

Vol. 278 Maria Luisa Maggioni, Amanda Murphy (eds.)
Back to the Future. English from Past to Present
250 pages. 2021. 978-3-0343-4273-5

Vol. 279 Luisa Chierichetti
Diálogos de serie. Una aproximación a la construcción discursiva de personajes basada en corpus
246 pages. 2021. 978-3-0343-4274-2

Vol. 280 Cristina Lastres-López
From subordination to insubordination. A functional-pragmatic approach to if/si-constructions in English, French and Spanish spoken discourse
258 pages. 2021. 978-3-0343-4220-9

Vol. 281 Eleonora Federici, Stefania Maci (eds.)
Gender issues. Translating and mediating languages, cultures and societies
500 pages. 2021. 978-3-0343-4022-9

Vol. 282 José Mateo, Francisco Yus (eds.)
Metaphor in Economics and specialised Discourse
354 pages. 2021. 978-3-0343-4048-9

Vol. 283 Nicholas Brownlees (ed.)
The Role of Context in the Production and Reception of Historical News Discourse
376 pages. 2021. 978-3-0343-4181-3

Vol. 284 Catalina Fuentes Rodriguez, María Ester Brenes Peña, Víctor Pérez Béjar (eds.)
Sintaxis discursiva: construcciones y operadores en español
396 pages. 2021. 978-3-0343-4306-0

Vol. 285 Dominic Stewart
Frequency in the dictionary. A corpus-assisted contrastive analysis of English and Italian
178 pages. 2021. 978-3-0343-4368-8

Vol. 286 Carla Bouzada-Jabois
Nonfinite supplements in the recent history of English
386 pages. 2021. 978-3-0343-4226-1

Vol. 287 Sofía Bemposta Rivas
Verb-governed infinitival complementation in the recent history of English
340 pages. 2021. 978-3-0343-4227-8

Vol. 288 Mirella Agorni
Translating Italy for the Nineteenth Century. Translators and an Imagined Nation in the Early Romantic Period 1816–1830s
182 pages. 2021. 978-3-0343-3612-3

Vol. 289 David Hirsh (ed.)
Research Perspectives in Language and Education
276 pages. 2021. 978-3-0343-4219-3

Vol. 290 Federica Vezzani
Terminologie numérique : conception, représentation et gestion
238 pages. 2022. 978-3-0343-4394-7

Vol. 291 Stefania M. Maci
Evidential verbs in the genre of medical posters. A corpus-based analysis
498 pages. 2022. 978-3-0343-4521-7

Vol. 292 Francisco J. Álvarez-Gil
Stance devices in tourism-related research articles: A corpus-based study
170 pages. 2022. 978-3-0343-4555-2

Vol. 293 Annalisa Baicchi / Stefania Biscetti (eds.)
The Language of Fashion. Linguistic, Cognitive, and Cultural Insights
192 pages. 2022. 978-3-0343-4428-9

Vol. 294 Ana Maria Piquer-Píriz
E-learning in EMI. Academic language for university students
228 pages. 2022. 978-3-0343-4589-7

Vol. 295 Geneviève Henrot Sostero (ed.)
Alle radici della fraseologia europea
638 pages. 2023. 978-3-0343-4645-0

Vol. 296 Klara Dankova
Les fibres textiles entre synchronie et diachronie: études terminologiques
288 pages. 2023. 978-3-0343-4587-3

Vol. 297 Marta Carretero, Juana I. Marín-Arrese, Elena Domínguez Romero, Mª Victoria Martín de la Rosa (eds.)
Evidentiality and Epistemic Modality. Conceptual and Descriptive issues
414 pages. 2023. 978-3-0343-3993-3

Vol. 298 Kim Grego, Alessandra Vicentini, Virpi Ylänne (eds.)
Age-Specific Issues. Language, Spaces, Technologies
280 pages. 2023. 978-3-0343-4411-1

Vol. 299 Giovanni Garofalo (ed.) Estudios de género asistidos por corpus.
Enfoques multidisciplinarios
290 pages. 2022. 978-3-0343-4548-4

Vol. 300 Giuseppe Palumbo, Katia Peruzzo, Gianluca Pontrandolfo (eds.)
What's Special About Specialised Translation? Essays in Honour of Federica Scarpa
298 pages. 2023. 978-3-0343-4411-1

Vol. 301 Raquel P. Romasanta
Probabilistic variability in clausal verb complementation in World Englishes.
374 pages. 2023. 978-3-0343-4703-7

Vol. 302 Giulia Adriana Pennisi
A linguistic Insight into Legislative Drafting. Tradition and Change in the UK Legislation
296 pages. 2023. 978-3-0343-4700-6

Vol. 303 Javier Fernández-Cruz, Antonio Moreno-Ortiz
Economic terms in the news during the Great Recession. A diachronic sentiment and collocational analysis
192 pages. 2023. 978-3-0343-4778-5

Vol. 304 Stefania Maci, Mark McGlashan (eds.)
(Critical) Discourse Studies and the (new?) normal. Analysing discourse in times of crisis.
400 pages. 2024. 978-3-0343-4767-9

Vol. 305 Ana Elvira, Ojanguren López
Predications in competition and the rise of serial verb constructions in English. The verbal and nominal complementation of Old English aspectual and manipulative verbs.
534 pages. 2024. 978-3-0343-4644-3

Vol. 306 Stefania Maci, Giovanni Garofalo (eds.)
Investigating Discourse and Text. Corpus-Assisted Analytical Perspectives.
372 pages. 2023. 978-3-0343-4753-2

Vol. 307 Víctor Pérez Béjar
Las construcciones suspendidas en español. Un paradigma en gramática del discurso
494 pages. 2024. 978-3-0343-4799-0

Vol. 308 Javier Calle Martín / Jeús Romero Barranco (eds.)
Corpora and Language Change in Late Modern English.
408 pages. 2024. 978-3-0343-4642-9

Vol. 309 Cristina Petras / Sonia Berbinski / Daciana Vlad / Raluca Balaţchi (eds.)
Marqueurs métalinguistiques : émergence, discours, variation /Metalinguistic Markers: Emergence, Discourse, Variation.
720 pages 2024. 978-3-0343-4908-6

Vol. 310 Micaela Rossi (éd.)
Néologie, terminologie et variation - Neología, terminología yvariación – Neologia, terminologia e variazione.
418 Pages. 2024. 978-3-0343-4696-2

Vol. 311 Sergio Maruenda-Bataller / Laura Mercé / Elena Castellano-Ortolà (eds.)
Discourse, gender, and violence: Insights from news and social media texts.
268 pages. 2024. 978-3-0343-4701-3

Vol. 312 Dario Del Fante
Migrating across times and cultures: Metaphorical images of migration in the U.S. and Italian newspaper discourse between the 20th and 21st centuries.
338 Pages. 2024. 978-3-0343-4659-7

Vol. 313 Francisco Alonso-Almeida / Begoña Bellés-Fortuño (eds.)
Corpus-based Studies in Specialized Discourses.
294 Pages. 2025. 978-3-0343-4261-2

www.ingramcontent.com/pod-product-compliance
Ingram Content Group UK Ltd.
Pitfield, Milton Keynes, MK11 3LW, UK
UKHW021836100926
8556IPUK00004B/382